LAST CHANCE IN TEXAS

LAST CHANCE

The Redemption of Criminal Youth

IN TEXAS

JOHN HUBNER

RANDOM HOUSE 🏠 NEW YORK

Published in the United States by Random House,
an imprint of The Random House Publishing Group,
a division of Random House, Inc., New York.

RANDOM HOUSE and colophon are registered
trademarks of Random House, Inc.

LIBRARY OF CONGRESS CATALOGING-IN-PUBLICATION DATA
Hubner, John.
Last chance in Texas: the redemption of criminal youth/by John Hubner.
p. cm.
Includes index.
ISBN 0-375-50809-0
1. Giddings State School. 2. Juvenile corrections—Texas.
3. Juvenile delinquents—Rehabilitation—Texas. 4. Juvenile justice,
Administration of—Texas. I. Title.
HV9105.T44G534 2005   365'.42—dc22   2005042892

Printed in the United States of America on acid-free paper

www.atrandom.com

2 4 6 8 9 7 5 3 1

First Edition

Book design by Jennifer Ann Daddio

TO ADULTS WHO CARE FOR
TROUBLED AND LONELY CHILDREN
EVERYWHERE;

AND TO MY OWN CHILDREN,
ALEXANDER SAM
AND
GWENDOLYN SARAH

"To enter one's ownself, it is necessary to go armed to the teeth."

—PAUL VALÉRY

AUTHOR'S NOTE

I spent nine months inside the Giddings State School, much of it behind a one way mirror in the Capital Offenders group room. The events described are based primarily on these youths' narratives. They are the best sources on themselves. I also had access to case files during daily meetings with psychologists, who read sections aloud as they were preparing for a group, or going over events that had occurred during a group.

Dialogue that appears in quotation marks is taken verbatim from the group room or was said directly to me. The youths' narratives of events were checked against police reports, trial transcripts, and interviews with parents and the victims of crimes. Steve Robinson, executive director of the Texas Youth Commission while I was in the Giddings State School, asked that I change the first names of students and alter the places where they committed their crimes. I have done both.

Citations for studies and statistics along with supporting material can be found in the notes section at the end of the book.

INTRODUCTION

"THE TOUGHEST PRISON IN TEXAS"

The way legendary singer-songwriter Billy Joe Shaver sees things, the town of Giddings (pop. 5,100) is "right there where the best is, smack dab in the heart of Texas."

Central Texas is post oak country, gently rolling savanna between the Colorado and Brazos rivers where the farmers raise peanuts and small herds of cattle graze on coastal Bermuda grass. Deer hide in cedar thickets, and deep in the night, coyotes work themselves into a frenzy. Here and there, rigs that look like giant grasshoppers suck oil from pockets deep in the earth. The area was settled by Germans and Czechs in the mid-1800s and is part of the "Barbecue Belt" that surrounds Austin, fifty miles to the east. Austin prides itself on being the Texas capital, the live-music capital of the world, and the high-tech center of the Southwest, but its influence doesn't extend to Giddings.

The town itself is a jumble of aging one- and two-story brick buildings, furniture stores, fast-food outlets, and gas stations, and like many another raw-looking Texas town, it makes up in friendliness what it lacks in charm. When people ask, "How you doin' today?" they actually want to know. "We like to think of Lee County as one big family," a deputy sheriff tells a newcomer during a conversation in the Wal-Mart.

The four-lane artery that runs between Austin and Houston, Highway 290, runs right through Giddings, and traffic pounds the town day and night. Except for five traffic lights, there is not much to stop for. Texas has some outrageous Victorian-era courthouses, and the Lee County Courthouse in Giddings is a redbrick monstrosity sprouting gables like malignant growths. The other landmark is City Meat Market, a hardcore, eat-it-with-your-fingers-off-butcher-paper barbecue joint where a big smoker turns brisket into gourmet fare and the smell is as heavy as the potato salad.

Most travelers blow through without noticing a lonely little green sign across from the Ramada Inn, pointing to an institution that, in certain circles, has made the name Giddings famous. Turn down a country road, pass a played-out oil field and a scrubby pasture where a few head of Brahma graze (there's a small herd of genuine Texas longhorns just up the road), and you arrive at the gate to the biggest employer in town. Almost four hundred people work at "the State School," or, as the locals say, with "those kids out there." Everyone in Lee County knows someone who works there, or has a relative, or maybe two, who does.

The Giddings State School gets "the worst of the worst," the four hundred most heinous youthful offenders in Texas. Across the country, the school is famous in juvenile justice circles for its aggressive treatment programs. Locally, the institution is something of an island, cut off from the town that gives it its name. On Friday nights in the fall the high school football team, the Giddings Buffalos, plays in a stadium that seats twice as many people as there are in town. Demand for tickets is so great the Buffalos sell reserved seats. In the two decades the State School has fielded a football team, the Giddings Indians have had only one losing season, a record that would make the coach the toast of any Texas town. But when Sandy Brown walks into the Texas Grill, a popular truck stop, no one recognizes the Indians' coach.

To Johnnie Christiansen, who has been cutting hair in his two-chair City Barber Shop for thirty years, the State School is like the Monday cattle auction, a local point of interest that long ago faded into the landscape.

"I never been out there myself, but I hear they take real good care of kids," Johnnie says. "I hear when they leave, most of 'em don't come back."

The Giddings State School is the flagship of the Texas Youth Commission, a chain of thirteen secure facilities scattered across the state that has around four thousand youthful offenders under lock and key. The State School does not look like a typical prison. Take away the fourteen-foot steel fence with motion detectors that surrounds the fifty-five-acre campus and it could pass for a classy southwestern prep school. The grounds are lush and dotted with oaks. Limestone walls shade carefully tended flower beds, water sparkles in a reflecting pool. The biggest building on campus, the high school, is shaped like a starfish, with corridors radiating off a glassed-in central area. The chapel has a dramatic, radically tapering steeple that pierces the sky like a lance. Rainwater running off copper roofs has stained rough-cut limestone facades green, giving the campus an aged, tradition-rich feel.

When it opened in 1972, the State School was intended as a facility where judges could send kids from broken homes, hoping they would stay long enough to earn a high school diploma. Above anything else, kids whose homes have been shattered hate it that they do not have a family. Some told themselves that this was about as good as things were likely to get and adjusted to the State School. But for a significant number who found themselves alone in the world, it did not matter how pastoral the setting was, or how caring the teachers were, or that the cottages were spotless and the food wasn't bad. Every day in a thousand ways, the State School kept reminding them they did not have a home of their own. A fair number took off running, as kids always have from orphanages, no matter how euphemistically they are named.

The locals kept complaining about the runaways and by the late 1970s, congregate-care facilities for youth who had no criminal records were becoming as outmoded as orphanages. Social workers scrambled to place orphans and abused and neglected children in long-term foster care, where they could grow up in conditions that as nearly as possible approximated those of a family of origin. In 1978, the Texas Youth Commission put up the fence and began transforming Giddings into a high-security institution. Youth who came from broken homes were replaced by youth who, through acts of violence, had broken up homes. The State School became a kind of barometer measuring one of the ugliest trends sweeping across Texas and the rest of America.

The juvenile crime rate began to rise in the mid-1970s, in Texas and the other forty-nine states. Some observers thought the cause could be traced to parents who came of age during the "let it all hang out" 1960s and failed to set limits for their children. Others pointed out that as young people experimented with hard-core drugs, heroin and methamphetamines were expanding far beyond their base in needle-using subcultures in inner cities.

The most alarming spike in violent juvenile crime occurred between 1984 and 1994, when arrest rates for juveniles charged with violent offenses like murder and aggravated assault jumped an incredible 78 percent. Criminologists like Alfred Blumstein and Richard Rosenfeld have traced these sharp increases to the development of the drug trade, in particular the crack cocaine market, on certain streets, in certain neighborhoods, in certain cities. Gang members armed with automatic weapons they had purchased from an array displayed in a car trunk fought running gun battles to control a street corner or a neighborhood. If a young man thought he was "dissed," he went home, got his gun, and went looking for the youth who had shown him up.

Dr. Linda Reyes, the Texas Youth Commission deputy executive director, was a witness to this deluge of violence. When Reyes arrived in the State School with a newly minted Ph.D. in psychology in 1988, there were about a dozen murderers on campus, most of whom had killed a family member, usually a mother or father. And then through the gate in ever larger numbers came youth who had committed "upon stranger" murders, the most terrifying crime there is. The carjacking victim has never seen his assailant; he turns over his vehicle and his wallet without a word, and the kid still kills him.

"The use of guns was increasing, gang-related murder was increasing, drugs, especially crack cocaine, were spreading—it was all happening at the same time," Reyes recalls. "There were ten to twelve murderers in the State School in 1988. In 1995, there were three hundred."

The epidemic of murder among the young peaked and passed in a decade. But "the worst of the worst" continue to come through the gate to the State School. From 1999 through 2003, the school received an average of thirty murderers a year. They enter a population of 325 boys and

65 girls, most of whom have been convicted of attempted murder, rape, or aggravated assault. So if Giddings looks like a prep school, it is a prep school in reverse. To get into Giddings, a youth has to have committed a violent crime.

The crimes are horrific. When she was fourteen, one girl suffocated her two-year-old nephew and five-month-old niece. A youth raped a five-year-old, and then gouged his eyes out so the little boy would not be able to identify him. A seventeen-year-old took a forty-year-old man into the woods, hit him over the head, doused him with gasoline, and set him on fire.

The young man who did the immolation is one of eighteen youths who are putting on jackets and lining up at the door in Cottage 5-A. Ten of these adolescents have committed a murder. Four were sentenced for attempted murder (two opened fire on police officers). The others were convicted of aggravated assault during a robbery, or assault with a deadly weapon. Each young felon counts as he crosses the threshold of the spartan, spotlessly clean cottage.

"One, sir."

"Two, sir."

"Three, sir."

The group forms two lines and halts on the sidewalk. Without being reminded, they perform an "arm check," extending a right arm and placing a hand on the shoulder of the youth in front to establish the proper marching distance. Then they move out.

"Left . . . left . . . your left," yells the young man calling cadence.

"Right . . . right . . . your right," the others chorus.

Minorities are overrepresented in this group, as they are in prison populations around the country. The youth are African-American, African-American-white, Jamaican-American, Latino, white, Latino-white, Vietnamese, Korean-American. Despite the different hues, they look very much alike. All have had their hair buzz-cut down to stubble; all wear loose-fitting blue pants with an elastic band ("prison pants"), an oatmeal-colored long-sleeved T-shirt or sweatshirt, a black sateen jacket, and a gray watch cap. Only the shoes differ, shoes being the only clothing the youth are allowed to select.

"Left, left, your left."

"Right, right, your right."

More than clothes or haircuts, what makes these young men appear so similar is how rigidly they march, and how drained their faces are of all expression. When a squad of incarcerated teenage girls marches past, usually a major event, the boys don't even glance their way. They could be conscripts going into battle. And in a way, they are.

The column turns left and proceeds to what might be a storage shed, a square, aluminum-sided, windowless building sitting on a concrete slab. The least interesting structure on campus, it has the most interesting function.

A staff member wearing jeans and a cowboy shirt calls for the column to halt and steps to the front of the line. He takes out a set of keys and opens a steel door. The youths file through a small hallway and enter an empty square room with a gray carpet, acoustic tile on the ceiling, and white fiberglass soundproofing on three walls. The young men have been hearing about this room for years and now that they have finally arrived, they stop to look around.

A one-way mirror runs the length of the back wall and the young offenders catch reflections of themselves in the silvery glass. Mirrors in the State School are burnished steel, like those found in service station restrooms, and offer only dull, hazy reflections. This is the best look these young men have had of themselves in years, but they don't want to be too obvious about it, so they sneak a glance or two and maybe roll a shoulder and then look away.

The staff member tells the young men to take gray plastic armchairs from a stack in a corner and place them in three rows. That completed, they sit down, working hard to keep their faces empty of any expression. But furtive glances and quick, jumpy movements reveal how apprehensive they are.

The outside door opens, startling the young men. They watch carefully as six adults file into the room and sit in a row of chairs facing them. Instinctively, their eyes land on a woman dressed in a black pants suit with light blond hair and dark brown eyes. Dr. Ann Kelley radiates professionalism and an athletic attractiveness, but good looks are not why she commands these young men's attention. A Ph.D. psychologist who has spent years on the Giddings campus working with violent youth, Kelley is now director of clinical services at the State School, someone who will carry considerable weight in determining the futures of these young men.

"Welcome to the Capital Offenders group. It's an honor for you to be here," Kelley says. The young men are too tense to smile or even nod. Kelley understands why they are shut down and ignores the blank looks.

"Since this is our first official session, let's be formal and introduce ourselves," Kelley continues. She introduces herself and the six therapists sitting with her do the same. The boys listen, sizing each one up and of course revealing nothing about their conclusions. When the therapists have finished, Kelley nods to a young man at the end of the first row, who cuts quite a figure as he gets to his feet. His waist can't be more than twenty-eight inches; his V-shaped chest flares into wide shoulders; his biceps must be half the size of his waist, and there is a black patch over his right eye. He fired a shotgun at a police officer, point-blank. The officer went down, wounded, and his partner returned fire, aiming at the young man's head. The bullet took out his eye and a small part of his eye socket. The young man has an IQ of 121. Intelligence counted for nothing that night on a Houston street.

The young felon closes his one eye for a moment to collect himself, and then in a quiet, soft voice delivers his "layout," which is how youth serving time in the TYC are taught to present themselves.

"My name is Jerome Evans. I am eighteen. My hometown is Houston, Texas. I am responsible for the attempted murder of James T. Edwards, a police officer. I am serving a fifteen-year sentence. I am currently a student confined to the Giddings State School. My phase is 3.2."

Kelley gives Jerome a slight nod and he sits down. The Vietnamese youth sitting next to him has two rows of self-inflicted cigarette burns on each forearm. He gets to his feet and recites his layout, and is followed by a pixielike Korean-American, who is followed by an angry-looking Latino whose neck is covered with tattoos. Coming fast and delivered with uninflected precision, these thumbnail sketches blend into a jumble of offenses and victims and deaths and sentences that stretch out into infinity. Kelley and the other staff members don't blink an eye, and neither do the young men. They have presented their layouts hundreds of times; the staff have heard thousands. It is a way for a youth to keep reminding himself, "This is who I am, this is who I hurt, this is what I am working on." But to keep hearing the word "student" repeated in the same sentence that contains the words "murder," "attempted murder," or "twenty-five-year sentence" is unsettling.

To the public, these young men are not "students." They are young thugs, "gangbangers," "teenage superpredators." But inside the fence, they are always "students," never "wards" or "inmates" or "prisoners," and certainly not "predators" or "psychopaths." From the State School superintendent to the kitchen employees, staff members refer to them as "the students," "the boys," "the girls," or, most often, "the kids," with all the love, annoyance, anger, and exhaustion the word "kids" connotes. A staff member may remember a multiple murderer as "the scariest kid I ever worked with," but discussing him with someone on the Giddings campus, he still refers to the young felon as "a kid."

Words like "students" and "peers," which is how students are taught to refer to one another, are not throwbacks to the institution's early days as a home for neglected and abused children. The young offenders are genuinely seen as students who have been sent to the State School to learn. The course they are enrolled in is called "resocialization," and it is rigorous and fundamental, as life-altering as it is grueling.

The belief that even "the worst of the worst" are students who can take their lives apart and become their own therapists, their own parents, really; who can go through emotional and spiritual experiences that will alter the trajectory of their lives, makes the TYC one of the most progressive youth commissions in the country. Putting this controversial premise to the test under extraordinary pressure in a specialized treatment program like Capital Offenders makes Giddings the TYC flagship.

That this institutional investment in the humanity of youth who have committed horribly violent acts should be happening in Texas, of all places, at first seems incongruous. The Lone Star State is, after all, the land where the Texas Rangers rode to enduring fame delivering retributive justice at the end of a rope, as swift as it was final. The Ranger spirit lives on. Texas is proud of the fact that it puts more criminals to death than any other state; one-third of all U.S. executions since 1977 have taken place in Huntsville. The Texas Department of Criminal Justice brags about running a prison system that has no air-conditioning. Until recently, the TDCJ posted the menu a death-row inmate chose for his last meal on its website.

But within the Texas Youth Commission, there is a treatment culture that has deep roots. The culture took hold in large part because of a landmark lawsuit filed in the early 1970s, and because for thirty years, the agency had two remarkable, forward-thinking directors. Go back further into Texas history and it becomes clear that the same frontier spirit that produced the harshest prison system in America also produced the TYC. The same cowboy who was deadly with a Walker Colt prided himself on being a gentleman around women, loving and playful around children, and a neighbor always willing to lend a hand. At its best, the cowboy myth is an expression of the idea that the strongest man is also the kindest. That ethic lives on in the TYC, where Butch Held, the State School superintendent, at times sounds more like an elementary school teacher than a warden.

"We're here to take care of kids," Held is fond of saying. "This is all about taking care of kids." He pauses for a moment and a small grin appears, then he adds, "And they don't want us to."

Held and the TYC are an anachronism early in the millennium. The first juvenile court was established in Chicago, in 1899, and was quickly followed by the creation of similar courts in every state in the country. They represent something of a landmark in human history. For the first time, a court was created not to punish; it was designed to rehabilitate. A century later, during the 1980s and 1990s, legislators in state after state were hard at work demolishing the juvenile justice system with wrecking balls, as if the courts were relics of a bygone era. The most important force driving the demolition was the violent crime wave among juveniles between 1984 and 1994. The spike occurred just as cable and the Internet were wiring the world. Images of unrepentant, tattooed young killers snarling for the camera came pouring into living rooms. It didn't matter if the crimes they were accused of committing happened in London, England, or a few miles away. These were not the "wayward youth" the juvenile court had been founded to reform. No stern but kindly juvenile court judge could turn these drug-addled, crazy killers around.

Politicians, with their acutely sensitive antennae, picked up on the fear. In states across the country, they rose to condemn the juvenile courts for coddling young criminals. "Teenage superpredators" were old enough to know the difference between right and wrong. Spending tax dollars on treatment programs was throwing good money after bad. We needed new laws to ensure that juveniles who commited adult crimes would do "adult time" in prison.

By the mid-1990s, the violent crime rate among juveniles was plummeting as fast as it had risen. Between 1994 and 2000, arrests for murder dropped 68 percent; robbery dropped 51 percent. In the year 2000, murder and robbery arrest rates among juveniles reached their lowest levels in twenty years. Criminologists attribute the declines to a strong economy; a market for hard drugs that was finally beginning to subside; a return to community policing in urban areas; organized efforts to keep guns out of the hands of juveniles; and community groups stepping in to mediate disputes between rival gangs.

But images of terrifying teenagers had become embedded in the public conscious. If the decline in the juvenile crime rate was noted at all it was usually by a prosecutor, who awarded credit for safer streets to the tough new sentencing laws. And so as the crime rates fell, state after state kept passing laws that sent more youth at younger ages directly into the adult criminal system.

The truth is, in most states the juvenile justice system deserved the wrecking ball. With a few exceptions, most institutions incarcerating juveniles do not rehabilitate. Indeed, they are not that much different from adult prisons. At best, they are holding tanks; at worst, they are finishing schools for career criminals.

"The harsh prisons that tough-on-crime types want are actually the easiest places to do time," says Stan DeGerolami, a former State School superintendent. "Putting kids in a prison, locking them away in a cell, that is easy time. All they have to do is sit there and feel sorry for themselves and convince themselves they have been wronged.

"Giddings looks nice on the outside. Inside, it is the toughest prison in Texas. Kids do hard time here. They have to face themselves. They have to deal with the events that put them here. They have to examine what they did and take responsibility for it. Kids who go through that do not go out and reoffend. That needs to be screamed out loud: they do not re-offend.

"The bottom line is public safety, and I can tell you, I'd much rather have a kid who has been through the programs at Giddings move in next to me than I would a kid who was just released from prison and is coming out meaner, angrier, and dumber than he went in."

Youth authorities in states around the country admit to recidivism rates over 60 percent. In fact, they are higher. In July 2004, the California Youth Authority ran recidivism rates for parolees from 1988 to 2001. Within three years of their release, 74 percent of all parolees had been re-arrested.

Treatment in the California Youth Authority is all but nonexistent. Texas puts kids through intense treatment programs, and those programs produce results. A three-year study that concluded in 2004 tracked graduates of the Capital Offenders program. After thirty-six months on parole, only 10 percent had been rearrested for a violent offense. Only 3 percent were rearrested for violent crimes in the year following their release.

These results cannot be attributed solely to COG, as the Capital Offenders group is called on campus. COG is like college; the young men in this room have been preparing for this moment for two, three, and four years. They are the products of the overall treatment system called re-socialization.

Resocialization is based on the idea that human beings, even those who may have committed the most inhumane crimes, are profoundly social creatures. Giddings is like a giant web where young offenders live under watchful eyes twenty-four hours a day. Every part of the school connects—the cottages, the therapy sessions, the high school, the vocational programs, the football team. Every behavior is "checked and confronted." If a youth talks back to the school librarian, his football coach hears about it. If two boys come close to blows in the dorm, they are separated and everyone grabs a chair and forms a circle and tries to figure out who did what to whom, and why.

To make it into Capital Offenders, a student has to have spent years in the general population, learning things he did not learn in his family of origin. How to communicate with words rather than with fists, a knife, or a gun; how to accept criticism rather than flare in anger; how to develop an introspection that will give him a split second to consider before reacting. The students have all reached at least phase two in the four-phase system. (Staff from all parts of the web—the school, the dorm, the treatment programs—meet once a month to assign a phase.) They must all have maintained this phase for at least six months, meaning that none has gotten into a fight or harassed a teacher or done anything that would cause him to slide in the rankings. Now that they have made it into this program, they will be watched even more closely. As soon as they were chosen for Capital Offenders, they became role models for the rest of the campus.

The eighteen students beginning Capital Offenders this particular autumn know they have a very good chance of leaving their criminal selves behind and living a productive life if they make it through the six-month program. But low recidivism rates are not the statistics these young men live and breathe. They get up in the morning and go to bed at night thinking about other numbers.

If a youth makes it through Capital Offenders, the odds that he will get an early release are almost 100 percent. Upon completing the program, youth who have been sentenced to twenty-five, thirty, and forty years have been released on parole, often after spending fewer than three years in the Giddings State School.

But if a student washes out of Capital Offenders, he is likely to find himself back in front of the judge who sentenced him, listening to a TYC official explain why he should be transferred to a state prison. When a youth leaves Giddings for prison, his days as a "student" are over. He becomes a number. And he will serve every day of his twenty-five-, thirty-, or forty-year sentence.

Housing young male and female offenders on the same campus creates endless headaches for the State School staff. The TYC does it so that girls as well as boys can go through the specialized treatment programs located there. Girls go through Capital Offenders, too, and the stakes for

them are the same as for the boys: Do well in COG and you will probably walk through the gate on parole. Fail COG and you will likely go
through the gate in a steel cage in the back of a van, on your way to prison.
And yet, inside the COG bunker, girls conduct themselves in ways that
are quite different from boys. Crime, it turns out, reveals a great deal about
the differences between the sexes.

This book follows a young man and a young woman as they go
through Capital Offenders. It is divided into two parts, "The Boys" and
"The Girls."

Part One

THE BOYS

"LOOKING LIKE PSYCHOPATHS"

"Tell us what you know about Capital Offenders," Kelley asks the group.

Up until this moment, the boys' reactions have been as uniform as their haircuts and clothing. Heads nodded when a yes was required, went sideways when the answer was no. Now, the masks are coming off. The youth with one eye breaks into a slow grin. A boy with peaked features and startling blue eyes in the second row waves his hand in the air. He looks up, surprised to see it there.

"Life Stories, miss. We'll be telling our Life Stories," says a small, somber black youth with large eyes. He inflects the words "Life Stories" in a way that makes it plain they are uppercase. Those two words are always capitalized in the TYC resocialization dialect these young men have learned to speak.

"You can't leave anything out! You go over it and over it until it's all out there in the open," adds a youth with a solid-gold front tooth, the symbol of a successful drug dealer.

"You can't be fronting. No way can you front your way through," declares a powerfully built young man in the first row. He is wearing granny glasses and could pass for a scholar-athlete if his forearms and biceps weren't so heavily gang-tattooed.

"You can't front empathy," agrees a slight, boyish Korean-American. "If it ain't real, you got to get real. You can't be hiding behind no thinking errors."

"Life stories." "Empathy." "Thinking errors." It turns out that human behavior and the programs designed to alter it are inextricably tied to language. The fact that the national debate over delinquency issues rarely, if ever, reaches a level where language is explored is one reason why the more lofty the setting—a mahogany-paneled legislative hearing room in a state capital; a Senate subcommittee room with chandeliers and marble floors in Washington, D.C.—the more ersatz the debate. Frontline treatment specialists in Giddings take little heed of congressional hearings such as "Is Treating Juvenile Offenders Cost-Effective?" The people who actually do the work tend to view splashy hearings as little more than a platform for grandstanding politicians, one-issue zealots, and academics pushing a thesis. On the front lines, that question has been settled: treatment works.

It is one thing to say that about programs in a state institution. Taxpayers are picking up the bills, and the outcomes, no matter how scientifically they are evaluated, remain suspect because state institutions collect their own data and measure their own results. It is quite another when the marketplace says that intense treatment changes the trajectory of troubled teenagers' lives. The best evidence of that is the "emotional-growth boarding schools" that have sprung up west of the Rockies in the last twenty years at a rate that rivals the growth of traditional prep schools in New England in the nineteenth century. These schools cater to teenagers who are so deeply into drugs and self-destructive behavior, their parents are terrified they will not live to turn twenty. The tuition at CEDU, the oldest of the emotional-growth, or "therapeutic," boarding schools (founded in 1967 in Palm Springs, California), is well over $100,000 a year. If the cost is astounding, so are the results. Families that can afford a six-figure annual tuition would not keep enrolling their children in CEDU if they did not see tremendous changes.

CEDU is at one end of the socioeconomic spectrum, Giddings is at the other. And yet the programs they operate are very similar. In both places, teenagers begin by memorizing a language they will eventually internalize. In both schools, the students come close to running the programs themselves.

The information the boys are practically shouting at Kelley did not come only from a manual or a lecture. Much of it came from their peers. They know so much about what is going to happen because after the eighteen boys were selected from the main Giddings population, they were transferred to Cottages 5-A and 5-B, where they moved in with a dozen students who had recently completed Capital Offenders. No introduction presented by a staff member, no matter how eloquent, carries the weight of a COG veteran who says, "Listen up, this is what they gonna have you do."

The eighteen boys in this room have spent the last two to four years immersed in the resocialization program that structures life in the State School. Resocialization is a rethinking of the oldest concept in juvenile justice—rehabilitation—and in some ways, the word is poorly chosen. It assumes that some early socialization occurred in the lives of these boys, and for a majority, that did not happen.

An average, functioning family acts as a crucible where children are socialized, i.e., civilized, meaning they learn to relate to others through the relationships they form with parents and siblings. Most of the boys in this room come from families where the adults were drunk, high, street criminals, or in prison. In their families, "socialization" too often meant getting together to shoot hard drugs.

Giddings is not an attempt to re-create the family. That never works, in institutions, group homes, or foster homes. Kids instinctively rebel— *This is bullshit! You're not my real dad!* Instead, Giddings is a gigantic bell jar where 390 young offenders are under intense observation sixteen hours a day. Over the past few years, these boys have spent countless hours in one kind of a group or another, acquiring skills that were not ingrained in their families of origin.

"Thinking errors" are at the heart of this process. Along with clothing, one of the first things a youth receives upon arriving in a TYC institution is *Changing Course: A Student Workbook for Resocialization*. As soon as he gets his layout down, he is told to turn to Chapter Three and memorize the list of nine thinking errors. They are: deceiving, downplaying, avoiding, blaming, making excuses, jumping to conclusions, acting helpless, overreacting, and feeling special. All of us employ these techniques at one time or another. These kids have used them in a way that has harmed others, and will allow them to keep on harming others, if their thought processes are not confronted and altered.

"Thinking errors are used to justify criminal behavior," says Linda Reyes. "The error is in the justification, not in the fact. A youth can state true facts: I was sexually abused. Therefore, I sexually abused my sister. The thinking error is not in the facts. It is in the justification based on the facts."

Do all newly incarcerated young felons hate memorizing thinking errors? They certainly do. Do they do it by rote, as if they were memorizing words in a foreign language? Of course. Learning a new language is like picking up a tool chest. The real work is learning to use those tools— sitting in a group and stopping a peer in midsentence with, "Hold on, right there. You just used a thinking error. Can you name it?" and then helping him see he is "avoiding" or "downplaying." This is an arduous practice, akin to a young musician learning the scales. It goes on and on and on, day after day. Walk into any cottage after dinner and the boys are likely to be sitting in a circle, conducting a behavior group. Typically, a boy has erupted in anger at a juvenile corrections officer—"Jay-Ko" in the Giddings vernacular—who ordered him to clean up his "PA," or personal area, a small clothes closet that sits at the foot of every bed. Instead of referring the boy to the security unit for being disobedient, the Jay-Ko called a behavior group. The group may spend hours in the circle, trying to help the boy understand why he got angry, and how anger feeds into his offense cycle.

The boys entering Capital Offenders are about to become archaeologists of the self, slowly and methodically sifting through their own lives. Each youth will spend two to three three-and-a-half-hour sessions telling his life story. At first glance, this does not seem daunting. Most of us, in one way or another, are telling one another our life stories all the time. But for these boys, the task is terrifying. They have soaked their systems in drugs and alcohol; shaved their heads and covered their bodies with tattoos; convinced themselves that they are hard, impossible to penetrate; surrendered their identity to a gang—all to hide themselves, from themselves.

When they were little, they were abused. They were defenseless; they were victims. As they got older, they vowed to be strong. Being strong meant inflicting pain. That is what the powerful figures in their lives did to them. Either/or, black or white, the preyed-upon and the predators. What is fascinating is, this "nature, red in tooth and claw" view of reality often butts up against an inner world that is pure fantasy.

The former drug dealer with the gold tooth? His mother was a crack cocaine addict who turned tricks on the corner. In fourth grade, he came out for recess and looked across the street to see his mother climbing into a van with a trick. "No boy should ever have to see his mother doing that," he blurted out one afternoon in a behavior group.

The short Latino in the front row covered with gang tattoos from his ears to his fingernails? Like his father, he has committed a murder. His father was in prison serving a life sentence when his conviction was suddenly overturned on a technicality. A few days after he got out, he found that his wife had taken up with another man while he was behind bars and promptly burned the house down.

A ten-year-old can't deal with a mother who is on the street, working as a prostitute. A twelve-year-old can't handle a father who gets drunk night after night, beats him and his mother, and keeps threatening to burn the house down—again. Sometimes, the only defense is fantasy, and these fantasies are often as delicate as they are elaborate. For years, the Latino gangbanger convinced himself that his dangerous, drug-dealing father was really an undercover agent for the DEA. His dad had infiltrated a gang of Colombians, and as soon as the DEA took them down, his dad was going to abandon the act and use his retirement money to buy his family a home on a hillside in Mexico, overlooking the ocean.

That fantasy is all the boy has left after his father was stabbed to death outside a bar in San Marcos. He cannot imagine living without it, just as he cannot imagine climbing out of the gang shell he has encased himself in. But in Capital Offenders, he will have to face the truth about his father, and the mother who never protected him, and his half dozen criminal uncles. This will require a great leap of faith, for like every boy in this room, he grew up knowing he could trust no one, least of all the adults entrusted with his care.

One word is used more often than any other in Giddings: "empathy."

Everything that happens on campus, from the behavior groups to the football team, is designed to foster empathy. It is ironic that empathy is a word that connotes soft, feminine feelings in "The Free," as the kids call the world outside the fence. Inside the fence, it describes a rigorous, demanding, life-and-death struggle.

"People tend to think that empathy leads to forgiveness, but forgiveness is too easy, way too easy," says Linda Reyes. "Kids say, 'I'm sorry for what I did, I forgive myself, I'm going to move past it.' Empathy is far more difficult. Having empathy means taking responsibility. It means making a choice: the things a youth has done to others will never happen to someone else because of him. In a sense, empathy means being your own father, your own mother."

The boys in this small, square room all ran. It is important to understand that. They stabbed or brutally beat someone, and took off running. They fired shots from a car into a house at the exact moment when every member of the family was home and then the driver floored it and the car fishtailed up the street. In a way, the prison system allows criminals to keep on running because it does not make them confront themselves. And when they come out, they are indeed angrier, meaner, and dumber than when they went in.

"In Giddings, they have to stop running," says Dr. Corinne Alvarez-Sanders, Linda Reyes's successor as the State School's director of clinical services. "Developing empathy holds them accountable in a very agonizing way. What's harder: being forced to look at yourself and what you did, or sitting in a cell day after day?"

Alvarez-Sanders is right. According to studies done by the U.S. Bureau of Justice Statistics, more than 75 percent of youth eighteen and under who are sentenced to terms in state prisons are released before they reach age twenty-two. Ninety-three percent of the population that are sentenced to prison while still in their teens complete their minimum sentences before reaching age twenty-eight.

Since violent young offenders are going to get out, society has to answer several questions: Do we want to try to treat this population before they are released and move in next door? Or do we want to keep sending them back to The Free, hardened and without a future? Without empathy? The answer seems obvious. And yet Texas, which loves its law-and-order image, is one of very few states that has intense, systematic programs designed to alter the lives of violent young offenders.

If empathy has a special meaning inside the fence, so does the word "thug." To the public, all 390 teenagers confined in Giddings State School are thugs—that is why they are there. But ask a veteran Jay-Ko, someone who has spent years working eight-hour shifts in the dorms, and she will search her memory before naming a kid who illustrates "the kind of young man prisons are built to hold," a kid who is "heartless," "cold-blooded," or has "nothing inside but ashes." Staff psychologists quote the *DSM-IV-TR*—the *Diagnostic and Statistical Manual of Mental Disorders*, the bible of the profession—on antisocial personality disorder, but in the end, their definition of "thug" is the same as that of the frontline staff: a true thug is someone who has no capacity for empathy; who will attack and hurt again and again, and regard each assault as a manifestation of how the world works.

"Fronting," or faking empathy, looms large in Giddings, particularly in Capital Offenders. A youth who is smart enough to realize he has no feelings for others is also smart enough to realize an early release depends to a large extent on his ability to demonstrate empathy. If he can't do that, he will try to front.

To get over, he will have to give a great performance, day after grueling day. The audience—his peers and his therapists—is as tough as the one in the workshops at the Lee Strasberg Theatre Institute, where the great method actors learned their craft. They will be watching and wondering and probing to see if the emotions a boy expresses are genuine.

"A kid had better be ready to be authentic in Capital Offenders," says Margie Soto, a veteran therapist. "He can try to front his way through, thinking, 'Oh yeah, I can play along. I can make stuff up and give them what they want and it won't touch me.' He can try, but it catches up with him.

"He can't hide from the group. Day in and day out, he is with the same people, in group and in the residence. The kids get to know what buttons to push, and when to push them. Day in and day out, he gets asked, 'What's going on? What's happening?' Pretty soon, that'll trigger a response that's real. The stories he's made up, the lies he's telling, the junk, the trash, the secrets, it will all come out."

Since Giddings gets "the worst of the worst," it seems logical to assume that a large percentage have full-blown antisocial personality disorders that no program, however intense, can touch. Most kids arrive acting like career criminals—"I did my crime, I just wanna do my time." It is common for a kid in an orange jumpsuit to throw down the list of thinking errors he has been told to memorize and shout, "Fuck this shit, man! Just send me to fucking prison! This is fucking bullshit."

But episodes like that do not mean a youth is a true thug.

"We have to be cautious about ruling out kids in the beginning," says Linda Reyes. "They all come through the gate looking like psychopaths. They're kids, they can develop, they can change."

Since the inception of the Capital Offenders program in 1988, Dr. Reyes, Dr. Alvarez-Sanders, and, currently, Dr. Ann Kelley have been clinical directors. Asked separately and at different times what percentage of the Giddings population they would classify as true psychopaths, each came up with the same figure: between 5 and 6 percent.

"Those who are devoid of empathy are a relatively small part of the Giddings population," Reyes explains. "That means we can work with ninety-five percent of the population. What happens is, they take the first step and begin to explore their feelings. They experience the range and subtlety of emotions. They connect with others. Having done that, they can no longer live in an antisocial world where everything is black and white and there is no concept of the other."

Back in the Capital Offenders bunker, a slight youth who shot his best friend to death has been waving his hand in the air. When Kelley finally calls on him, he says, "Crime stories, miss. We'll be telling our crime stories."

"We have to tell everything that we did, right from the beginning," adds a tall youth with a deep voice and heavy eyelids. "We can't be skipping over anything."

After each boy narrates his life story—a process that will take months to get through—a dramatic change comes over the COG bunker. Life stories are about what was done to these boys; the next step—crime stories—will be about what they did to others. A therapist will drape an arm around a boy and stroke his head when he breaks down and sobs while telling his life story. When he tells his crime story, that same therapist turns very tough. She will go after him, and stay after him, until he faces the horrors he has inflicted.

A tall youth with a narrow face and deep-set, penetrating black eyes stands up, tucks his sweatshirt into his elastic-band prison pants, sits down, and raises his hand. His name is Ronnie and he was part of a gang that did a home invasion and assaulted an elderly couple. They ended up kidnapping the couple, intending to drain their checking account. If the elderly gentleman had not escaped, Ronnie would have killed him.

"We're supposed to be telling everything about ourselves in here. Well, what if we tell things about our parents and they're not exactly what you'd call 'prosocial' types?" Ronnie asks. "What if we tell things that could get them locked up?"

"Thank you, thank you for asking," Kelley replies.

"And what about our own selves?" Ronnie interjects before Kelley can continue. "Know what I'm saying? What if we get into things we maybe did that maybe haven't come to light? What if we tell things we can be arrested for?"

"Let's go through this carefully, so we all know where we stand," Kelley says slowly.

Kelley outlines the multiple roles therapists play in a correctional institution. They are not just caretakers, helping damaged youth put their psyches together. They are also evaluators who have to decide if a boy is on his way to becoming someone who can live in society, or if he is a manipulator trying to front his way through and is likely to commit a serious offense if released.

Therapists are also mandated reporters. If they discover a boy is planning to assault someone, or planning to hurt himself, or actively planning to escape, they are duty-bound to stop it.

"If you were abused as a child and the perpetrator is endangering another child, we have to report that. Is that understood?" Kelley asks.

The boys are listening too closely even to nod.

"A lot of the things you did, you didn't get caught for," Kelley continues. "Part of Capital Offenders is accepting responsibility. We want you to tell us what you have done. We want you to be honest."

Kelley goes on to explain that therapists are required to report crimes that have not come to light. If a boy divulges the exact details of a crime, things like the date, time, location, and the names of accomplices, the therapists are required to report it. But Kelley also stresses that uncovering and reporting crimes is not what COG is about. This means the boys and the therapists will walk a fine line. Tell the truth about what you did, but not in such detail that a therapist feels compelled to call the cops back in your hometown.

No doubt inventorying their criminal careers, the young men think this through in silence. Kelley waits and then asks, "What have you heard about role plays?"

A Latino sitting in the front row waves his hand back and forth, begging to be called on. Kelley does and he breaks into a huge, infectious grin.

"Miss, I hear role plays are real scary. Like, if you got whupped as a kid with a belt, miss? They, like, pretend to hit you with a belt."

Kelley's eyes search the group until they land on a powerfully built African-American wearing standard-issue TYC glasses with huge black plastic frames.

"Josh, you were in the last group," Kelley says. "What can you tell us about role plays?"

Most of these young men were born into families where Chaos, the most primitive god of all, reigned supreme. But they also share at least one piece of good luck: they committed their crimes in Texas. Josh may be the luckiest of all.

There is a mechanism in the sentences these young men are serving that puts the decisions about a youth's future in his hands, and in the hands of the professionals who know him best, the treatment staff at Giddings. If a boy washes out of Capital Offenders, he will almost surely be transferred from Giddings to the Texas Department of Criminal Justice, the adult prison system. During the previous Capital Offenders group, Josh became so incensed at a peer he thought was "withholding"— refusing to reveal the truth—he punched him in the face during a break.

He was, of course, immediately removed from the group and taken to the security unit, where a hearing was held. Josh was placed in a behavior management program, meaning he ate, slept, and went to school in the security unit. Meanwhile, Giddings officials were trying to decide what to do with him.

They contemplated filing assault charges and starting the machinery that would send Josh to prison, where he would spend the next twenty-five years. Finally, they decided that after thirty days in the security unit, Josh could come back to the general population on phase zero, starting all over again in an orange jumpsuit. Last year, Josh was the best player on the football team. This year, because of the punch he threw, he is not eligible to play. It took Josh six months of near-flawless behavior to work his way back up to phase three and join the next Capital Offenders group in this room.

"A role play is an experience that's out of this world," Josh says, a sense of wonder in his voice. "One moment, you are in the room. The next moment, you are back there as a kid. You're really there!"

"Role plays are about connecting thoughts with feelings," Kelley comments. "A lot of you haven't let yourselves feel. That's dangerous. If you can't feel for yourself, you won't feel for anybody else. You'll go out there and reoffend."

Any therapist who specializes in working with troubled adolescents knows that there is no one best way to reach them, no silver bullet that will hit a youth between the eyes and turn his life around. The best programs are eclectic and pragmatic, trying out approaches borrowed from sociology, psychology, and biochemistry, using them all, betting hunches, hoping to get lucky, seeing what works. This is especially true of Capital Offenders.

When Linda Reyes arrived in Giddings in the late 1980s, how a youth behaved while incarcerated did not count for much. If he did not commit a serious assault on a staff member or another youth, the TYC had to release him the day he turned twenty-one, no matter how serious his crime or how likely the State School staff thought he was to reoffend. As Giddings began to fill up with young murderers in the late eighties, Reyes scrambled to create a program that would somehow lower the risk that violent youth would turn back to violence after they were released. The program had to be high impact, and the impact had to happen fast. Many were nearing their twenty-first birthdays.

"Imagine the feeling, listening to a young murderer describe his crimes, asking him, 'You did what, how many times?' and trying to not let anything show on your face," Reyes recalls. "You're thinking, This kid will be back on the streets in a year or two if he behaves. We don't have the luxury to do talk therapy for a year or two. These kids are going to get out."

Reyes knows that in order to survive the trauma of his childhood, a youth begins to think like a warrior, equating being stoic with being strong; being hard, closed off from yourself, with being a man. Two feelings predominate: anger and the drive for power.

"Listening to their stories, I saw a lack of empathy in these kids," Reyes recalls. "They were full of anger, hostility, aggression, resentment, and they refused to accept responsibility. The more stories I heard, the more that empathy seemed to be the critical thing. Empathy keeps you from doing something that might harm someone. We had to find a way to build empathy."

Reyes hit upon the idea of having youth reenact the key events in their lives. Drama, she thought, might be a way for them to reach back and relive events. Reenacting key scenes in their lives in a setting that is safe gives them a chance to experience the emotions they have kept walled off inside. Drama is a way to break through that "I'm tough, nothing touches me" shield they erect. If they can fully experience the events that have shaped them, they will, in effect, begin to discover their own humanity.

"When victimizers numb their feelings, it is a global shutdown of emotion," Reyes says. "You can't choose which feelings to shut down; if you shut down, you shut down everything. Psychodrama is one of the quickest ways to get a youth back in touch with his emotions. Once he has done that, he can go on to explore the forces that led to incarceration."

For these reasons, at the end of every life story and every crime story, the COG bunker turns into a stage as bare as the ancient Greeks used. The boys and their therapists become actors. While the boy who has just finished his narrative slumps in a corner, the group huddles with the therapists in an opposite corner or out in the hall, where they choose the incidents to reenact, assign roles, create dialogue. The acting in the makeshift dramas is usually stilted in the beginning, but quickly becomes very real. The most minimal presentation can convince a boy his past is unfolding before his eyes. As Josh said, "You're really there!"

There are two role plays at the end of every crime story. In the first, the boy plays himself, reenacting his crime exactly as it happened. In the second, an exercise in empathy that can be terrifying, the boy plays his own victim.

Kelley explains that taking part in a role play is going to be difficult. You are going to be asked to play an abusive father, and you may have a father who beat you, she says. You are going to be asked to reenact a murder, and you may be responsible for taking someone's life. Don't try to back out if you are feeling overwhelmed and think you can't do it. Tell yourself, This is for my peer. I'm doing it to help him.

Kelley pauses for a moment and focuses on the tattoos on the arms of the young man wearing granny glasses in the front row.

"How many of you are gang involved right now?" she inquires.

Gang activity is confronted from the day a youth enters the State School. So that they will get beyond their gang identities and learn to deal with one another as individuals, youth from rival gangs are intentionally placed in the same dorm. To their astonishment, rival gang members often end up as best friends. Exploring why a youth joined a gang and put his future in jeopardy is a big part of Capital Offenders.

One hand goes up slowly; then two, three, four. Now that it's safe, another four raise their hands.

"You wouldn't mark up your body if you didn't have a lot of affection for your gang," Kelley says. "We expect you to get in there and work on that. But let me warn you: if we find you are involved in gang-related incidents, there will be immediate consequences. Gang involvement will not be tolerated."

Kelley asks the therapists if they have anything to add; all six shake their heads no. They already know the boys well, having spent the past six weeks putting the group together. They've assessed personalities and

mixed gang affiliations. They've balanced ages and races; seriousness of offenses and sentence lengths; time served with release dates. They took the
boys on a "trust walk," an exercise in which a blindfolded boy must rely
on another boy, often the very person he has identified as trusting the
least—the person he thinks is most likely to hurt him. A trust walk forces
the boys to face those fears and makes them begin to rely upon one another. It also gives the psychologists a peek at the dynamics of the group,
an insight into how the boys will interact when the work begins.

The psychologists have divided the eighteen boys into two groups of
nine—nine being the maximum number for therapy this rigorous. Each
group will have a Ph.D. psychologist, an experienced therapist, and an intern therapist. There is a husband-and-wife team among the therapists,
Frank and Margie Soto. Frank will be in Capital Offenders Group A,
Margie in Capital Offenders Group B. They have been working at Giddings in various positions for seventeen years and are Capital Offenders
veterans, but they are nervous, as they always are when a new group is
starting.

It is not so much the physical danger, although that concern is always
present. It is more the realization that for the next six months or more,
they are going to be sharing their lives with kids who have been through
hell and gone on to inflict hell on others. It is knowing that every night,
they will climb into the cab of their Ford pickup and drive home, physically and emotionally spent.

Linda Reyes knows all about that. After she developed Capital Offenders and worked in Giddings for seven years, Reyes was promoted to
the TYC main office in Austin, where she is now the deputy executive director, the agency's number two position, a job that does not require her
to get into a bunker with eight or nine murderers. Reyes loved the work
she did at Giddings; but after so many years, she was exhausted.

"I felt like I was descending into hell to save their souls," Reyes says.
"The bodies begin to stack up in the psyche. After a while, there isn't any
more room."

Kelley warns the boys that Capital Offenders gets off to a running
start. She tells them that each nine-member group will be meeting in the

cottage that very evening to decide who will be the first to tell his life story.

"Think about it before you volunteer," she cautions. "It isn't going to be as easy as you might think."

Capital Offenders typically gets off to a rocky start. A boy who volunteers to go early usually has a macho "What's the big deal? I can do this" attitude. He begins his narrative; the group and the therapists consider it sketchy and start to probe, and suddenly, the boy finds himself up against events he has spent years trying to forget. He falters, halts, starts again, falters, and finally stops. The therapists keep jump-starting him, all the while warning the group, "See, it isn't easy. When it is your turn, you better be ready."

Ronnie, the boy who kidnapped the elderly couple, is wondering about volunteering to go first. When he went out for football, it was the first time he had participated in an organized activity other than a drive-by shooting. The first day of practice, he put his shoulder pads on backward. Now, he is a team leader and is learning how good it feels to accomplish something. He is thinking that if he goes first, he will get the same feeling in Capital Offenders. But that isn't the main reason why he is considering going first.

"I want to talk about all the shit that's happened in my life," Ronnie says. "I just really want to get it all out there. I've gotten really tired, dragging it around."

2.

"I WANT TO RUN AND
GET A KNIFE"

As things turned out, Ronnie was not the first to tell his life story. The Capital Offenders Group A treatment staff made an obvious choice, opting to begin with Johnnie, the Korean-American. Johnnie is something of a mascot for the group, small-boned and sweet-natured with a disarming cuddliness that is rare among teenage boys, especially those who are incarcerated. The boys had Johnnie pegged as a victim, someone hurt so many times in his childhood he finally lashed back. And so they listened with wide eyes and, occasionally, dropped jaws as Johnnie described the abuse he had heaped on his grandparents.

Johnnie's grandparents lived in Mineral Wells, a town of seventeen thousand in the Hill Country due west of Ft. Worth. They were unable to have children—the fertility procedures available today were still in the experimental stage in the mid-1960s. After exploring different possibilities, Johnnie's grandparents decided to create an instant family by adopting twin, two-month-old sisters from Korea. Adopted children can go through a profound crisis, no matter how loving their adoptive parents. Emotional-growth schools like CEDU are full of teenagers whose adoptive parents could not have been more attentive, and yet when they reached their teens the children spun out of control and became dangerously self-destructive. Inside, the adopted child is telling herself, "Sure, they love me, but I must not be worth anything because my real parents didn't want me," or, "Sure, they love me, but this isn't really where I belong." A lot of other things must have gone wrong for the twin sisters in Mineral Wells, because in their early teens they turned into party girls, eventually evolving into cocaine addicts and, finally, high-price call girls.

Johnnie was three years old the evening his mother dropped him off at his grandparents', promising to be there to pick him up first thing the next morning. She disappeared into the Dallas–Ft. Worth metroplex. Johnnie's grandparents hired a private detective to track her down and deliver a simple message: Please call home. She never did.

For this, Johnnie never forgave—his grandparents. Every day, over and over again, he asked, "When's my mom gonna come back?" Every day, he got the same answer: "We don't know, Johnnie. But we love you, Johnnie." He hated them for that. His grandparents were old and sick and smelly, easy to hate. His mother was a beautiful lady with a big smile, holding Johnnie on her lap in the picture he kept next to the radio by his bed. Johnnie couldn't hate her. Johnnie wanted her to come back and be his mom.

When Johnnie started school, he quickly established himself as the perfect target. He was the smallest kid in class, the only Asian, and it was easy to make him cry. "They called me Chink," Johnnie told the group. "They beat me up." Five mornings a week, he hid under the covers and squeezed his eyes shut with all his might. When his grandmother tried to get him up, he kicked her black and blue. His grandfather had to come in and jerk him out of bed by the ankles and fight him into his clothes.

"They never asked why I didn't want to go to school and I never told them," Johnnie said. "When I asked where my mom was at, they had no answer. I was scared that if I told them what was happening at school, they wouldn't have an answer for that, either."

As Johnnie got older, his rage at his grandparents and his desperate need to be accepted kept growing. Johnnie had some friends over one afternoon and they got rowdy around his grandfather's pool table, undercutting balls to arc them off the felt. Johnnie's grandmother came in and told them to stop and he threw a pool ball at her head, as hard as he could. As the other boys rushed for the front door, Johnnie went after his grandmother. She had emphysema and got around in an electric cart with an oxygen tank strapped to the back. Johnnie stood on her oxygen tube and stayed there until she was gasping for breath. Another time, he bit holes in the tube.

By his early teens, Johnnie was the perfect gang wannabe. In other words, the perfect chump. Johnnie did anything gang members told him to do and took all the shit they could hand out and it didn't matter because they let him hang out with them. His grandfather was in a hospice dying of cancer the night two gang members ordered Johnnie to steal his car. Johnnie went right out and did it. When he got back, the two guys piled in and told him they were going to do a drive-by. Johnnie was thrilled. They trusted him, they were even letting him drive.

The shooter emptied a nine-millimeter into a party on the lawn of a rival gang member's house, hitting a twenty-year-old in the head, killing him instantly. The victim was a college student, a youth from the neighborhood who was not gang-affiliated. Three days after it happened, Johnnie's grandfather died.

The boys going through Capital Offenders are required to record their impressions of each session in a journal. They turn their entries in to the therapists at the beginning of each session. The therapists read them for content, not style, and return them at the end of the following session. Johnnie's final three-and-a-half-hour session ended with role plays of two scenes from his life story. After the scenes were enacted, the boys sat on the floor, their backs against the walls.

It is at this point that the boys are asked to express the thoughts they have been recording in their journals. When each boy has had his say, the therapists take their turns. This final round is called "feedback." As with so much else in Giddings, feedback is a measure of empathy.

The therapists listened carefully, gauging the impact Johnnie's story had on each boy, and were particularly impressed with the quality of Tran's insights. You thought of yourself as a victim, Tran told Johnnie in eloquent, if choppy, English. Your mother left you and that wasn't fair. The other kids beat you up and that wasn't fair. You wanted to be in a gang so bad because you wanted to feel safe and strong. Other people would be afraid to mess with you. You wouldn't be a victim no more. But the gang didn't care about you. They had you get your grandfather's car because it was easier than stealing one. You are their victim, Johnnie.

The therapists decided the lone Vietnamese in the group was ready, and Tran went next.

Seven of the nine boys in Capital Offenders Group A have been abused in ways that seem unimaginable until you grow familiar with this population. They have been living alone with the thought that no one has ever been hurt as badly as they have. When they heard Tran's story, they realized that not only were they not alone, someone else had had it even worse than they had.

Tran was five the night he heard his aunt screaming and rushed out of bed and into the kitchen to see his uncle knocking her around, a moment Tran recalled with startling clarity.

"My aunt is on the floor. She says, 'Why are you doing this?' My uncle says, 'I'm the man of the house! I do what I want! I can go out, I can drink! I don't give a fuck!' "

"What did it feel like, standing there, watching?" asked Frank Soto.

"Like chicken skin," Tran replied. "Like when you walk in a cold place. Goose bumps."

"I feel like I want to whup him but I'm too small!" Tran wailed. "If I try to tackle him, he gonna beat me up! I have to stand there and watch my aunt get beat up! I start to cry. He sees me and runs over and kicks me in the hip, boom! I stumble forward, he smacks me in the head, pow! I'm confused. Why did he hit me? He shoves me into a corner, he pushes down on my shoulders, makes me kneel on a rice mat. He says, 'You gonna stay here two or three hours! If you move, I'll put you on your knees four or five hours!' I stay there and try to hold everything in. I'm too scared to get up. I get up, he gonna run over and kick my little bitch ass again!"

After that night, Tran's uncle chained him to a table every morning, leaving him alone in the empty house until late afternoon, when he'd return and unlock the chains. The first thing he did was kick Tran because there was always a pool of urine on the floor. As he told his story, Tran kept referring to "my chain," a description Dr. Sherry Whatley found appalling.

"Your chain, Tran, your chain?" Whatley inquired. "A dog has a chain, not a human being!"

Tran was trying so hard to stanch his tears, his body was quivering. Frank Soto quietly asked him which boy in the group he was closest to. Tran thought for a moment and then named Dwayne, a tall, taciturn youth sitting beside him. Dwayne rocked back in surprise when Tran made his choice.

"Dwayne asks if I'm okay, if I'm doing all right. Dwayne makes me feel safe," Tran told the group.

"Would it be okay if Dwayne moves his chair closer to you? If he put his arm around you?" Soto asked.

The idea terrified Tran.

"No! I'm fucked-up! My life's fucked-up!" Tran yelled. "I didn't have nothing but that wall, man! When I was chained up, that wall was my only friend! I built my own wall, man! So thick, nobody comes around! Don't come to me now with that! I don't deserve it!"

"Why don't you think you deserve it, Tran?" asked Jackie Urbach, the intern therapist.

"My mother should have come in for me; my father should have been there. It never happened, so I don't deserve it! All my life, nobody ever came up to me and said, 'How you doin', baby?' Nobody ever done that for me!"

When Tran finally allowed Dwayne to put an arm around him, Tran let himself cry and his body convulsed as he sobbed. Dwayne was one of the most closed members of the group, never contributing unless a therapist asked him to, and even then the therapists had to labor to extricate what Dwayne was thinking. During Tran's feedback round, Dwayne was more animated than anyone had ever seen him, going on about how good it felt to help his friend. Seeing an opening, the therapists decided Dwayne would go next.

Dwayne told his life story, followed by Tim, and then Antonio, who spent three solid sessions telling his. By the time Antonio finished, the group had coalesced. They were about to stack the chairs at the end of Antonio's feedback round when Frank Soto focused on Ronnie.

"You'll go next," Soto said. "Be ready."

Ronnie nodded, solemn as a marine whose CO has just ordered him to undertake a dangerous mission.

On Wednesdays and Fridays, the days Capital Offenders does not meet, the boys have "core group" with their caseworker. Caseworkers serve as a bridge between the JCOs, the frontline dorm staff, and the Capital Offenders therapists. Caseworkers shepherd students through the State School and prepare them to return to The Free. In a core group, a caseworker helps the boys thrash through emotions that surfaced in the last Capital Offenders group and prepares them for the next meeting.

During the session that followed Antonio's life story, Daryl Liedecke, the caseworker running the group, asked Ronnie if he felt ready. Ronnie said he didn't know. When Liedecke pressed him, Ronnie mumbled, "I don't want to tell it, but I know it has to be done."

"Why don't you want to tell it?" Liedecke asked.

"There's things I don't want to see," Ronnie answered.

"Are you ready to look at them?" Liedecke asked.

Ronnie shrugged and retreated into monosyllables, finally letting his head hang between his legs and nodding yes and then no. He stayed shut down through the weekend, speaking to no one but his mother, who called Sunday afternoon. On Monday, Liedecke told the Capital Offenders therapists that Ronnie was either gearing up to tell his story or burrowing so far down in a hole, it would take days to dig him out.

It is cold, windy, and wet the morning Ronnie begins his life story. Capital Offenders starts at 7:30 A.M. and the therapists always spend a half hour together before it begins, so it is pitch-black when Frank and Margie Soto arrive. Dr. Sherry Whatley's big gray Buick pulls into the parking lot moments later, followed by Jackie Urbach's car. The therapists hurry across the wind-whipped grounds to the social services building, where they pause inside the door to shake off the damp cold. They spend a few minutes in their offices checking e-mail and reading the overnight report, and then Urbach and Frank Soto walk down the long hallway to Whatley's corner office.

"I hope Ronnie is warmed up; it's too cold to have to jump-start him," Soto jokes as he sinks into a large Naugahyde chair. With his lean build, thick black hair, and mustache as big as his smile, Soto cuts a handsome figure. He usually wears Wranglers, cowboy shirts with bright blocks of color, and boots—his favorite pair are fashioned from soft, supple anteater.

"I can't get warm, either!" Whatley agrees, rubbing her upper arms. She is sitting at her desk, degrees from several Texas universities on the wall behind her, leafing through Ronnie's case file, which must be eight inches thick. The childhood of an average youth is recorded in a family album full of snapshots that capture birthdays, Christmases, picnics, and vacations. By the time a boy like Ronnie lands in Giddings, he has put together a case file that is the exact opposite of a family album. Every antisocial event that comes to the attention of the authorities is recorded in these pages.

When they were putting the Capital Offenders groups together, the therapists read through every boy's file. Now, before each group, they review the file of the boy who is telling his story and discuss strategy. Whatley reads the basics aloud—where Ronnie was born, who raised him, how far he got in school, that he was poly-drug-addicted at the time of his arrest, as are a vast majority of State School youth. Whatley notes the significant findings in the psychological evaluations that were performed in the Marlin Orientation and Assessment Unit, the TYC intake center. He was abused as a child, but a TYC psychologist in Marlin ruled out post-traumatic stress disorder, a condition that afflicts many students in Giddings. Whatley breezes past his psychological diagnosis—conduct disorder—because the term is basically clinical jargon for heavy-duty juvenile delinquency, and because the State School is as much a destination for teenagers with this diagnosis as Austin, fifty miles to the east, is for aspiring musicians.

"There's a lot of denial here," Whatley points out. "He blames his three co-actors for his offense. And he says he wouldn't have done it if he wasn't messed up on fry."

The criminal argot is a strange blend of street language and law enforcement terms. Cops, prosecutors, and therapists use words like "perpetrators" and "perps" and just as often use "actors" and "co-actors," terms favored by the actors themselves, the criminals. "Fry" is a street term for marijuana that has been soaked in embalming fluid. Embalming fluid, or "water," as it is called on the street, contains PCP and turns marijuana into a powerful hallucinogen.

"I wonder if he'll start and then go to denial?" Jackie Urbach muses.

Soto calls Cottage 5-A and asks the JCO to have the boys ready, then leaves to collect them. Urbach and Whatley gather their coats and the boys' journals and go back outside, hugging the cafeteria wall to avoid the wind and saying little, saving their energy for the group.

The boys file into the square group room, arrange the chairs in a circle, and sit down. Whatley waits for them to settle in before going through the bookkeeping that always begins a group. How did the weekend go? Anything happen in the cottage that we need to talk about? Has everyone turned in a journal entry?

Whatley has large, expressive brown eyes set in a round face, light brown hair, and pale skin, and wears sweaters over print dresses. She has a big, warm smile and looks like a schoolteacher who sings in a church choir (she does). The boys have typed her a "Goody Two-shoes," something she knows and uses to her advantage. Sometimes, she plays to type, embodying the voice of society, letting the boys know what a housewife in a mall is thinking when she comes upon a pack of gangbangers. Other times, she plays against her stereotype, employing street terms in an easy, confident way or discussing a sex act in a quiet, analytical voice. Her eyes seem to dance as they move around the circle, hovering over each youth before landing on Ronnie. Whatley studies him for a moment before her face blossoms into a smile. Slowly, she nods her head. This is the moment group really begins.

"How you feeling, Ronnie?"

Ronnie nods. He's okay.

"You feeling ready?" Whatley asks.

Ronnie nods again.

"What's the earliest thing you remember?"

Physically, Ronnie resembles the descendant of poor dirt farmers, one of those pinched, angular figures in a Dorothea Lange photograph. He is tall and gaunt-looking, with a narrow face and a broad forehead. His eyes are black, set deep under a sloping forehead. At seventeen, his hairline is already receding and his skin is pockmarked, but put him in a cowboy hat and he'd be good-looking in a rough-and-tumble way. Ronnie takes a deep breath and stares at the carpet.

"My mom abandoned me and my little brother to my grandparents when I was six."

There is hurt in his deep, quiet monotone. This is going to cost Ronnie something, but he is going to throw himself into his life story the way he is learning to throw his body at opposing linemen on the football field.

"Where did this happen?" Frank Soto asks.

"In Oklahoma. My mom was nineteen when I was born, my dad was twenty. He's white, she's Hispanic. That was part of the problem, right there."

Ronnie was born in Frederick, a town in southwest Oklahoma, fifteen miles north of the Red River, which forms the border with Texas. Frederick is the Tillman County seat. Its population is 4,636; Tillman County has a population of 9,419, down 965 from the 1990 census. Three of those who left were Ronnie, his mother, and his little brother.

Frederick is in the Great Plains, short-grass country where they raise cattle, cotton, and wheat. People out there seem to develop a special love for their towns, perhaps because they are small and isolated. Like many other towns across Oklahoma, Frederick went through a "de-aluminizing" period in the 1990s, stripping off the siding that was put up in the 1950s to protect buildings against the hard winds. The town fathers wanted to return the town to the way it looked in the first half of the twentieth century, giving it a more "authentic" feel.

Frederick has broad, clean streets and neat frame houses—and a drug subculture. Sometime during the 1960s, methamphetamine arrived in the Great Plains, probably riding in on a motorcycle. Meth took up residence, right next to the traditional mind-bender, "shine," or "white lightning." In "Choctaw Bingo," singer-songwriter James McMurtry records the connection:

Uncle Slaton . . . cooks that crystal meth cuz his shine don't sell
you know he likes that money, he don't mind the smell

Griffin, Ronnie's father, was a frame carpenter who moonlighted as a carpet installer. In high school a lot of kids did crank, now and then. Griff never did. After they graduated some of his friends became long-distance truckers and sheetrockers and turned into regular users, doing lines the way a guy with a desk job drinks coffee. That was certainly how things were on the carpet crew. It is no fun going into a bank a few minutes after it closes at 5 P.M., knowing your boss has signed a contract that guarantees the place will be recarpeted by the time it opens for business the next morning at nine. But it is fun if you go in all cranked up and concentrate so hard on cutting every curve just right, you look up and are shocked to see rosy-fingered dawn breaking across the plains.

Griff never used. He felt stretched to the limit and was afraid using speed would send him flying through space, like a rubber band when you let go. Griff had a secret. Not a secret, really. Everyone in town knew about it. But no one in town talked about it, at least not with him. Two of his brothers had committed suicide.

Marina was living with a brother and sister-in-law in a small apartment house in downtown Frederick. She was just starting her senior year in high school. Griff had graduated the year before and was living in the apartment upstairs. Marina had a secret, too. That was what drew them to each other, what turned them into a couple.

Both came from huge families; Marina was one of eleven children, Griff one of twelve. His people were dry-land farmers. Marina's father was a Pentecostal minister who had a small congregation. In the pulpit, he led his flock through hail, fire, and brimstone to salvation. At home, he *was* hail, fire, and brimstone.

"My dad was very abusive to my mom," Marina recalled in an interview that took place after Ronnie completed his life story. "He'd throw her to the ground and kick her in the face and head and legs until she bled. I remember once when I was little, he beat her with a stick and left her lying on the floor in a pool of blood.

"The sexual abuse started when I was eleven or twelve."

Marina had nine brothers and a younger sister. The little girls used the bathroom together, and when they did, their father watched. He had bored a hole in the wall and when it was their turn in the bathroom, he went into the bedroom he shared with his wife and pulled up a chair. No one ever spoke of it. Marina and her little sister knew they were not to try to plug the hole with a washrag or a towel. They tried to stay out of the line of sight.

Marina's father began visiting her bed, night after night. She knew it was happening, and yet a part of her didn't know. It was like a dream and when she thought about it later, she could recall only bits and pieces of what had happened. Her mother contributed to this strange feeling that things weren't real. Marina kept telling her what was happening, and she kept saying Marina was lying.

"She'd say, 'No, no, no! He's not doing that! You're making things up!' I thought that there were too many of us for her to bother with me. I started sleeping with my little brothers so my dad wouldn't come around."

When Marina was twelve, thirteen, fourteen, and fifteen, there were times when Dad did "come around." The older she became, the more obsessed her father became. He started following her to school. When the last bell rang and she went out the door, he was parked across the street, watching. She still isn't sure why she did it. Being sexually assaulted over and over again for years had to be the reason, of course. But how creepy it was to be followed by her father, the reverend, had a lot to do with it, too.

"One day, I just decided I wanted to talk to the worker at the school. I told her what was happening and she drove me to the hospital for an examination. We went back to the school and she called my mom. When my mom came into her office, she was crying and she was mad at me. She kept asking me, 'Why are you lying?' "

Later that afternoon, a patrol car stopped in front of Marina's home and two deputy sheriffs politely asked her father to go with them. He spent a night in jail and then he was out. The district attorney had decided it was better for all concerned if this case didn't go before a judge. A daughter testifying against her father, that was the worst thing that could happen to a family. Yes, the tests showed the girl had been penetrated, but who knew, maybe she had a boyfriend she wasn't telling anyone about. Her father was a man of the cloth with a pretty good following, and he was swearing up and down he'd never laid a hand on her, hadn't even kissed her since she became a young lady. Best thing to do was get the girls out of that home, make sure they were safe, and let things follow their course.

Marina and her younger sister were sent to a state home for juvenile girls in Taft, a dusty little hamlet outside Muskogee. It is the kind of institution that, thanks to lawsuits from watchdog organizations, no longer exists. Judges sent girls who had committed violent crimes to the Taft Juvenile Center. Girls who were adjudicated on "status crimes," crimes that can be committed only by a minor, like running away or being beyond the control of their parents, also went to the Taft Center. (And why were they running? If the authorities had looked, they would likely have found the girls were being abused, physically, sexually, or both.) To Taft, they also sent girls like Marina and her sister, who had never been formally charged with anything.

It was horrible. Big and cold, institutional through and through, full of angry, unhappy girls. Marina and her little sister were there two years. When they got out, each girl went to live with an older brother. Their brothers were not willing to pull the girls out of Taft earlier because they thought their sisters had lied about their father, or were angry that Marina had gone to the authorities. If she had told one of them, they could have taken care of it within the family.

"When I left, they closed that book," Marina recalled. "My father started having heart attacks and when I got back, he was on dialysis. Somebody would call and say, 'He's real sick, we need you to come over.' Usually, I wouldn't go. If I did he'd look at me and I'd get feelings and I'd leave. I couldn't be there. Even now, it's still not too good with my mother. I just wish she would talk to me about it. I just wish she'd tell me she knew what was going on but couldn't do anything because he was beating her so bad. I want her to say something. But she won't."

Griff had left his family and moved into his own apartment "to try to get his head on straight." A brother he was especially close to had just committed suicide.

"One brother hung himself in a trailer house, the other brother hung himself from a tree," Marina said. "Griff's people were like hillbillies. They were pretty low-class."

Griff hung out with guys who spent nights racing down red dirt roads that followed section lines, downing beers and firing pistols at empties in the ditch. But he wasn't a testosterone-crazed, crank-snorting animal whose idea of the most intense pleasure life has to offer is a fistfight. Griff was quiet and very polite. Marina was exceptionally pretty, tall and slen-

der with long black hair that curled as it fell down her back, and eyes that
sparkled simply because she was out of Taft and living apart from her father. She had a wide smile, breasts that attracted a man's attention, a slim
waist, and long legs. When she and Griff passed on the apartment steps,
he dropped his eyes and touched his hat and said good morning. When
they finally struck up a conversation, Marina discovered he was someone
she could talk to.

"That meant a lot," Marina recalled. "We weren't doing drugs, neither
of us even smoked. It just felt right, being together. We'd both been
through a lot."

Now, instead of roaming the country roads with his buddies, Griff
took Marina on long rides outside of town, but not before roaming the
side streets and finding a car he could siphon gas from.

The summer after she graduated, Marina worked as a clerk in an
appliance/rental equipment store a block off Main Street. She wore sleeve-
less blouses that left her navel exposed and tight jeans, and the contractors
loved her sweet disposition. They joked among themselves about coming
in just to get their "daily look." Griff did a lot of framing for one of the
larger contractors and on the Fourth of July, he invited them both to a
barbecue at his home. Marina and Griff literally bumped into each other
in the deep end of his swimming pool. Griff proposed and she accepted.

They had a lot of fun together, in the beginning. Griff picked Marina
up after work every day and they went riding or out to dinner. Some
nights, they sat out back and watched a storm come in, thunder booming
and lightning crackling across the sky, as if an army were invading. Marina did not want a church wedding and Griff's parents wouldn't have attended if they had one. They were bigots who hated everything Mexican
except the food at Taco Bell and ignored Marina when Griff brought her
to their home.

One Friday the two left work early and went to the courthouse, where
they filled out the papers for a marriage license. A week later they returned and were married by a justice of the peace. Marina made reserva-
tions in a hotel in Port Aransas on the Gulf. She had always wanted to see
the ocean. But they were exhausted by the time they made it to the
Ft. Worth–Dallas metroplex and Griff checked them into a motel in Ar-

lington, near the Texas Rangers ballpark. They ended up spending the weekend there. They kept promising themselves that one day, they'd jump in the pickup and roll down to the Gulf, but they never did.

When Griff announced he was married, his father said he knew Griff was dumb, but not so dumb he'd go off and marry a Mexican. That hurt, but it also helped weld him to Marina. He had problems with his family, she had problems with hers; they would create a life all their own.

Marina kept her job and Griff was working steady. Then Griff decided he would build a home for Marina and the family they were planning, and the couple bought land on the edge of town from one of his uncles. Griff was completely absorbed in the project. He spent night after night roughing out drawings in a three-ring notebook. He bartered with his buddies for their services. A backhoe team dug the foundation in exchange for a huge barbecue picnic Griff threw on the site. He joked afterward that they drank so much beer, it would have been cheaper just to pay them. Two brothers who ran a masonry business poured the basement. Griff framed a bedroom one of the brothers was adding to his home and they called it even.

Marina and Griff spent every weekend working on the house. Marina got pregnant with Ronnie and quit working. Eighteen months later, Kenny arrived. And with the children problems developed with Griff's mother and father that Marina could not ignore. "They were always butting into our business," Marina recalled. "They'd come over and tell Griff I was raising the kids all wrong. I got to the point where I couldn't take his family telling me this, telling me that. Griff was never abusive, he never hit me. But his mother didn't like the kids and she used to hit them a lot, especially Kenny."

It became clear that Griff would have to decide between his new family and his old family. Marina thought the choice had already been made and was surprised at how miserable Griff was. One Easter Sunday morning, he announced he was going to spend the day with his parents. Marina was upset—she had a ham ready to put in the oven. Griff apologized—relatives were coming from all over the state and he had to be there.

After that, it seemed to Marina that Griff was courting his parents. He stopped by their house almost every day and stayed for longer and longer periods. There was always an excuse—his father was ripping up the old deck out back and needed Griff's help. The Oklahoma Sooners–Oklahoma State Cowboys basketball game went into overtime. Marina found herself wishing Griff were having an affair. If there was another woman, they might have a fight and Griff would come back to her. But who'd ever heard of a guy breaking up with his parents?

One night, Marina waited for Griff until eleven o'clock and then picked up the phone and called his parents. His mother's voice was as icy as the February winds outside. Yes, he's here. No, he wouldn't be coming home tonight, not any night, as far as she could tell. Griff had made up his mind he was going to stay right where he was. He'd be by to pick up some things in the morning, when she wasn't there. Marina stayed in the apartment until the end of the month, when the rent was up, and then did something she absolutely hated doing: she moved back into her parents' home.

"My dad left my mom because his family was prejudiced against Hispanics," Ronnie tells the group. "Actually, I think he had some of that, too, but mostly, it was his family. They put so much pressure on him, he went toward their beliefs. They only lived a few houses from my maternal grandparents, where we went to live, but my brother and I never went to visit. My dad's family didn't want to see us kids because we were mixed."

"How'd you feel when your dad left?" asks an intensely interested Josh, whose alcoholic father had disappeared before he was born, leaving Josh with a massive father problem. As a toddler, Josh would wander up to a stranger and call him Daddy.

"How'd it feel when your dad didn't show you no love?" Johnnie asks when Ronnie does not answer Josh.

"I felt angry about it. He was supposed to be my dad and he wasn't there," Ronnie replies, his voice flat.

"What was it like when he was there?" asks Daniel, yet another youth with a father problem. Daniel is smart and articulate and prides himself on his blunt honesty. He describes his father as "a womanizer. He had a white woman stashed away in an apartment waiting for him when he left my mother." Daniel's father paid next to no attention to him after he moved out.

"My dad would go to work," Ronnie replies. "That's all I remember."

Ronnie's brow has deep furrows and he does not look up, even when replying to a question. It is almost as if he is watching his life story on a television hidden in the carpet and narrating what he sees. Now, it seems that he is seeing the day his mother packed up and left Frederick.

Ronnie was five the morning he woke up and wandered into the kitchen, where his little brother was already in his high chair, eating Cheerios with both hands. Ronnie dug into his own bowl of Cheerios and failed to notice that his grandmother did not say good morning. After a few moments he sensed that something was off and got up and went to the front door, where he spotted his mother in the driveway, loading things into the trunk of their car. Ronnie threw open the screen door and dashed outside.

"What are you doing, Mommy?"

"Putting clothes in the car. I'm going to the Laundromat," his mother replied.

"Can I come, too?" Ronnie asked.

"Sure. I wouldn't go to the Laundromat without my little man."

Marina went into the house and collected Ronnie's little brother. As their grandmother stood behind the screen door watching, Marina strapped the boys into their car seats, got behind the wheel, and backed out of the driveway. Without even glancing in her mother's direction, she drove off. She went through downtown Frederick and kept on going.

"This Laundromat is way far away, isn't it, Mommy?" Ronnie said as they turned onto Highway 183 and headed south toward Texas.

"It's a long, long way, Ronnie," Marina agreed, "and it's going to be a long, long time before we get there. Try to take a nap, okay?"

Marina was, in fact, on her way to Amarillo, to move in with her little sister. It was the only thing she could think to do. She was trapped in a town in the middle of nowhere. Her father was sick, aging rapidly, and mellowing, but she still could not stand to be under the same roof with him. Every guy she met knew Griffin; none of them would ask her out.

Even if she did happen to meet someone who didn't know Griff, he probably wouldn't date her after he found out she had two little boys.

"My sister called and said, 'You're separated and Roberto's in prison, come and stay with me for a while. She had three kids and she'd been through a lot of abuse. Her husband hit her a lot and one time when she left him, he kidnapped her, took her out into the country, threw her down on the road, and raped her right there. She went back to him and they got into a fight and he cut her from the end of an ear halfway across the throat with a knife. They were out one night and he stabbed a man for dancing with her. He went to prison for that."

Marianne lived in a flimsy duplex that was too small for her family and was barely getting by on welfare and food stamps. But to Ronnie, his aunt's crowded apartment was way better than being back in Frederick. He loved chasing his cousins in and out the back door and playing games they made up on the spot. He loved settling into the big brown corduroy couch to watch television and pass a bowl of Trix from one kid to the next. Ronnie kept asking, "Mom, we're not going to go back to Grandma's, are we? We're going to stay here with Aunt Marianne, aren't we, Mom?"

Marina loved living in the barrio in Amarillo. Frederick had always defined reality, and she didn't know how suffocating it was until she escaped.

"I felt like I was related to just about everybody in Frederick," Marina recalled. "I'd never been around so many Spanish people and I was feeling free and single. I got a job as a waitress and I started dating. And then I made the biggest mistake of my life. I met Jimmie."

Jimmie had a cowboy's build, tall—Marina has a weakness for tall men—slim, and narrow-hipped. He had caramel-colored eyes flecked with brown and beautiful teeth that flashed when he smiled. He oiled his black hair and combed it back on the sides and into a big pompadour in front. Jimmie was an air-conditioning mechanic who bragged about being able to fix anything. He kept coming into the restaurant and sitting at a table in Marina's section. One day, he asked if there was a man in her house. When Marina asked why, Jimmie said, "Just curious. If you need anything fixed, let me know. I can fix anything." The next time he came in, Jimmie asked her out.

"We got drunk, really wasted. We went to one last club, one of those big old cowboy places that has a band and a big dance floor and stays open as late as they'll let 'em. We're sitting in a booth and I knew I was really drunk. Jimmie pulled a little bottle out of his pocket, poured something on the back of his hand, and snorted it. I asked him, 'What's that? What is it you're doing?'

" 'You're fixin' to go to work in a few hours. You're going to need something. Give this a little try and see what you think.'

"He poured a line on his hand and I did it. It woke me right up! I said, 'Oh, wow! What was that stuff?'

" 'You like it?' he asked, and this big old smile spread across his face. 'Coke,' Jimmie said. 'It's cocaine.'

"After that, it was nothing but coke. Coke, coke, coke. I was going to college, I wanted to be a registered nurse. I had grants, every two weeks I got a check for five hundred dollars. We used that money to buy drugs. We'd sell some, to get more money to buy more drugs."

Ronnie barely noticed that his mom was going out every night. There was so much to do and she never left until he was in bed and was always there when he woke up. But one morning, his mom wasn't there. He asked Aunt Marianne where his mom was and she said she didn't know. She seemed kind of mad about it. Ronnie went outside and sat down on the concrete slab in front of the door to wait. Finally, just before noon, a car pulled up and his mom got out. Ronnie raced down the sidewalk and wrapped his arms around her legs and wouldn't let go. "Ronnie, Ronnie," she sighed, patting his head. "I'm too tired for this. Let me get a little sleep."

Marina went up to the bedroom she shared with her sons and locked the door. She went out again that night and the next morning, she wasn't there. She didn't come home the next night, or the next. Ronnie was terrified and asked his aunt where his mother was about a hundred times every day. He sat on the slab outside the front door for hours, going back into the house when it became too hot to stay outside, or when his cousins begged him to come in and play. But every time he heard a car pull to the curb, he raced out front.

"I had kids too young, I wanted to have my own time," Marina explained later. "I met Jimmie and thought I'd fallen in love. I wanted to be with him. I felt like my kids were intruding on my relationship. Ronnie would cling to my legs and cry, 'I miss you!' and it didn't matter. It was drugs. I'm not saying Jimmie made me do drugs. I did it because I liked it. It was a way to be who I wanted. I wanted to be in my own little world. I didn't care about nothing. I just wanted my way."

When his mother did come back, Ronnie did not let her out of his sight, clinging to her leg like a baby chimp. Marina had to keep prying him off. Ronnie and Kenny were sleeping on a piece of yellow foam beside their mother's bed. But now, Ronnie wouldn't let his mother sleep alone, and Kenny wouldn't sleep on the floor without his brother, so the boys ended up in their mother's bed, one on either side. If Ronnie felt her move, he threw an arm across her and pressed down with all his strength. Still, there were mornings when he woke up to find she was gone. And now when she left, Marina was staying away for weeks at a time.

"I kept asking my aunt where my mom was and my aunt kept saying, 'She went out to buy you cookies and candy. She'll be back,'" Ronnie says, slowly and carefully. "I'd wait all day and no Mom. The next day, no Mom. The next day, no Mom. Every day I asked my aunt, every day I got the same answer. When my mom finally came back, I raced to her. My first question was, 'Mom, do you love me?' My second was, 'Where's the cookies?' My mom said, 'What cookies?'"

Ronnie's aunt fixed their meals and made sure they took their baths and got to bed. Sometimes, she'd say, "Your mom shouldn't be doing you this way," Or, "It's not right, what your mom is doing. You kids need her here." Ronnie knew Marianne had a temper—he had seen her jerk his cousin up by the arm and slap his face with an open palm until he managed to wiggle and kick free. But he wasn't afraid of her. She had never hit him.

One hot, windy afternoon, Ronnie and his favorite cousin were hugging the shade of the apartment building, playing in Marianne's flower bed. She loved her flowers; they were the only things that were really hers and when she had a free moment, she spent it there. Ronnie and Sammy had seen a TV program about an off-road race that went all the way from Tijuana to the tip of Baja, and they had re-created it in the flower bed, complete with jumps and canyons. They were happily racing their Hot

Wheels when Ronnie looked up and saw terror on his cousin's face. He followed Sammy's gaze to the back porch, where his aunt had appeared, holding a green plastic bag full of garbage. She had one rule and she recited it to the children, over and over: Never, ever play in my flower bed. Quick as a cat, Sammy was on his feet, running for the front of the house. Ronnie stayed where he was, staring up at his aunt. She dropped the garbage bag, stooped to pick up a rope the boys used as a lasso when they were playing cowboy, and descended on him.

"What are you doing in my flowers?" she screamed. "Didn't I tell you, never go in my flowers?"

She struck Ronnie with the rope, across his back, his arms, his bare legs. Ronnie was screaming, as much in shock as in pain.

"Shut up, goddamn you, shut up! The neighbors will hear you, you little shit!" his aunt hissed. She started whipping Ronnie around the mouth, trying to get him to stop screaming. He fended the rope off with his hands and kept shrieking. His aunt picked up a long flower stake and used it to beat Ronnie into submission.

"Quit crying or I'll hit you more!" Marianne warned as she brought the stake down across Ronnie's back. He wanted to stop; he tried hard to get control of himself, but he couldn't and his aunt kept hitting him.

Finally, she jerked the five-year-old to his feet and rushed him into the house and down the hall to the bathroom, where she threw him to the floor. Ronnie's aunt ran a scalding-hot bath, picked up the quivering boy and lifted him over the tub, then dropped him in on his back. Ronnie remembered his screams echoing off the blue tile on the walls around the bathtub, and then he remembered nothing.

"The next thing I knew, it was nighttime and I was in bed, hurting all over. My body was full of abrasions and I was hurting real bad."

A week after the beating, Ronnie's mother finally came home. He raced up the sidewalk to hug her and she looked down and saw the welts, abrasions, and bruises.

"Ronnie! What happened!" Marina asked, dropping to her knees to look him in the eyes.

"Auntie! Auntie beat me up, Mommy! She hit me with a rope and then with a board! Look, look at this here!"

Ronnie pulled down his pants to reveal an ugly blue-red blotch on his hip. Marina glanced at the house and saw her sister standing inside the door. She took Ronnie by the hand and led him up the stairs to the house. Marianne opened the door without a word.

"What happened?" Marina asked when they were inside.

"Oh, you know how it is: Sammy and Ronnie got into it. They went after each other with my garden stakes. Boys will be boys, I guess."

"That's not true, Mommy!" yelled Ronnie. He put everything he had into each word. "We were playing in her flowers and she came out and Sammy ran but I didn't! She beat me with a rope and then she hit me with a board. Just look! Just look at me, Mommy! Look what she did! She's mean and I hate her and I don't want us to live here anymore! When you go, take me with you. Please, Mommy, please!"

"Just look at Sammy," Marianne countered. "He had to have three stitches, right over his eye."

"She's lying!" Ronnie screamed. "Sammy was chasing Hector and he ran into a door! She had to take him to a hospital! You can go to the hospital, Mommy! You can ask the doctor that fixed him! He'll tell you what happened!"

Marianne shrugged. "I had to separate them or they'd have killed each other."

Ronnie pauses and looks up and the group room is still. Finally, Antonio, the hard-core gangbanger, asks, "What'd your mom do?"

"Nothing. My mom believed my aunt," Ronnie replies, his voice heavy with resignation. It is clear his mother refusing to believe him hurts more than the beating from his aunt. He stares at the floor and then finds the thread of his narrative.

"My mom promised she wouldn't leave after that, but that same night, my mom left again, she snuck out. After that, when my mom was there, I wouldn't let myself fall asleep because I knew she would be gone when I woke up. If I fell asleep, she'd get up and get dressed. I'd wake up and race across the room and grab her legs and wouldn't let go. I'd really get a grip on her. I was so terrified of my aunt!"

Marianne must have crossed some kind of internal barrier when she beat up Ronnie. The little boy must have come to represent everything she hated about her big sister, about raising kids, about her own life. After that first beating, she beat her nephew for everything he did wrong, and almost everything Ronnie did was wrong. If he was playing, it was the wrong time to be playing. His aunt hit him. If he was laughing, he was laughing too loud, and she hit him for that. If he didn't eat his potatoes, she beat him.

Ronnie began spending his days wedged between the wall and the big corduroy couch. Sammy and the others jumped on the couch and peered over the back and pleaded with Ronnie to come out and play. Ronnie stayed behind the couch, where it was safe.

Sleep should have been a blessed escape, but it was not. Ronnie kept having the same nightmare, over and over. It was not about his aunt hitting him with a closed fist or striking him across the knees with a wooden baking spoon. In his nightmare, his mother rose from the bed like a beautiful ghost and floated backward, blowing him kisses as she went. She melted through the closed door, and outside in the hallway, Ronnie heard her saying, "Good-bye, little boy. You'll never see your mother again." And then she laughed, and it sounded like chimes, tinkling in the wind.

Wedged between the wall and the couch, Ronnie had all day to think about that dream. He kept asking himself, "Why is she always going?" Finally, he found the answer. And the answer wasn't, I feel alone and scared because my mother keeps leaving me and doesn't protect me from my vicious aunt. It wasn't, It's my mom's fault, she's a lousy mother.

No, Ronnie found the answer where troubled children almost always do. It was him: he was the problem. A child lives at the center of a very small universe. If something is really, really wrong in that universe, the fault has to be his.

"I asked myself, 'Did I do something wrong?' " Ronnie tells the group. "Finally, I decided I must have. I blamed myself."

"But it wasn't your fault, Ronnie," Whatley implores. "You were a little boy! You were innocent!"

Working with a violent adolescent at this stage often entails telling him, over and over again, that it is not his fault. The harm he inflicted later, that is his fault. But he is not responsible for the hurt inflicted on him when he was small and defenseless. Whatley is trying to awaken feelings Ronnie shut down way back when he was living with his aunt.

"Kids learn at a very young age to turn off the hurt, the fear," Whatley explained later. "They shut those feelings down and learn to be hard. They stop feeling anything but anger. It's a survival mechanism. We ask them to go back and relive those experiences so they can track where the anger comes from. So they can get a feel for who they are today. We ask them to go back and experience the very things they've spent their whole lives defending against."

Beatings and the anger they generate are one thing. Abandonment and the guilt it creates are quite another. A little boy like Ronnie lives a kind of secular Calvinism. He is unworthy of his mother's love, therefore he is unworthy of love. His mother doesn't love him, therefore he has no value. Guilt and feelings of worthlessness mix with anger to form a toxic, volatile stew.

A memory is surfacing, and as it does, Ronnie stirs in his seat, crosses his legs, uncrosses them, rests his forearms on his knees, and leans forward. It seems that one night, Ronnie woke up just as his mother was creeping out the door. He did what he always did at this moment—bolted out of bed and wrapped his arms around her legs. Asking her to stay was no good, Ronnie had learned that, so he had begun begging his mother to take him with her.

"Please, Mom, please, please, please, can I please go with you?"

It had never worked before and Ronnie had no hope it would this time. So he was astounded when his mother sighed and said, "All right, just this once."

Ronnie got into his shorts and shirt and sandals as fast as he could, and to be sure his mother wouldn't leave him behind, he took her hand and let her lead him out to their old Ford Taurus. Ronnie sat in the front seat, quivering more from excitement than the chilly night air. He wanted to ask where they were going and what they were going to do but was afraid if he did, she would turn around and take him back to his aunt's, so he sat very still and tried to be a good boy. If he proved he could act like a big boy who didn't bother his mom, maybe she would take him along every time she left.

They drove for what seemed like a long time, down streets that got darker and darker. Every time a car passed, Ronnie caught a glimpse of his mother in the headlights. Her hair was swept back and pinned in a braid down her neck and she had on lipstick that was so brown, it looked black. She was wearing a black dress and a white sweater with little pearls that caught the light. Ronnie thought she looked very pretty and was proud to be there beside her.

Marina pulled into a large circular driveway and found a place to park. The house they were about to enter filled Ronnie with awe. It was long and low, with lights hidden in the bushes. Marina opened a polished wood door and they stepped into a room full of music and people talking and laughing. She led Ronnie down a long hallway. One side was sliding glass doors that opened onto a patio that had soft lights along a rock wall. People were sitting at tables with umbrellas and were swimming in a pool that had underwater lights and dark blue tile. If Ronnie had been capable of speech, he'd have asked his mother if he could go swimming.

Marina led Ronnie into a room that had the biggest couch he had ever seen—cream-colored leather with plump, soft-looking cushions. It made a big U and beautiful women with lots of hair and lipstick were sitting on the couch, holding drinks. Ronnie saw they were wearing fine dresses like his mom, blue dresses, red dresses, white, yellow, and they were all looking up at Marina and Ronnie.

"Hey, everybody," Marina said gaily. "This is my main man. This is Ronnie, my oldest."

"Hi, Ronnie!" "Hey, Ronnie!" the women chorused. And then he heard one of them coo, "*Ooohh,* he's so cute!"

"Wherever have you been keeping this handsome young man?" a lady asked.

"How come you haven't brought him around before?" asked another.

A black woman with very short hair that formed a curl in front of each ear got off the couch. She was wearing a tight red dress and she took little, mincing steps right up to Ronnie.

"You come over and sit by me," she commanded, removing Ronnie's hand from his mother's.

"Oh no, you don't," one of the women on the couch said. "He's not going to sit on that end way over there by you. You put him down right here in the middle. That way we can all get our fair share."

The black lady sighed in mock resignation and led Ronnie to the center of the couch. Two women moved over so he could sit between them and then scrunched up close.

"Tell us your name again, baby."

"How old did you say you are? Five? That can't be right. You're way too big and strong for five."

A woman with long blond hair had begun stroking Ronnie's head.

"Your hair is so soft, I just can't stop myself. You let me know if I'm bothering you."

"I was loving it," Ronnie tells his peers. "All that attention? I'd never gotten attention like that."

A lady picked up a silver plate that had candies on one side and mixed nuts on the other and put it on a glass table in front of Ronnie. When he couldn't decide what he wanted, she took green paper off a toffee and put it in his mouth. His mother had left but Ronnie didn't care. These ladies liked him so much, he was planning on asking them to ask his mother to bring him here every night.

"Were they prostitutes?" Daniel asks.

Daniel is the scholar-athlete, intense and intelligent-looking in his granny glasses. Tattoos look right on the other boys; on Daniel, they seem jarring, out of place. Daniel is a defensive end on the football team; Ronnie lines up beside him at right tackle. On the field, they have learned to trust each other. But it is different in Capital Offenders. Ronnie is vulnerable, revealing his deepest secrets. He gives Daniel a long, penetrating look, trying to gauge where his football friend is coming from. Is Daniel trying to put him down? Is he looking for information he can use if they happen to clash in the dorm—*You ain't shit! Your mom's a hooker!*

"I don't know, I never asked. I never pushed it," Ronnie finally replies.

Before Daniel can decide whether to let it go, Ronnie forges ahead.

"All of a sudden, there's screams coming from another room. A man runs in and there's these strings hanging from his stomach." Ronnie is staring straight ahead, picturing what he is relating. "Those strings were his intestines."

In vivid detail, Ronnie remembers what he saw as a five-year-old. The man had long black hair and was wearing a long black leather coat. He had on a blue shirt that was soaked in blood. The "strings" he was trying to hold in were his intestines wiggling around his fingers. Ronnie screamed and leapt off the couch and headed across a sunken floor to an empty fireplace. There he cowered like a terrified animal.

"Another guy came in," Ronnie continues. "His head and face were soaked in blood. So much blood. He couldn't even see. A woman out on the patio had grabbed a brick and used it to split his head open. He was staggering around. And then this lady in a black jumpsuit came running in and she was holding this knife and yelling, 'I'll kill that motherfucker! I'll kill that motherfucker!'

"My mom came running into the room; she intervened. She went up to the lady with the knife and told her, 'Stop it, it's not worth it!' I was still screaming but my mom didn't come over to me, she ignored me. She stayed with the knifer, calming her down, getting the knife away from her. Another woman came over and picked me up. She held me and said, 'Ronnie, it's okay. It's okay.'

"We heard a *pop pop pop.* Somebody was shooting a gun in another room. Everybody grabbed their things and left, real fast. We passed an ambulance and cop cars on the way home. We heard a whole lot of sirens."

Ronnie pauses and when he continues, he is so engrossed in the memory that his narrative seems to turn into an internal monologue.

"I had nightmares about those strings hanging from the man's stomach for a long time. But what I really remembered from that night was the knife, and the nightmares didn't stop me from thinking about that knife. The knife is the turning point. I felt the way that lady felt. I wanted to do what she did. I started fantasizing about stabbing my aunt."

"When you were thinking of stabbing her, you were getting some power back. Weren't you, Ronnie," Sherry Whatley suggests.

"It made me feel bigger, not like I was a little kid," Ronnie replies. "It made me feel like I was actually doing something."

For a year, Ronnie's aunt continued to beat him almost every day, and he had nothing to defend himself with but fantasies. He would do something to trigger her wrath and run to his room and cling to a pillow. His aunt was always right behind him.

"Whenever my aunt would hurt me, I'd think, I want to run and get a knife and put it in her stomach and watch her cry the way she was making me cry," Ronnie recalls. "I don't want to say it took away the pain, but it was kind of a shield. The only way to make me stop crying was to think of inflicting the pain on her she was inflicting on me. It made me feel good."

Did the pivotal points in Ronnie's life really happen the way he related them? Does his mother accept his version of events? Did the stabbing he recalled so vividly really happen?

"It did," Marina confirmed. "The party took place at Jimmie's cousin's house. It was not a house of prostitution. I've done a lot of things, but I never did that. A fight started and Jimmie's cousin got stabbed and somebody hit somebody else with a brick from the patio. Jimmie comes from a very troubled family. They stab people, they kill people. Two of his uncles were shot and thrown in Dumpsters. No one ever found out who did it."

Do the therapists accept Ronnie's version of his childhood as reality?

Yes, and no.

There was a pretty complete version of Ronnie's life in his case file. Various authorities have interviewed his mother on different occasions, and the therapists can pick up a phone and check Ronnie's version of events against Marina's. Unlike a majority of the parents of youth in Giddings, she was still in Ronnie's life. Every time she called, Marina said, "I want to have a relationship with you. I know it's hard, but I can change, too, and I really want to try." There was nothing about Ronnie witnessing a knifing in his case file, and his mother had never mentioned it. And that is the point. The whole idea behind Capital Offenders is for youth to reveal things they have never told anyone.

Youth are by far the best sources on their own lives. Next to a boy's version of himself, school reports, police reports, and psychological evaluations all pale, like faxes from a machine low on ink. Delinquents get typecast as chronic liars, largely because they lie to the cops. Delinquents do lie to cops—or rather, try to lie. Kids are incompetent liars—a capable cop will always break them down. And kids of course lie to themselves, creating fantasies to paste over years of abuse, abandonment, or neglect.

More often than not—and this is the case with Ronnie—therapists and the group do not have to work all that hard to get a pretty good picture of the forces that have shaped a boy's life. Put teenagers in a safe setting and they will relish revealing what has happened to them. They have an almost desperate need to talk about themselves. And that is understandable, because no one has ever listened to them.

Capital Offenders is not so much about uncovering reality as it is revealing a kid's perception of reality. Therapists and group members probe those perceptions, more to test their validity than their factual accuracy. The group room is not a courtroom, where prosecutors and defense attorneys establish a dialectic and a jury decides which version of events is the most credible. The therapists work with a youth's impressions, and that is as it should be, for in the end the impressions we take from events matter much more than the literal truth of what really did, or did not, happen.

Teenage offenders are the most complex creatures evolution has presented us with. Quantum physics, with subatomic particles constantly in flux, comes closest to capturing their ever-unfolding state. Ronnie may think that witnessing a stabbing led him to fantasize about stabbing his aunt, and that in turn led to his criminal behavior. But a whole constellation of factors had to come together to turn Ronnie into a violent young offender.

Criminals, the teenage variety as well as adults, feel they have a right to commit crimes. Confronting that thinking head-on is not effective, a fact all too often revealed at a sentencing hearing when a victim faces her assailant and says, "I just want to hear you say you are sorry." And the thug replies, "*Sorry* is a sorry word."

Telling his life story, Ronnie was beginning to explore the forces churning inside him that had erupted in violent behavior. If he kept dig-

ging, he could begin to recognize what triggers those forces, and eventually, hopefully, learn to control them. If that happened, the inner fires
would begin to cool. The volcano would stop spewing molten rage.

"After you have been victimized, anger becomes a force. It is a source
of strength," says Linda Reyes. "Expressing anger in a therapeutic group
setting is a way to begin to get rid of it. It's like treating an infected
wound. You'll always have the scar, but the wound won't hurt.

"But anger is too easy for these kids," Reyes continues. "You want to
get to the feelings behind the anger. You want to ask, 'What are you
thinking? What are you feeling?' That's the toughest part, getting in touch
with the feelings behind the anger. It's painful, kids don't want to do it.
But those feelings are deep down inside and they are going to come out
and hurt somebody—a wife or someone else—unless they get dealt with.
Feelings will continue to have power until they are expressed."

"A STRANGER PASSING BY"

"I began to stand up to my aunt," Ronnie announces to the group. "When she beat me, I wouldn't cry anymore."

The beatings ended the night a norther was pounding Amarillo. All over town, residents were digging out their rain gear and weather clichés. Someone would say, "The only thing between Texas and the arctic is barbed wire." Someone else was sure to add, "And the fence is down."

Ronnie was in his mother's bed with Kenny, his little brother. She was gone again; had been gone, in fact, for days. Maybe it was the wind howling and sheets of rain hitting the window so hard Ronnie was afraid the glass was going to break. Maybe it was Aunt Marianne getting mad and ordering them both to bed. Everything. Ronnie figured it had to be everything. That's why Kenny had started crying and couldn't stop.

Kenny was in his chocolate brown Dr. Denton's. His eyes were wet and shut tight, his fists were clenched, and his breath kept catching. He'd gasp for air three or four times and then start bawling again, real loud. He'd let out a sigh and start all over again. Ronnie wanted to hit him but knew that would only make it worse. He thought of putting his hand over Kenny's mouth, but Kenny was crying so hard he was already having trouble breathing and Ronnie was afraid he might smother him or something. Ronnie had tried putting his head under the pillow; he had pulled the pillow over his ears. He still heard Kenny. He was wondering if he should ask Kenny if he wanted a glass of water. Kenny might nod okay and Ronnie would get up and go to the bathroom and by the time he came back, Kenny would be sniveling and rubbing his eyes. Or maybe he should try to tell Kenny a story. Just start telling it and maybe Kenny would stop.

Ronnie didn't have a chance to try anything. The door slammed open and the lights went on, blinding Ronnie for a moment. Kenny gasped and Ronnie closed his eyes. He opened them to see Aunt Marianne in the doorway. The wind gusted, rattling the window. Marianne ran straight to it, making Ronnie think for a second that somehow the window had opened and she was hurrying to shut it. Aunt Marianne jerked the window up as far as it would go. Cold night air rushed in, blowing a stack of Ronnie's drawings off the dresser and billowing the curtains at the other end of the room. Before Ronnie could get his hands up in defense, his aunt was hovering over the bed. She surprised Ronnie by reaching across him and grabbing Kenny by his Dr. Denton's and lifting him out of bed. When Kenny realized he was in the air, he let loose with a shriek and kicked and punched and tried to bite his aunt, who held him away from her, like a dog she had pulled out of a fight. She rushed Kenny to the window, swung him back behind her hip, and sent him headfirst out the first-floor window, into the rain.

Ronnie jumped up on the bed and put up his six-year-old fists.

"Fuck you, bitch!" he yelled at his aunt. "Fuck you!"

Marianne knocked him down, grabbed a fistful of his hair, yanked him out of bed, and jerked him to the window.

"She picked me up and threw me out, just chunked me out, then she closed the window," Ronnie recalls, his voice flat and matter-of-fact.

Ronnie hit the rain-soaked grass with a splat and looked up to see his little brother sitting there, staring up at the window, as if trying to figure out what had just happened. Ronnie jumped to his feet and ran as fast as he could to the front of the duplex. He skidded around the corner, stubbed his toe on the concrete slab, and was just opening the screen door when he heard a lock click. His aunt had beaten him to the door. He tried the shiny brass knob—it didn't move. He banged on the hollow-core door and screamed for his aunt to open up. He pressed his ear to the door but all he could hear was the rain and wind. He thought of Kenny and ran around to the back.

His aunt had never had a dog, but there was a doghouse in the back. The people who lived there before must have had one. Ronnie got Kenny to his feet and led him to the doghouse. He got in first and reached out and took Kenny by the wrist and pulled him inside. He made Kenny lie down and had him scoot back as far as he could, away from the entrance and the sharp wind. Ronnie got down next to Kenny and wrapped his arms around him, trying to get him warm.

Kenny fell asleep, but Ronnie never did. He listened as the wind tapered off and the rain played out, and then he listened to the very still night. Finally, he heard what he had been waiting for: a car stopping at the curb and his mother's laugh echoing in the night air.

"My mom came home drunk that night, laughing with a guy," Ronnie remembers. "I came running out of the doghouse. She said, 'Ronnie, what happened? Why are you out here?' I said, 'Aunt Marianne threw us out of the house!' My mom said, 'She did *what*?' "

" 'She chunked us out the bedroom window, me and Kenny! Kenny's out back in the doghouse. I took us there!' "

" 'In the doghouse? Out back? There's a doghouse in back?' "

A man worked his way out of a black Pontiac Firebird and came around the front. His black hair was combed back on the sides and into a big wave in front. He was wearing a red shirt under a black Windbreaker. He placed a hand on the fender to steady himself and looked at Ronnie and smiled. Then he frowned at Marina and asked her what a little boy in pj's was doing outside in all this weather. Marina put an arm on his shoulder and eased him back around to the driver's side. When they got there, he pushed her arm away.

"You got a situation here?" he asked, swaying gently on the heels of his cowboy boots. "You got something I need to look into?"

Yes, yes, yes, say yes! Ronnie silently begged his mother. Let me tell him everything my aunt did. Maybe he's got a knife.

"It's my sister. I can handle it," Marina said.

The man stood there, looking past Marina to the front door. Then he gave his head a quick shake and looked at her. "Aw, hell. I'll just mind my own damn business."

He started the car and drove off. Marina watched him go and then Ronnie took her hand and led her back to the doghouse, where they collected Kenny and climbed the steps to the back porch. Ronnie was surprised the door was not locked. He was surprised to see Aunt Marianne in the kitchen, arms folded, leaning against the sink.

"What are you doing to my children?" Marina challenged.

"What do you care what I do? You don't take care of your own children!"

"I don't throw them out a window into the rain!"

"You don't care nothing for your children! All you care about is yourself! Yourself and partying!"

"Don't you get into my life! My life is my own business!"

"Your business? You call what you're doing 'business'?"

"You stay out of my life!"

"I'm the only one who's here! Who do you think takes care of your kids when you take off?"

"You stay out of my life!"

"That's what you call it? A life?"

"You stay out of it!"

"You think I don't have a life?"

"I don't have to take this shit no more! Not from someone as fucked-up as you!"

"Good! I don't want you or your goddamn kids here! I'll load them in your goddamn car myself!"

"I'll load my goddamn car myself!"

Marina grasped Ronnie by the shoulders and spun him toward her.

"Take your little brother upstairs and get you both into some dry clothes. I'll be right up."

Ronnie did as he was told and his mother arrived moments later, kicking a cardboard box through the door. She pulled two suitcases out from under the bed and began throwing in clothes. What wouldn't fit in the suitcase went into the box. Marina carried everything downstairs and tossed it into the trunk of the car. She hurried the boys into the backseat and gave them the comforter she had torn off her bed. Marina jumped in the car and floored it in reverse, backing out the drive and hitting the brakes so hard, Ronnie and Kenny spun off the backseat onto the floor. She gave the wheel a hard spin and headed in the direction she had come from, a year earlier.

"We went back to Oklahoma and moved in with my grandparents," Ronnie tells his peers. "I told them about my aunt's abuse. My grandmother comforted me. She said, 'Nobody is going to hurt you again.' My grandmother asked my mother about my aunt abusing us. She denied it at first, then she minimized it. Pretty soon she found an apartment and we moved there."

Ronnie looks around the circle, searching the group for questions. The boys are leaning forward, forearms across the armrests, hands folded, the balls of their feet vibrating on the floor. Surprisingly, none is curious about Ronnie's aunt—What happened to her? Did he ever see her again? Did she ever get what she deserved? Most of them have had someone like her in their lives, someone who handed out never-ending abuse. They know that when an evil figure disappears, that is all that matters—she is gone. Her impact on Ronnie is something they will explore later. Right now, they want to hear more.

Marina got her old job back at the appliance/rental equipment store. Every morning she dropped the boys off at their grandparents', and Ronnie spent the day worrying she would not come back. But every evening, she arrived to pick them up. The fall came and Ronnie started first grade and quickly discovered he loved school. All you had to do was what the teacher said. She didn't hit you or yell at you and you could count on her being there every morning, sitting at her desk and smiling. Everyone's name was listed in alphabetical order on dark blue paper on the corkboard at one side of the classroom. If you were good, she put a silver star by your name. If you did something really good, you got a gold star. There were rows of gold and silver stars behind each name, and Ronnie's row was as long as anyone's. The first thing he did every morning was check the stars; if he got a new one, the thrill lasted all day.

One day after lunch, he found a small, white envelope on his desk. Someone had written his name on the front in purple ink. Inside was a

card. A little cowboy on a pony was lassoing another little cowboy standing by a fence. In the same color ink, someone had written "T.J." by the
cowboy in the saddle, and "Ronnie" by the cowboy on the ground. On
the back was more writing. T.J. was rounding up all his friends for a birthday party. Ronnie was invited to a party!

"I was so excited! This was really big for me!" Ronnie tells the group,
and, for the first time, he is smiling. But the smile quickly dead-ends into
a frown. "My mom drove me to the party," Ronnie continues, back to
staring down at the carpet. "She pulled up in front of the house and asked
if I had my present. I showed it to her. She said, 'Ronnie, I love you.'
Then she said, 'Be sure to take care of your little brother.'

"I knew what that meant," Ronnie says, his voice heavy. "My mother
was going to leave. I watched her drive away. I went inside but I couldn't
enjoy the party. I knew my mom was gone. Sure enough, the party ended.
Everybody went home and I was still there. The lady was going, 'Where's
your mother? Is she coming for you?' I kept saying, 'I don't know.'

"My mom never came. I didn't see her for four years."

Ronnie and Kenny moved in with their grandparents. Ronnie told the
group his grandmother "cried a lot. She was always saying she was going
to pray for us. When she'd talk about Mom, I wouldn't want to listen. I'd
get up and go do something else. She'd always wanted to hug us, but I
wouldn't want to. I wanted the whole cake, not a piece of it."

There is a long silence. Finally, Josh clears his throat. His voice is so
deep, it rumbles.

"When your mother left your aunt's house, she didn't do it to protect
her sons. She did it to protect her own business."

Josh nods his head, reflecting on the righteousness of his observation.

"Was your mom on drugs?" he asks.

"She was using coke," Ronnie replies.

Daniel is eyeing Ronnie from behind his granny glasses, preparing a
question he has asked before. "Was your mother a prostitute?" Startled,
Ronnie straightens up in his chair to look at Daniel.

Daniel prided himself on asking the questions he thinks other group
members are too timid, or not smart enough, to ask. Daniel did ask penetrating questions, but he was self-centered to the point that when his

name popped up in a conversation among the therapists, the word "narcissist" was almost always sure to follow. Daniel had a way of making everything that was happening about himself.

"I don't want to see her that way," Ronnie finally says.

"She's using coke. What's she doing to get it?" Daniel shoots back.

Ronnie is glaring at Daniel, as if he is about to "charge him up," a phrase the kids use to describe how a fight starts. But then Ronnie suddenly does something that boys and girls going through Capital Offenders often do in a moment like this. He tries to fold himself into a clam, covering his face with his hands and burying his head in his knees.

"You guys have done it. You know what it's about," Daniel pushes on. "You give a girl something, you want something in return."

Ronnie covers his ears with his hands.

"What's your real feeling about your mother?" Daniel asks. "What are you trying to cover up?"

"The truth is there," Josh thunders. "Dope is not for free!"

"My mother was on drugs, just like yours," Johnnie, the Korean-American, adds quickly, trying to soften Josh's and Daniel's assault. "She left me, just like your mom did. I wanted my mom, just like you wanted yours. Now, I don't know if I want to see my mom."

The boys wait for Ronnie to respond.

"Talk to us, Ronnie!" Josh yells. "How do you feel?"

"Don't hold it in," Sherry Whatley urges quietly.

"I'm scared," Ronnie cries through his knees. "I can't trust nobody!"

When the group ends, Ronnie and Johnnie meet in the center of the room and hug, unashamedly holding on to each other. Aged, sickly grandparents did their best to raise these boys. Both Ronnie's grandparents suffered from kidney failure and were on dialysis; Johnnie's grandmother had severe emphysema. Both boys did not want to be seen with smelly, withered oldsters. Both grew up thinking they were the only ones who hated their grandparents for being kind. Both had just discovered they were not alone. It is moments like this that take two battered, angry young men out of their isolation and open them up.

"I think they were feeling guilty about the way they treated their grandparents, that's why they hugged each other so hard," Sherry What-ley observes later as the therapists walk slowly back to the social services building. "That's good! They've been so angry, they haven't been able to see that."

Ronnie has been so consumed with longing, he has not been able to develop the distance he needs to see his mother for who she was. Like the other boys, he has been acting out the dynamics the relationship gave birth to, without exploring them. If not forced to, Ronnie would never explore them. He'd spend his life acting them out. On their own, teenagers—or adults, for that matter—cannot deal with a mother who abandons them, or a father who beats them. As bad as abandonment or beatings are when they occur, the real killer is their legacy: a tape loop that endlessly repeats—*My dad didn't love me enough to stop beating me up. My mom didn't love me enough to come back.*

There are thousands and thousands of uncounted, mute heroes who have endured childhoods as horrible as Ronnie's, and yet, they did not turn violent, as he did. Why didn't they? And why did Ronnie? No one knows for sure.

"The abuse impressed me the most. It is so horrendous and so pro-longed," Linda Reyes says, summing up her years at the State School. "But it's not just the abuse; it's how you learn to respond to the abuse. There's an imprecision in our ability to predict that. Who will turn out to be the doctors and the therapists, and who will be the killers? You learn that after the fact.

"But there are indicators," Reyes continues. "The big one is failure of empathy. Victims who go on to victimize have shut down their feelings. They have no empathy, for themselves or anyone else. The person who grows up to be the caretaker retains the ability to empathize with his 'vic-tim self' and not hold himself accountable for that. He tells himself, 'What was done to me was wrong,' and he lives to minimize that past."

Ronnie was telling his life story in order to do exactly that. To get some perspective on his past so he can develop some empathy for himself, and begin to heal. Without help, young men like Ronnie will typically try to bury the message that they are not worthy of love in anger, violence, drugs, the testosterone-soaked camaraderie of gangs, but the tape loop is always running. That is why the hair trigger that sets off a violent youth is often an innocuous reference to his mother—*What'd you just say about my mother? What'd you just fucking say?* It's not because she is incredibly dear to him; quite the contrary. Getting into a fight is easier than facing who your mother and father really are, and what their effect has been. But to grow, Ronnie will have to remember.

A group of adolescents is very good at making him do this. In fact, after the session, the three therapists worry that the group has been applying too much pressure. If Ronnie feels assaulted, he'll shut down. But if he isn't challenged, insights won't develop. Josh asked the right questions, but he could be so condemnatory. Daniel was so eager to wield a scalpel, he could come off as cruel. The therapists don't want Ronnie to denounce his mother, as Daniel and Josh seemed to be demanding. They want him to see her for who she was. Ronnie's mother—and Johnnie's —both vanished, but they are still the only mothers these boys have. And when it comes to parents, the therapists must tread lightly.

"Kids have extreme thinking," Frank Soto muses after he sinks into the big chair in Whatley's office. "One day, Ronnie says he hates his mother. The next day, he'll come in saying he loves her. Things are all black or all white.

"We try to get kids to merge the two extremes, to integrate, to see their parents as they really are. We're not here to tell Ronnie his mother was a terrible mom and that he needs to hate her. She's his mother, she's all he has. She has her own problems. It is easy to hate the parents, until you hear their stories.

"The parents are there. They're broken. We're all broken. We can work together to put ourselves back together."

Soto thinks that what goes for the children must also go for the parents. If Ronnie is capable of change, then his mother has to be, too. If Ronnie is not beyond redemption, then neither is Marina. Change is easier for adolescents, who are still in the developmental process and are locked up in a structured setting designed to foster change. But sometimes, a sentence in the Giddings State School can trigger changes in a parent.

Frank Soto's wife, Margie, is a therapist in Capital Offenders Group B, which meets concurrently in an identical room across the hall. Unable to have children of their own, Frank and Margie have spent the last seventeen years doing what all dedicated parents do, carrying on an endless conversation about children. The only difference is, the Sotos' children are the kids going through Giddings. The Sotos have had a variety of positions in the State School; they have worked with every type of teenage offender imaginable, and met all kinds of parents.

"A long time ago," Margie said, "I stopped thinking in terms of 'good parents' and 'bad parents.' I think of parents as 'healthy' and 'unhealthy.' "

A healthy parent is someone who is willing and able to enter the healing process. An unhealthy parent is someone terminally addicted to drugs, violence, a criminal lifestyle.

At the next session, Ronnie resumes his narrative with a memory that has haunted him for a decade, which is a long time when your eighteenth birthday is still six months away.

Every morning when he left for school, Ronnie had a choice. He could turn right and walk four blocks to school. Or he could turn left and take the long way. Every morning, Ronnie took the long way.

His paternal grandparents, the dry-land farmers who wouldn't let him in the door because he was half Hispanic, lived in a redbrick house on Gladstone Street. Every morning, his father was on the front porch, his feet perched on a small round table next to an ashtray. His chest was concave and the sleeves on his T-shirt were much too large for arms that were as thin as the water pipes under a sink. He always wore a faded blue baseball cap over his long hair and he was always smoking a cigarette.

"Something happened to him after we divorced," Marina explained years later. "He was fine when we left Frederick. Then he started drinking real heavily. I'd hear about him walking down the street with a beer bottle. He was in a state institution for a while. I guess he went kind of crazy."

Every morning, when Ronnie walked down the street and spotted his stick-figure father on the porch, his heart started racing. He walked on reciting his own private mantra: *Look at me, look at me, look at me, look at me, look at me.*

Every morning, his father did.

"He'd go like this," Ronnie says, lifting a wrist to mime a weak, despondent wave. "I was like a stranger passing by."

That tepid wave combined with his mother's vanishing act to create disastrous results for Ronnie, his little brother, his grandparents, his schoolmates. The days when Ronnie earned silver and gold stars were over.

"I'd be so angry when I got to school. I'd pick on kids, get into fights," Ronnie explains. "I was angry at home, too. I beat up my little brother. I took it out on somebody else."

"You could have got to school a different way," Johnnie points out. "Why'd you keep going by your dad? You were only hurtin' yourself."

"I didn't want to give up on him," Ronnie replies, his voice weary.

Frank Soto is not an analytical man. He does not have a Ph.D., is not versed in psychological theory. But he does have years of experience and finely honed instincts. Everything Soto has learned about violent youth tells him that this was the crucial time in Ronnie's life. This was the period when he went from being a victim to being a victimizer. Ronnie is ready, Soto decides, to look at that pattern. He knows Ronnie will erupt—kids always do when you confront them with the violence they have inflicted on others—so he readies himself for Ronnie's response before he asks the question.

"I can see why you were hurting," Soto says. "But why did you think you could take it out on your little brother and the kids at school? What did they do to hurt you?"

Soto gets the reaction he expects. Ronnie's eyes flash and his words come in a torrent. The anger was there all along, flowing beneath the surface like an underground river.

"Life wasn't fair to me, so why should I be fair to them?" Ronnie snaps. "I got beat up by my aunt and didn't deserve it. Why should it be any different for my brother or the kids in school?"

"But, Ronnie, your brother, those kids who were your classmates, they were innocent," Soto persists.

"So was I, and I got beat up!" Ronnie fires back, his voice rising. "I was pissed off! My mom and dad didn't care about me! Why should I care about anybody else?"

After working together through many groups, therapists develop non-verbal communication and the ability to play off each other that is similar to a jazz trio. In a split second, Whatley and Soto exchange a glance that says Soto is ready to yield the floor and she will push Ronnie further.

"Do you see what you were doing, Ronnie?" she asks, leaning forward, trying to establish eye contact. "Do you see how you were taking your anger and inflicting it on others?"

Ronnie narrows his eyes until they are slits. His face is so utterly devoid of expression, it brings to mind an ancient Greek war mask. He slowly opens and closes his fists, as if getting ready to fight. If subconsciously he is trying to intimidate the therapists, it doesn't work. They ride right over the signals.

"Look at it, Ronnie," Jackie Urbach insists. "Don't get mad, look at it. What's your thinking error?"

A long moment passes. Just when it seems he is not going to answer, Ronnie spits out, "Feeling special."

This is no academic exercise, as it was when Ronnie arrived in the State School in a steel cage in the back of a white van and was almost immediately told to memorize a list of thinking errors. This is a triumph of resocialization over Ronnie's past. He didn't act on the anger surging through him; he reflected on it, however ruefully. Later in her office, Sherry Whatley explained that the hallmark of the antisocial personality disorder, which defines most career criminals, is their emotional and spiritual distance from the rest of the human race. *I am an individual; you are not. I am driven by wants; you are clay I can use or destroy to fulfill my wants.* At first, Ronnie did not shut down his feelings; he was filled with love for his mother and longing for his father. But by age eight, he was already becoming dangerous, inflicting pain on schoolmates and terrible abuse on Kenny, the little brother he once heroically defended. If a youthful offender is to be redeemed, this developmental trajectory has to be altered—and the youth has to do that himself. Otherwise, he will end up in a prison cell.

Slowly, one piece at a time, Ronnie is revealing the blueprint his life has followed. If he takes what he discovers out of the bunker and applies his insights to daily life, he will be able to create a new blueprint for himself.

"Insight is not enough," Ann Kelley is fond of telling youthful offenders. "Insight has to be put into action. If we've got a motto at Giddings, that's it."

Ronnie spends a very long time staring at the carpet. When he finally looks up, his brow is no longer furrowed and his fists are unclenched. His eyes are misted, his lips quivering, and he is sliding his hands down to his knees, as if trying to find something to hold on to. He has just been confronted about hurting people because he was angry. Now, the anger appears to be gone, swept away by another feeling. Guilt.

"Telling a life story is all about a kid connecting with pain. He has shoved it way down deep and kept it there with anger," Larry Reue, a veteran of nineteen Capital Offenders groups, explained later. "You want him to get to the sadness beneath the anger. You want a kid to have guilt. You want him to feel awful about what he did."

What Ronnie is beginning to see—what he doesn't want to see—is how his little brother's protector became his torturer. It was a matter of size and proximity more than Kenny provoking Ronnie. Kenny was in fact sweet-natured. The more Ronnie hit him, the more he tried to hide behind a big smile. But just by being alive, he enraged his big brother. Ronnie begins telling the story with a mixture of gloom and resignation.

One Saturday morning when Ronnie was in second grade and Kenny was six, their grandmother was downtown at the hairdresser's and their grandfather was in his office at the church, working on his Sunday sermon. The boys were in the living room, watching TV. Kenny was small for his age and full of energy, forever begging Ronnie to play Chinese checkers or wanting him to start on the fort Ronnie promised they'd build in the chinaberry tree out back. Now, Kenny was happy to be with his big brother, watching *The Bugs Bunny Roadrunner Show*. When it ended, Kenny wanted to watch *The Adventures of Tom and Jerry*. Ronnie wanted to watch *Doug* on Nickelodeon and immediately changed the channel. A squabble began, drearily similar to millions of others in homes with children and televisions and a remote control.

"We always have to watch what you want," Kenny complained. "How come you always get to choose?"

"Shut the hell up," Ronnie warned.

"Why don't you shut the hell up?" Kenny retorted.

Usually, a parent is around to intervene and use the episode as a "teaching moment." But Ronnie and Kenny were alone and even when their grandparents were home, they were too old and feeble to be effective. So Ronnie was free to react like a king whose divine right has been challenged. This was no mere personal affront; it was a violation of the order of things.

"Shut up and watch," he growled.

"I don't want to," Kenny replied.

Ronnie leapt off the couch, a clenched fist extended behind him, and hit Kenny in the stomach. Kenny went *"ouff"* and doubled over. Ronnie hit him as hard he could in the face, a left, a right. The feel of his fists striking flesh and bone felt good, very good. Ronnie kept hitting Kenny until his little brother pitched himself out of the easy chair and lay facedown on the burnt-orange shag carpet.

"I told you: you better do what I tell you to do, or else," Ronnie said as he kicked his brother in the ribs. "I told you. You should have done what I said."

As Ronnie recalls this moment, he shakes his head slowly, as if having difficulty believing the things he did to his little brother.

"If he didn't do what I wanted him to, I'd punch him in the face. He always had bruises, he grew up with bruises. Bruises on his back where I kicked him, bruises all over his face. Black eyes; sometimes two black eyes, sometimes one. He was extroverted. He had all these bruises and he'd act like a normal kid, like nothing happened. It was like he had to work extra hard so people would like him. He'd take flowers to school.

"I couldn't stop hitting him. I hit him all the time. He'd start crying and I'd tell him to stop. He wouldn't and I'd hit him more. I turned into a person I didn't want to be, a person I didn't like."

"Didn't your aunt tell you to stop crying when she was beating you?" Sherry Whatley points out.

"It's a pattern," Daniel adds eagerly. "You've got no control over your mom; you do have control over your little brother. I was that way. They'd make me watch my little brother and I resented that. I took it out on him, I beat him up. My little sister came along, same thing. I ended up holding a gun to her head."

Ronnie jerks back in surprise and looks at Daniel for a moment. He is thinking of telling him something when Josh's voice comes booming across the room.

"Your aunt took your childhood away, you took Kenny's," Josh declares.

"She took your innocence away, you took his," Whatley echoes.

"Didn't your grandparents know? Didn't they try to stop it?" Jackie Urbach asks.

"They couldn't stop it. He didn't want to do things with me anymore. He told them that and I called him a tattletale and hit him more," Ronnie says.

Ronnie surveys the group, letting a moment pass to prepare the group for what was coming next. Then he says, "It started getting worser."

One night, Ronnie and Kenny were in their beds when Ronnie heard paper crinkling and looked over to see Kenny unwrapping a Tootsie Roll. He noticed Ronnie watching and tried to sneak the wrapper under the pillow, inadvertently letting Ronnie know there was more candy where that came from.

"Give me some!" Ronnie demanded.

"No," Kenny replied. "I bought it with my own money."

"You better give me some!"

"No!"

Ronnie leapt out of bed, grabbed his brother by the pajamas, and threw him to the floor. He jumped on top of him, put his forearm across Kenny's throat, and pushed.

"Ronnie, stop! Please, stop! I can't breathe!" Kenny managed to plead.

Ronnie was grinding his teeth and pressing down harder. Kenny's face turned red and then got darker. The bedroom door flew open and the grandparents rushed in. The grandmother, a large, heavyset woman, tried to pull Ronnie off.

"Ronnie! Stop! Please, stop!" she screamed.

His grandmother couldn't pull him off. His grandfather picked up a broom and whacked Ronnie across the shoulders with the handle until he rolled off Kenny. He held the broom menacingly over Ronnie while his wife fell to her knees to cradle Kenny and sob and say a prayer.

"When your brother was saying, 'Ronnie, stop, please, stop!' it was like he was saying, 'Ronnie, it's me! I'm your little brother, I love you!' But you didn't stop," Frank Soto observes. "Why not?"

Ronnie falls silent. When he replies, it is apparent that he was putting things together.

"Things were never the way I thought it should be. I was angry, angry with myself. It wasn't any particular thing. I was just mad and I'd just do things. I was always asking myself, 'What's wrong with me? Why ain't there nobody that can love me?' I couldn't have a mom, I couldn't have a daddy. I had to live with my grandparents and I didn't like it.

"It's like, fuck everybody else," Ronnie continues, looking across the room at Soto, silently begging for understanding. "My mom wasn't there. I didn't get nothing from her, she didn't call. She's not gonna be here for me, why should I care? I knew that guy was my dad. I walked by because I wanted to catch his attention. I wanted him to love me, I didn't want him to push me away. But he didn't call to me, he didn't talk. It was just that little wave. After a while, it was, Fuck him, man."

"You forget your little brother went through everything you did," Daniel points out.

"Beating up your little brother, did that make you feel powerful or something?" asks Antonio, who knows what it is like to feel powerless. The day his father torched their house, Antonio came home to a smoldering ruin and couldn't stop asking about his pet. "Where's my lizard at? Where's my lizard at?" His father finally told him, Shut the fuck up and be a man. Antonio kept asking and got a beating.

"I couldn't stop myself," Ronnie replies, looking at Antonio.

"Your brother felt he couldn't trust anyone, just like you couldn't," Johnnie observes. "You beat him just like your aunt beat you."

Ronnie winces and that tells Jackie Urbach that Johnnie's point has hit home. She decides he is ready to hear the truth.

"You felt you had no one. You had your little brother, Ronnie," Urbach says, her voice rich with feeling. "He loved you and you ended up victimizing him, over and over again. You chose to feel anger and abandonment and distrust. You made your brother feel all those things. You could have stopped; you didn't."

Ronnie begins crying.

"He didn't deserve it! I'm sorry!" Ronnie says through his sobs.

"You didn't care then. You care now?" Urbach asks.

"I'm ashamed of myself. I see him with bruises all over his face. I'm ashamed!"

"You put him in his place; he was below you and he'd better remember that," Daniel observes. "Being beaten up all those years, that had to have an effect. My little brother remembers. That's why I don't like going to visitation. He wrote me a poem that made me cry."

It has taken Ronnie almost four years to get to a place where he can tell this story. In his thick file, there is a psychological diagnosis that in three words puts a neat label on the themes in his story: "oppositional defiant disorder." And yet, Ronnie's definition of this behavior is far more succinct than the three pages it takes to describe this condition in the *DSM-IV, The Diagnostic and Statistical Manual of Mental Disorders.*

"Regardless of what anybody said, I was going to do what I wanted to do," Ronnie tells the group.

This applied most especially to beating up Kenny. One of Ronnie's uncles, Adam, was the last to leave home. He was a senior in high school, counting the days until he got his diploma and joined the Marine Corps. When his grandparents couldn't keep Ronnie off Kenny, they turned to Adam.

"They told me to stop messing with my brother, so I didn't. I'd make excuses, like 'He hit me first.' I had more respect for my grandparents than my uncle. They would ask me to do things they had a hard time doing for themselves—'Could you go get me some water?' and I'd do it. My uncle would tell me to do something, I wouldn't do it. I felt like he always had to have control. I always had to do what he told me to do and I wouldn't do it. He'd spank me and I'd bite and spit in his face and yell, 'Leave me the fuck alone, you can't tell me what to do, you're not my daddy!' He'd put me in my room. I'd sneak out the window.

"It was like I was practicing at home for what I could do at school."

Ronnie's best friend in third grade was T.J., the same boy who had invited him to his birthday party in first grade. Every day, they played together at recess. But when T.J. triggered the rage inside Ronnie, that friendship meant nothing.

They were playing on the monkey bars, happily swinging from level to level. Ronnie was up near the top and T.J. was near the middle when T.J. started singing a song that went, "Momma didn't like you/Momma didn't like you." Ronnie scrambled down the bars and kicked T.J. in the head. He kicked him again and T.J. dropped to the ground. He picked himself up and ran for a teacher.

"I felt like the song was about me, that's why I kicked him in the head," Ronnie explains. "The teacher came running up and asked what happened. I lied, I covered up. I said I slipped. I was always getting into fights but this time I didn't get into trouble. The teacher told me to be more careful.

"My friend T.J. didn't believe me. He mistrusted me after that."

Four years went by without Marina once calling to ask how her sons were doing. Every time a car went by, Ronnie checked to see if his mother was inside. She never was, but Ronnie never stopped watching.

It was December, a few days before school would let out. Coming home after school, Ronnie was thinking this was going to be another Christmas without his mother. He turned a corner and was walking up the street when he saw a black car parked in front of his grandparents' house, a car that had never been parked there before. There was something familiar about it, too. Ronnie's heart was beating faster. He got closer and saw it was a Firebird, like the one his mother was riding in the night he and Kenny were shivering in the doghouse. He got closer still and saw a guy behind the wheel, a guy smoking a cigarette who had black hair combed back on the sides and high in front. Before he realized what he had done, Ronnie had cut across the lawn, taken the porch steps two at a time, and thrown open the front door. He halted at the threshold.

His mother was sitting on the couch, an arm around Kenny. She had on a loose white blouse and black toreador pants and to Ronnie, she was as pretty as ever. She squealed, "Ronnie!" and jumped off the couch and raced to hug him.

"Look at you, just look at you," Marina said, holding him at arm's length before wrapping her arms around him again. "You've gotten so big! You're a little man now."

She kissed Ronnie on the forehead and led him to the couch. She sat down between them and put an arm around both sons. Ronnie had rehearsed what he would say to his mother and what she would say to him over and over again. He thought he knew exactly how he would feel. But now that it was actually happening, he was too shocked to feel much of anything. He couldn't even see very clearly. He knew his grandmother was in her chair and his grandfather was shifting uneasily on a dining room chair. His uncle Adam, home on leave from the Marine Corps, was standing near his grandfather, leaning against a wall, both hands in his pockets. Ronnie didn't even notice the huge pile of gifts on the floor at one end of the couch until Kenny said, "Now that Ronnie's here, can we start opening our presents? Can we, Mommy?"

"You sure can, Kenny. And since you've been such a good boy and so patient, you can open the first one. Try that big one over there with the big shiny red bow."

Kenny leapt off the couch and attacked the wrapping paper.

"A drum set! A whole drum set!" Kenny marveled, lifting a snare drum out of the big box. "There's an even bigger drum inside! And I see cymbals!"

"Your turn, Ronnie!" Marina smiled. "Open the long one."

It was a Fender guitar, a Squire, the starter Stratocaster.

Ronnie had just opened his third present, a Daisy BB gun, when Adam pushed himself away from the wall, strode across the room, ripped the gun out of Ronnie's hands, and threw it on his sister's lap.

"I can't believe how obvious you are! You walk out on your kids. You dump them here for four years and never so much as call. We don't hear word one and then out of the blue, you sweep in to play Santa Claus! Well, you can't buy their love and I'm sick of seeing you try. So gather up all these bribes and get the hell out of here! Go back outside and get in that car and you and that dirtbag just go on and drive back where you came from."

"Don't you call him a dirtbag! That man out there's my husband!"

Ronnie and Kenny exchanged surprised looks.

"Okay, I'm sorry. Now, why don't you just go on back through that door, back where you came from. With that *scumbag* behind the wheel!"

Marina gave her brother a long, smoldering look. Then she got up and walked out the door without saying a word. Ronnie, Kenny, their grandparents and uncle followed and stood on the porch, watching as Marina went down the sidewalk and opened the passenger door.

"He ruined it!" she shouted, pointing back at Adam, who was standing at the top of the stairs. "He says I should take the presents back! He says I'm trying to buy their love!"

The man leaned across the front seat.

"Thanks a lot, asshole!" he shouted at Adam. "She's been workin' on this for weeks!"

Adam bounded down the steps and ran down the sidewalk and around the car to the driver's side. Marina hopped in and slammed the door shut and rolled up the window. Jimmie, Marina's husband, managed to get his window three-quarters up before Adam arrived.

"What'd you call me? What'd you call me, you fucking lowlife?" Adam yelled.

Without taking his eyes off the young marine, the man reached out and started the engine.

"Get out of that fucking car and I'll kick your ass all the way back to Texas," Adam yelled. "Come on, get out here! You can be my Christmas present!"

"Move it, Jimmie! Go! Go! Go!" Marina yelled.

Ronnie raced off the porch. The window on his mother's side was down just far enough for him to get his fingers in and get a grip. He held on, running alongside the car as it moved up the street. Marina yelled for Jimmie to stop and he did, but Ronnie still held on.

"Mom! Mom! Promise! You'll come back! Promise!" Ronnie pleaded.

"I won't, honey. I'm never coming back. But you can come and see me. You and Kenny can come to Amarillo and be with me when Easter break comes. I promise, honey. I won't let you down, not this time."

"You promise, Mom? You really promise?"

"I really promise. Now, let go. We have to leave."

Ronnie let go and Jimmie floored it and burned rubber all the way up the street. Ronnie watched and then went back inside, where presents and wrapping paper littered the floor.

"I always had to take action to be with my mother," Ronnie tells the group. "If I hadn't of grabbed hold of that Firebird, that would have been the last time I saw her."

4.

"NO AFFECTION OR CONCERN
UNTIL I GOT LOCKED UP"

The three Capital Offenders therapists knew they were in for a long haul when they met in Sherry Whatley's office early in the morning before Ronnie's second session. Ronnie had established a nice rhythm: he would move forward and falter; they'd push and he'd move forward again. Still, Ronnie had a lot of ground to cover before he completed his life story, and as soon as he was finished, they would do his role play. They discussed extending Ronnie's life story to a third session but decided against it. To have maximum impact, a role play has to be done at the end of a life story. So, the role play was going to happen today, no matter how long the session went.

As lead therapist, Sherry Whatley also had to consider the overall schedule. Capital Offenders is supposed to take six months to complete, but the groups invariably run longer. Some go on for as long as nine months—a student bogs down telling a life story or crime story; a student gets sick (the rule is, if one student is too ill to attend, the group does not meet); therapists have to leave the campus to attend training sessions; a grandparent or a parent dies. The administrators who monitor the program in the TYC central office in Austin understand this and tend not to crack a whip if a group falls behind schedule. Still, Whatley and the other therapists are keenly aware that they are not in private practice. Taxpayers in the Lone Star State are picking up the tab for hundreds of hours of psychotherapy, and the therapists are grateful for the chance to treat a population that goes untreated almost everywhere else. So they spent the half hour before group roughing out the role play, suggesting scenes that could be enacted and students who might play certain roles.

"What were things like, after your mother left just before Christmas?" Frank Soto asks, looking at Ronnie and liking what he sees. Ronnie is fresh and eager to begin. Remove a boy from the chaos he's managed to survive, place him in a setting where he feels safe, and he will be eager to trust, as Ronnie clearly is. He has never had this much attention, and Ronnie craves attention. Having this many people listen to him, this many people care about him, feels very good. Since no one has ever listened to him before, he has never learned to listen to himself. Now, both are happening.

"I kept on hurting my little brother," Ronnie begins. "Once after I beat up Kenny, my uncle Adam sat us down and told me, 'This is your brother. This is all you have left. You and him have to stick together.' That worked for a little bit. Then I started hitting him again.

"At school, I didn't have a friend you could call a friend. They never knew what to expect. I'd start cussing the teacher, 'I don't want to do this shit!' I was pushing the intercom button that went to the principal's office and saying stuff like, 'You can't tell me what to do!' I was playing with pencils, flipping them off the edge of my desk. They'd send notes home and I'd tear them up so my uncle wouldn't see them."

"You're angry. You're angry at your mom," Soto observes. "Did you ever think of getting back at her?"

"No," Ronnie replies, sadly shaking his head. "I still loved her. I'd see the kids in school. They got moms."

"Were there times when you felt care and concern for others?" Jackie Urbach asks.

"I felt sorry about beating on my brother at first but after a while, I stopped caring. I didn't care about myself or about what people thought. I got into a not-caring attitude. I was about eight or nine."

A "not-caring attitude" is about as good a definition of alienated, angry depression as any. Add righteousness to "not caring"—"Nobody cared about me; why should I care about anyone else?"—and you get the classroom bully Ronnie was at ten, and the violent young offender he would become by fifteen. Jeri Pamp, a psychologist with an office down the hall from Whatley's, has learned to recognize this pattern in the case files she reads, the psychological evaluations she performs, and the stories she listens to in Capital Offenders. Pamp, like other State School therapists, is almost evangelical in her belief that agents outside the family have to step in before this condition sinks roots deep in the soul. If teachers, counselors, principals, police officers, social workers, and judges understood the forces that are at work in the children who disrupt elementary school classrooms, they would intervene.

"Anger is the depression a kid sends into the world," Pamp says. "Anger is a drug. Anger energizes; it gets things pumped up. Anger creates high drama. Anger makes pain and injury grow dimmer and dimmer.

"We ask them to set aside the best defense they have, their anger," Pamp says, summing up her work at the State School. "We ask them to set aside enormous injury and go ahead and have a life. We ask a lot."

Not the least of these requests is asking Ronnie to stop rejecting his life. A youth can absorb only so much hurt before he reverses the process. Ronnie rejected his grandparents and his uncle, and violently spurned his brother. He defied authority figures like teachers and principals and held on to the hope that his mother or father would reach out to him. But one day he walked down his father's street, got the same lame wave for his effort, and never walked that way again.

"I had to stop," Ronnie tells his peers. "It made me so angry."

At the dinner table one evening, Ronnie noticed Adam watching him closely. Adam left Ronnie and Kenny pretty much to themselves, unless Ronnie's grandmother or grandfather asked him to intervene. Focusing on Ronnie could only mean Adam was going to demand they have "a little talk," and that always meant trouble. Ronnie would defy him, Adam would knock him around and send him to his room. Ronnie would zip out the window. But as the evening moved along, Adam didn't approach him and Ronnie started thinking maybe he was reading the signs wrong. He and Kenny were in their beds when Adam appeared in the doorway. Ronnie picked up a Spider-Man comic book and pretended to read.

"Guess who I saw today?" Adam said, a grin beginning to play on his lips.

Kenny looked up, interested. Ronnie focused on Spider-Man.

"Your dad," Adam said.

Kenny used his hands to scoot himself up in bed.

"You did? Where? Where'd you see him? At his house?" Kenny asked.

"Downtown at the drugstore. Outside the drugstore, actually. He was smoking a cigarette, waiting for a prescription."

Ronnie put the comic book down. Adam got to the point.

"He said he'd like to see you guys. Maybe take you out somewhere. He mentioned Hackberry Flat. Spring migration is starting, birds are on the wing. You'll see all kinds out there."

"I'll go, I'll go!" Kenny said. He was almost jumping up and down in bed. "When can we go? When?"

"He was talking about this weekend. How 'bout you, Ronnie? You up for it?"

Ronnie threw the comic book on the floor, turned on his side, and pulled the covers up to his ear. "I ain't goin'."

"Why not?"

"Don't feel like it."

"I can't believe this. You been walking by your dad's house for I don't know how long, hoping for just a glimpse. Now he finally makes a move. He's up for doin' something and you're gonna say no?"

"Yeah, Ronnie, come on!" Kenny cried. "This is our chance!" He was afraid that if Ronnie didn't say yes, he wouldn't get to go.

"You shut up!" Ronnie yelled. "You shut the hell up!"

"Knock that shit off! Stop it before it gets started!" Adam roared. He waited a moment, and in a much softer voice continued, "Come on, Ronnie, lighten up. Go have a little bit of fun."

"It won't be fun! I ain't goin'!"

Ronnie didn't go, but Kenny did. When he got back, Ronnie didn't ask where they went or what they did or what their dad was like. The first chance he got, he beat Kenny black and blue. Their father never asked either boy to do anything again.

"He wasn't there when I wanted him, so I wasn't going to go with him then," Ronnie explains, eager that his reasoning be accepted. Whatley is gazing at Ronnie and slowly nodding her head.

"You were getting some of your power back," she tells him. "You said, 'I'm going to reject you. You rejected me.' "

Ronnie gave Whatley a smile as slight as it was rare. Gaining power over his dad. Yes, that was what he was doing.

Throughout this period, Ronnie kept a close eye on the religious calendar in the kitchen, counting off the days until Easter. He tried not to let his hopes get too high—his mother had never kept a promise—but somehow, he knew this time she would. He came home from school one day just as his grandmother was hanging up the phone. It was the third time she had talked to his mother that day, she told Ronnie. Everything was set. Adam would drive the boys out to Amarillo; he'd be back at the end of the week to pick them up. His mother had really changed! She was finally acting like a mother!

As it turned out, following through on the Easter visit hadn't been Marina's idea; surprising the boys with a Christmas visit wasn't hers, either. Both had come from Jimmie.

"Love was dying," Marina explained years later. "He was tired of taking me out all the time, but he wanted me around, too. So one day he up and says, 'Let's go get the kids.' He was thinking, She'll have to stay home with them. I'll go out alone."

This time, it was Adam who did not get out of the car when he stopped in front of a single-story, flat-roofed house guarded by a barbed-wire fence and shaded by three small willow trees in the country outside Amarillo. Four cars were scattered along the driveway, including a black Pontiac Firebird. Ronnie's heart leapt when he spotted it.

Marina burst through the door to hug the boys but did not acknowledge Adam, who kept his hands on the wheel and his eyes straight ahead. She was skinnier and had more hair than Ronnie remembered. Kenny had to go to the bathroom and Marina hurried him into the house. Adam yanked the suitcases out of the truck and set them by the fence. He got back in the car and Ronnie watched as he turned around and drove back past the house. As soon as he went by, Marina, Kenny, and Jimmie appeared. Jimmie picked up the suitcases and carried them into the house.

Inside, it was evident Marina and Jimmie had done nothing to prepare for the boys' visit. Big, torpid flies buzzed around a lazy ceiling fan.

Dirty dishes were piled in the sink. A small mountain had formed at the top of a big gray plastic garbage bin. Next to it were two steel bowls. There was no water in one bowl and no food in the other, but kibble was scattered everywhere. Outside on a feces-laden patio, the boys' arrival had sent Jimmie's two German shepherds into attack mode and they were barking and banging against a filthy sliding glass door. Jimmie yelled at them to shut up and the dogs went even wilder. Empty beer cans and liquor bottles were scattered everywhere—there was an especially large pile next to an expensive leather recliner that faced the biggest TV the boys had ever seen.

Marina led her sons down a hall to a small bedroom, where twin beds faced a rectangular window that overlooked the patio. The room was clean but the air was stale and smelled of dogs. Marina helped the boys unpack, stuffing their clothes into an unpainted dresser. Then she disappeared into the bathroom.

"You two ever hear of Route Sixty-six?" Jimmie asked when Ronnie and Kenny came back to the living room. He opened the refrigerator door, peered in, and fished out a Lone Star longneck. He grinned when Ronnie and Kenny shook their heads no, they hadn't.

"Just what I thought! Listen to this, I got it cued up."

Jimmie went to the one pristine thing in the house, a rack of thin, black sound equipment with tiny lights glowing red, amber, and green. He pressed a button and Ronnie and Kenny jerked back as sound exploded all over the room. It was the Rolling Stones' version of the oft-recorded "Route 66": *Well, it winds from Chicago to L.A., more than two thousand miles all the way . . .*

"Two thousand four hundred and forty-eight miles, to be exact!" Jimmie shouted above the music. "Ain't this great? It's why I like it out here. You can crank it up and it won't bring the neighbors around to give you shit."

Jimmie explained that old Route 66 became Sixth Street in Amarillo and promised he was going to personally take the boys to a diner down there that had the best damn burgers and the best damn jukebox. "It's got pretty much everything Buddy Holly ever done on it. Buddy, he was from Lubbock, but hell, we forgive him for that!"

Marina came out of the bathroom; Jimmie excused himself and went in. She asked if the boys were thirsty and made a show of pouring apple juice. She seemed tense and avoided looking at them.

"Palo Duro Canyon! That's another place we're goin'!" Jimmie yelled, emerging from the bathroom, eyes gleaming. "The Grand Canyon of Texas! Last Indian fight ever in Texas, where do you think it was? Out there in Palo Duro. Hey! Maybe we'll hunt arrowheads!"

Marina tried to say something, but Jimmie put up a hand.

"Cadillac Ranch! You boys will be seeing Cadillac Ranch! You like cars? Ah hell, what am I askin'? All boys like cars! Cadillac Ranch is a whole bunch of big ol' tail-fin Caddies stuck in the ground, all at the same angle, all in a row. Damnedest thing you ever saw!"

The boys did indeed have hamburgers in a retro diner on Sixth Street. They did visit Palo Duro Canyon, and they saw the Cadillacs buried in a field. They watched movie after movie on the big-screen TV and heard a lot of classic rock. And before the week was over, Jimmie had changed his mind about the boys staying to keep their mother occupied. He wanted them gone. They cramped his style. He had a business to run. This place wasn't just his home, it was his office.

As Ronnie would phrase it, he and Kenny wanted "the whole cake." They were determined not to let their mother get away again.

"I had this idea of the way I thought it would be with my mom," Ronnie informs the group. "I thought we'd be all loving."

"What was your mother doing? Was she working?" asks Tim, a small youth with dark skin, large eyes, and a perfectly round head. Tim was a great cat burglar. He went into an air duct the way a needle goes into a vein.

"My mom worked as a nurse's aide in a nursing home," Ronnie replies with obvious pride.

"Even though she was doing coke?" Tim asks. "That's what they was doin', right? When they kept going into the bathroom? That's how it was in my house."

"My mom was using, but she still worked."

"And Jimmie?" Tim asks. "Did he work?"

"Self-employed. Drug dealer," Ronnie says. Hearing his description, he has to smile.

Marina promised Jimmie that when Saturday arrived, the boys would be packed and ready to go. But when a hungover Jimmie stumbled out of the bedroom, the boys were rooted on the couch and the TV wasn't on. Jimmie went down the hall to the bedroom and sure enough, their clothes were still in the dresser. Marina was outside on the patio, smoking a cigarette. Jimmie went out there and starting yelling, stooping every now and then to pick up an empty beer can and throw it at his common-law wife. Marina finally ran into the house and locked herself in the bathroom.

Adam and the boys' grandmother arrived late that afternoon—their grandfather was too sick to travel. When Grandma couldn't talk the boys into leaving, Adam got out of the car, marched into the house, and jerked Kenny off the couch. Kenny screamed and fought and Adam finally let him go. Meanwhile, Jimmie was in the kitchen, pacing with his fists clenched, careful to stay away from Adam.

Marina and Jimmie went into their bedroom and Jimmie yelled at her. The boy's grandmother was crying. When a drawn-looking Marina finally emerged, her mother was sitting on the edge of the couch, dabbing her eyes with a handkerchief. She pulled herself together and looked at her daughter.

"I can't see my way to leaving the boys," she told Marina. "That man in the bedroom is a bad influence. Just look how you two are living! This ain't no place for boys. Let me take them back. When you decide you can take care of them, you can come for them."

"You think you can do right by them? You think you did right by me?" Marina shot back, leaning toward her mother.

"I'm just saying what I think is best for the boys."

"Don't you tell me what to do!"

Seeing Marina edging close to her mother, Adam stepped between them. He took the old woman by the arm and led her to the car. He opened the door and helped her in and got behind the wheel and they drove off alone. Ten-year-old Ronnie and eight-year-old Kenny were finally reunited with their mother.

"It didn't turn out to be the way I thought it would," Ronnie informs the group in his characteristically understated way. "She wasn't there to see us grow up and she didn't know what to do. She was distant. She was weird, real weird."

Angry that he had lost the tug-of-war, Jimmie refused to let the boys eat at the same table he did. Marina made macaroni and cheese and heated up TV dinners and the boys carried them down the hall to their room. One afternoon Kenny got hungry and climbed up on the counter to get a loaf of Mexican sweet bread he had seen his mother put in a cabinet over the sink. Jimmie came in just as he was reaching for it. Jimmie made Kenny sit down at the kitchen table and stay there until he had eaten the whole loaf.

Marina says she felt trapped. If she tried to stick up for her kids, Jimmie hit her. If she didn't, she felt guilty. But there was a way out, and Marina took it every chance she had.

"I was on drugs, living day to day for the high," Marina explained. "That was the way I wanted to be. We spent all our money on drugs. Whatever we got, even my income tax refund check, we'd use to buy drugs. My boys didn't mean anything to me. I'd take the boys shopping and say, 'Pick one.' They got one pair of pants, one shirt, one pair of shoes. That was it. The rest of the money was going to drugs.

"It got bad to where I started smoking crack."

Ronnie awoke one night to hear his mother screaming and things breaking in the kitchen. He jumped out of bed, crept down the hallway, and peeked into the kitchen. Jimmie had his fists wrapped in his mother's long hair and was banging her head into the wall. He got one hand free and backhanded her across the mouth, then slapped her across the face. Then he stepped back and watched as Marina sank down the wall to the floor. Ronnie thought about crying out, but somehow, he didn't.

"I gave myself excuses," he explains. "I told myself, 'She shouldn't have been bitching so much.' They were arguing all the time. I told myself, 'This is just the way they are.' "

There was more to it than that. Ronnie was starting to reject his mother, as he had his father. Ronnie was who mattered most now. He didn't defend his mother because he didn't want to mess things up with Jimmie.

"The way I felt was, I liked the lifestyle. I didn't ask her if I could go anywhere, I just went. She never said nothing about it. I could do what I wanted. I didn't have no one telling me what to do."

Ronnie became a nomad, roaming the streets of Amarillo at will. Every morning he scoured the apartment for loose change to buy Slurpees and hot dogs. He knew the merchandise in every resale shop on Sixth Street, and when a car moved off a used-car lot, he noticed. Some days, he did not bother going to school. Other days he showed up but left at noon. No truant officer came knocking or swooped down as Ronnie walked a street alone in the middle of a school day. The few times he made it to class, Ronnie was so disruptive, school officials may have been glad when he wasn't there and let it go at that.

One Saturday morning, Jimmie had everyone pile into the Firebird and they drove out to his parents' spread, a run-down, ramshackle ranch full of rusting farm equipment an hour west of Amarillo. It was the annual family reunion and to Jimmie, it was better than New Year's Eve and the Fourth of July rolled into one. Ronnie was amazed. Kids his age were dipping into buckets filled with ice and pulling out cold beers. Out in a field, adults were setting off firecrackers, big ones, not those dinky little inchers or sparklers for sale at roadside stands. A firing range was set up out behind the barbecue pit and three men and a couple of women were blasting away at bottles, cans, rocks, prickly pear cactus—anything that presented a target—with pistols and large-bore automatic weapons.

Ronnie assumed drinking, barbecuing a side of beef, firecrackers, and firing weapons was all the entertainment anyone could want, until he found out there was more.

"Come 'ere, I want you to meet somebody," Jimmie said.

Jimmie had been drinking and loading up on drugs since he stepped out of the Firebird. He threw an arm around Ronnie and guided him around the huge bonfire. They stopped with Ronnie face-to-face with one of Jimmie's cousins, a boy about his age. He had brown skin and a buzz cut and small, narrow eyes that looked straight at Ronnie and did not blink.

"This here's Ronnie," Jimmie said. "Ronnie, this here is Tyler. Tyler, Ronnie's been going around all day saying he can kick your ass."

"No, I ain't!" Ronnie yelped.

"You ain't?" Jimmie said, feigning surprise. "Well hell, then, that makes one of us a liar."

Jimmie reached down and grabbed Ronnie's left hand and used it to throw a jab at Tyler. Tyler moved back a step. "See what I'm saying, Tyler? All day long he's been wanting to fight you."

"I'll fight him," Tyler said, his voice quiet and flat.

"Ronnie's from up there in Traileroma," Jimmie taunted. "Think you can put a whooping on a boy from Indian Territory?"

"If he wants, I'll kick his ass," Tyler replied.

"Ronnie? You want in this family? Fastest way is fighting your way in."

"I ain't gonna say no," Ronnie said.

"Ohh-wee!" Jimmie yipped. "Everybody, gather round! We got ourselves one!"

"Something going on!" a voice shouted in the dark.

"We got one going!" someone else cried.

A circle quickly formed around the boys. Tyler got the first lick in, surprising Ronnie with a shot to the nose that drew blood. Rage hit and Ronnie suddenly felt twice his size. He charged, head-butted Tyler and drove him to the ground. The two boys rolled in the dirt, exchanging punches. And then a woman's voice cut through the night air.

"Stop it! Stop it right now, goddamnit!"

The boys kept fighting but people in the crowd were distracted, looking around to see who had yelled. Marina stepped forward and grabbed Ronnie by the sweatshirt and jerked him to his feet.

"What the hell's wrong with you?" she yelled at Jimmie. "Can't you tell the difference between a boy and a pit bull?"

"What the fuck is wrong with you?" Jimmie countered. "Can't you have no fun no more?"

It turned out that Ronnie was on Jimmie's side.

"My mom was really mad, but I liked fighting," Ronnie tells the group. "I liked the attention."

What he liked best, though, was being home alone, searching the house, finding stuff, trying things out.

Like lighting up a marijuana roach and taking a quick hit.

Like the tiny white granules scattered on the glass coffee table. Ronnie collected them on a wet finger and rubbed his finger across his gums, the way he had seen Jimmie do. He knew it was a drug and it was called cocaine, but he didn't understand why it was such a big deal. All it did was make you feel like you'd gone to the dentist and he'd stuck a needle in your gum and made it numb. Why would anyone want to feel like they had just been to the dentist?

The best discovery of all took place on the day Ronnie finally got the nerve to explore the closet in Jimmie and his mother's bedroom. Long, gray steel boxes were stacked at one end. Luckily, none was locked. Ronnie lifted the top one—it was heavy—and got it down to the carpet. Afraid to breathe, Ronnie undid the snaps and opened it. It was full of tools, so many different tools. Ronnie figured Jimmie used them when he was working on air conditioners. Ronnie opened the second and third boxes. They were full of tools, too.

What Ronnie saw when he opened the last box took his breath away. Inside were two plastic bags, both half filled with a white powder Ronnie knew right away must be cocaine. Nestled next to the baggies, terrifying, ominous, thrilling, was a Ruger Mark II .22 pistol.

Ronnie had found porn magazines in a drawer on the nightstand on Jimmie's side of the bed and had returned numerous times to study the images. But he had never looked at anything as long and hard as he did that gun. The barrel was gleaming stainless steel; it appeared no one had ever touched it. The grip was ebony, made to fit right into your hand. Ronnie reached out to pick the weapon up but held back. He focused on the trigger, perfectly positioned inside its guard. He imagined his finger squeezing, squeezing, squeezing, until, *Boom!*

Ronnie finally reached down and lifted the pistol out of its box, slowly, as if he were removing a puppy from its litter. Its weight surprised him. He pointed the gun at the wall across the room and tried to figure out how to look down its sights. He waved the pistol in the air a couple of times, then stood up and jammed it under his belt. He looked at himself in the mirror. He tried different poses. He liked what he saw.

Ronnie sat down on the bed and turned the gun over and over in his hands, testing its weight. How did it load? The part behind the barrel looked as if it might move. Ronnie held the gun away and pulled the bolt back. So that was how you cocked it!

Ronnie stood up. He studied himself in the mirror, holding the pistol at his knee. Then he left the room. He was looking for his little brother. He was not entirely sure, but he thought he might kill him.

Larry Reue, the veteran TYC psychologist, is the son of a building contractor, and he prides himself on having "a blue-collar mentality."

"If you go to a doctor, he asks where does it hurt and you tell him it's your arm," Reue says. "If he jerks the arm around and you scream, you're not saying you don't want him to fix it. You're telling him he's found the place where it hurts."

Ronnie had shown the therapists where he was hurting. Now, they had to decide how best to address that pain. If there is a philosophy that underlies the TYC treatment programs it is this: There is no magic bullet. There are only tools.

Psychotropic medication, for example, is one tool. Ronnie was on an antidepressant when he arrived at Giddings. A doctor at the TYC assessment center in Marlin had decided he was depressed—why would he not be?—and had put him on Prozac. As he settled into life in Giddings, got three solid if unexciting meals a day, eight hours of sleep, and regular exercise in the gym and weight room, a psychiatrist who spent one day on campus a month took Ronnie off the antidepressant. Ronnie didn't notice the difference, and that was the usual pattern in the State School. At any one time, 20 percent of the students in Giddings are on antidepressant medications. A majority of those, like Ronnie, are in their first year to eighteen months on campus.

"Antidepressants can help a student achieve the chemical balance he needs to plug into treatment," Reue explains. "It would be ridiculous to say medication is the only way, or group therapy is better than medication, just as it would be ridiculous to stand at a building site arguing that a saw is better than a hammer. If you want a hole, get a drill; if you want to drive a nail, get a hammer. You can't build a kid with just one tool. In TYC, we've got the whole toolbox."

With an hour left in the second session of Ronnie's life story, the Capital Offenders therapists were about to pull the role play out of their toolbox. Role plays are delicate. It is one thing to narrate a life story, as Ronnie has. It is another to experience the emotions connected to those events, feelings a youth has not allowed himself to experience. A role play is a trip back to childhood, but it is healing, not traumatizing, as the childhood was.

"It's a regression in a safe way in a safe setting," Sherry Whatley explained earlier. "It's a way to get in touch with feelings and issues that led to incarceration."

Whatley and the other State School therapists are true believers in this practice, but regression is controversial, especially among mainstream psychologists. By the mid-1990s, outcome studies were showing that Capital Offenders graduates had remarkably low recidivism rates, and Linda Reyes decided the evidence was solid and compelling enough to make public. She and her staff spent weeks preparing to present the program at the 104th Annual Meeting of the American Psychological Association in Toronto, in 1996. Reyes was thrilled to learn that so many registrants were interested, conference planners had moved her program to the main ballroom. She was all but certain that once the professionals understood what was happening in Texas and examined the statistics, they would push legislators in their home states to establish similar programs.

It didn't work out that way. The audience was skeptical—this wasn't the traditional one-on-one or group therapy psychologists were used to—and they were especially alarmed by role plays. Therapists getting out of their chairs and playing roles in mini-dramas? Where's the objectivity? The professional detachment? How can you control a youth's response? What happens if you regress a kid and he doesn't come back?

Reyes and her staff answered every question, but they felt the audience had stopped listening. The psychologists seemed more interested in convincing one another that a population they were not treating could not be treated, at least not in an innovative, aggressive way.

"We're up, we're moving around, we're reenacting trauma, and that's controversial," says Ann Kelley, who attended the Toronto conference. "They don't teach working with the fringes in graduate school, and murderers are the fringe. They are, by definition, not redeemable."

"The people in the profession are the hardest to convince," Larry Reue says when asked about that afternoon in Toronto. "Part of it is, we're coming from inside the penal system, where people in the profession pretty much agree that nothing works. But what are the psychologists who are actually working with these kids supposed to do? Teach them to be good inmates?"

There is a famous story about Jean Cocteau, the artist, poet, and film-maker, visiting his childhood home outside Paris as an adult. Cocteau had been gone for so many years, he could not relate to the setting where he had spent the first ten years of his life until he picked up a stick and ran it along a picket fence, something he was fond of doing as a boy. The sound broke a dam and Cocteau was flooded with childhood memories.

Something similar happens in the COG bunker. The therapists look for triggers—the smell of crack cocaine, the sound of a belt hitting an open palm, the feel of blood on fingers—that will send a youth spiraling back into childhood and reexperience what happened. That is a big step beyond recalling events at a distance, as if they had happened to someone else.

"Role plays are especially effective with adolescents because they are close to their childhoods. Kids have fewer barriers and defenses," explains Corinne Alvarez-Sanders. "I never saw hardness inside these kids. I saw it as a level of clothing that could be removed. Underneath it, there is soft-ness, and where there is softness, there is hope. It's the hope that keeps you going, that and knowing that a role play is a cleansing process. We're energized when we're part of a cleansing process."

The boys have stacked the chairs and are huddling in a corner while Ronnie sits alone in a corner diagonally across the room, looking like a patient waiting for a shock treatment. His back is straight, his body rigid, his face is as ashen as the walls. Ronnie senses that the barricades he has built against his past are going to come tumbling down. And he lives in terror of his past.

There is a great deal riding on a role play, both for the boy it is about and for the "actors." Therapists keep close track of how willing a youth is to perform a role, especially a demanding one, like playing an abusive father. A youth who is willing to undertake this to benefit a peer is perceived by the therapists to be developing empathy. A boy who cannot convince a set of tough-minded therapists he has empathy is most likely on his way to prison.

The Progressives who created the country's first juvenile court in Chicago at the end of the nineteenth century were men of their era and they based the new court on the patriarchal premise that a stern but compassionate judge could help redirect the lives of wayward youth. A century later, the powers invested in that father figure in a black robe have been stripped away in state after state.

Since 1992, almost every state has eliminated the judge and other important gates that youth have to pass through before being seen as adults in the eyes of the law. The new laws have different names: Georgia's SB440, California's Proposition 21, New York's Juvenile Offender Law, Oregon's Ballot Measure 11, Massachusetts's Juvenile Justice Reform Act. And they each work in a slightly different way. But the end result is the same.

The laws redefine the boundary between childhood and adulthood in ways that have little parallel elsewhere. Across the country, youth must be eighteen to vote; in many states, they cannot drive until they are sixteen and they must be eighteen or twenty-one to purchase tobacco and alcohol. Yet, legislation allows youth who are too young to drive or get married or join the military—youth as young as age ten in some cases—to be tried, convicted, sentenced, and imprisoned as an adult. All told, nearly one in five offenders under age eighteen is prosecuted as an adult. In essence, the pathways from the juvenile to the adult system have become wider, steeper, and much more numerous:

- At least twenty-nine states limit or completely eliminate the traditional role of the juvenile court judge by excluding certain youth and certain crimes (ranging from serious violent crimes to lesser drug offenses) from juvenile court jurisdiction.
- At least fifteen states and the District of Columbia give the prosecutor the discretion to bypass the judge and move juvenile cases directly into adult court.
- Since 1997, at least thirty-one states have enacted "once an adult, always an adult" statutes, meaning that a youth who is convicted in adult court will typically remain in adult court, no matter how small and insignificant the subsequent offense.
- Most dramatic of all, thousands of youth under age eighteen are automatically excluded from the juvenile justice system—not because of the severity of their crimes and not because they are violent or habitual offenders, but solely because of their age. At least thirteen states have discounted the traditional age of eighteen and established a lower age of adulthood for youth who commit any crime, major or minor, significant or insignificant. The majority of these sixteen- or seventeen-year-olds have committed nothing more serious than minor property or drug offenses, but are sent into the adult system simply because they are legally defined as adults under state law.

Several interwoven factors came together to bring about this drive to send more youth and younger youth into the maw of the adult system. Between 1984 and 1994, arrest rates for juveniles charged with violent offenses jumped 78 percent. Politicians—some motivated by the always present need to be reelected, some genuinely shocked by high-profile crimes in their districts—acted promptly by introducing a raft of "adult crime–adult time" legislation. Some justified their actions by saying that the rehabilitation offered in the juvenile court system would be wasted on the new breed of "superpredators," who were beyond help. Others on the get-tough bandwagon faulted the juvenile system as being too lax, without the legal muscle to hold teenagers accountable and to apply appropriately tough sentences.

As early as the mid-1990s, the overall violent crime rate among juveniles plummeted. Between 1994 and 2000, the overall juvenile arrest rate declined 13 percent with even larger decreases in violent offenses. For example, during that time period, among juveniles arrests for murder dropped 68 percent; 51 percent for robbery, 33 percent for burglary, and 42 percent for motor vehicle theft. By 2000, murder and robbery arrest rates for juveniles had reached their lowest levels in twenty years.

And while the concept of childhood was being narrowed in the juvenile courts, researchers were using state-of-the-art medical technology to prove that youth differ from adults in their ability to make decisions and to understand the long-term repercussions of their actions. Certain parts of the brain—particularly the frontal lobe and the cable of nerves connecting both sides of the brain—are not fully formed in many adolescents, contributing to a large extent to teenage impulsivity and mood swings. As Jay Giedd of the National Institute of Mental Health explains, "Teenagers don't utilize inhibitory pathways as well as their parents do to moderate their impulses."

Psychologist Michael J. Bradley, author of *Yes, Your Teen Is Crazy! Loving Your Kid Without Losing Your Mind,* makes the same point: "There's neurological evidence that an adolescent's brain is going through a period of massive reorganization. We've recently learned that the most critical part of the brain develops ninety-five percent of its capacity in adolescence—it doesn't even begin to develop until you hit eleven or twelve, and it doesn't finish until you're nineteen or twenty. It's the part that has to do with making good judgments, moral and ethical decisions, and reining in impulsive behavior."

Acknowledging this biological difference is not meant to excuse criminal behavior, or to suggest that youth should not be held accountable for their crimes. But it does mean that youth can sometimes be considered less morally, ethically, and cognitively developed in the same way that offenders with developmental delays and brain damage are sometimes seen by the court as less legally responsible for their actions.

Because the brain is still forming, drug treatment, education, vocational training, and anger management for adolescents can have a major impact. Indeed, studies indicate that the influence of a mentor—just one consistent and caring adult—can be the difference between a teenager who succumbs to drugs and gangs and a teenager who avoids negative influences.

In recent years, a growing number of people—from youth advocates to correctional personnel to judges and lawmakers from all points on the political spectrum—have begun to combine the punitive aspects of the adult system with the traditional rehabilitative focus of the juvenile court. One of the most popular combinations among reformers is called "blended sentences," which, as the name implies, combine the juvenile system with the adult criminal courts.

Today, at least twenty-two states have enacted some form of blended sentencing. In theory, this legal procedure allows judges faced with the task of sanctioning juvenile offenders to choose between juvenile and adult correctional sanctions—or sometimes to impose both at the same time—rather than restricting them solely to one system or the other.

In Texas, a blended sentence is known as a determinate sentence, and Texas is more creative in its application than other states. A determinate sentence gives a youth a chance to determine his own future, and hands tremendous power to the staff at a TYC facility like the Giddings State School.

The nine boys in Capital Offenders Group A all have determinate sentences. At twenty-five years, Ronnie's sentence is about in the middle. Mark's is the longest, forty years for murdering his sixteen-year-old girlfriend. Daniel's is the shortest, eight years for a string of armed robberies. Judges sentenced these young men as adults and imposed long prison sentences. But instead of sending them into the Texas prison system in Huntsville, which could have the same sign over the gate as Dante's *Inferno*—"Abandon hope, all ye who enter here"—the judge gave them the opportunity to redeem themselves in the Giddings State School.

Juveniles, particularly those who have lived chaotic lives and committed crimes, are notorious for not thinking beyond the moment. A determinate sentence forces youth to consider long-term consequences. It also allows the treatment specialists who know a youth best to play a pivotal role in deciding his future.

If the treatment staff decide that a youth has successfully completed the programs in the State School, if the psychological evaluations they perform suggest he has a low risk of reoffending, they will recommend he be released on parole. Youth serving sentences of forty, thirty, and twenty-five years are routinely released from the State School after only three years.

Every Wednesday at 8:30 A.M., a committee meets behind drawn blinds in a conference room across from the administration building. The committee has the kind of euphemistic name that often cloaks power—the Special Services Committee. Chaired by Ann Kelley, it includes the school principal; program administrators; an institutional coordinator in charge of placing youth who are leaving Giddings in group homes or halfway houses; and the on-campus victim representative (should they choose to, victims may also appear before the committee). This committee has the power to recommend that a youth be released on parole or transferred to a state prison to serve his entire sentence. It also has the authority to summon a youth and tell him that if he does not change, they will recommend he be transferred to a state penitentiary.

The nine boys in the bunker all know youth who were sent to prison for fighting, gang involvement, using drugs, or failing to pass Capital Offenders. They all know how important it is to participate in role plays.

The boys have gathered in a corner of the room with the therapists and there is much whispering and animated gestures. Meanwhile, the forlorn Ronnie waits in the opposite corner.

Finally, Frank Soto breaks away from the group and walks slowly to Ronnie. Soto will not be enacting a part, but he has perhaps the most important role in the drama that is to come. Soto will be doing the "processing" with Ronnie, speaking into his ear, telling him what is going on, asking what he is feeling, prompting and then guiding Ronnie's emotions. Soto kneels beside Ronnie and begins talking softly. Ronnie buries his face in his hands.

Meanwhile, Whatley and Urbach continue to rehearse the scenes they want to reenact, going over dialogue and taking suggestions from the boys, who are intent upon making sure they know exactly what they will be doing. Josh with the mighty voice will be playing Ronnie's abusive aunt; Daniel is going to be Ronnie; Mark is Ronnie's mother. Johnnie and

Tim, the two smallest boys, will play Kenny and Ronnie's little cousin, with Dwayne playing the older cousin. Tran is playing Ronnie's grandmother.

The boys take a certain pride in playing female roles. Like actors everywhere, they are proud of their range.

Finally, the group splits up. Soto takes Ronnie by the shoulders and gently turns him to face the action. The boys take four chairs off the stack in a corner and use them to create a "car" in the center of the room—two chairs in front, two chairs in back.

"Look, Ronnie, look at what's happening!" Soto urges, leaning close to Ronnie's ear.

"Let's go, Ronnie!" says Mark, playing Ronnie's mother.

"Where we going, Mama?" asks Daniel, playing Ronnie.

"To the Laundromat! Come on, get in the car!"

The actors playing Ronnie, Marina, and Kenny get in the car and Mark/Marina mimes driving. A highly agitated Ronnie begins to rock back and forth as he casts terrified glances at the car.

"It's taking a long time to get to the Laundromat, isn't it, Mommy? Are we almost there?" asks Daniel/Ronnie.

"We're not going to the Laundromat, Ronnie."

"We're not? Where are we going, Mommy?"

"To your aunt Marianne's house. You take a nap. We'll be there soon."

"Do you remember what the car smelled like, Ronnie?" Soto asks. "You were there. You were in a car seat. Do you remember what you felt like, strapped in your car seat all those hours?"

Suddenly, Ronnie pitches himself out of his chair, landing face-first on the carpet, sobbing uncontrollably. Soto quickly lies down beside him and drapes an arm over his shoulder. "Look, look what's happening now, Ronnie," Soto urges.

Ronnie lifts his head and cranks it around to the stage. The car has vanished. Now, Daniel and Tim, playing Ronnie and his cousin, are on the floor, making believe that blackboard erasers are toy trucks. And then Josh's thunderous voice echoes across the room, so loud even the one-way mirror seems to tremble.

"What are you doing in my flower bed!"

The real Ronnie yelps like a dog who has been hit by a kick he did not see coming. His body arches and lurches one way and then another. Soto struggles to keep his hold around Ronnie's shoulders. Josh/Marianne runs to Daniel/Ronnie and mimes hitting him with a rope, slapping his hands to simulate contact. Every time Josh/Marianne slaps his hands, Ronnie flinches.

"Stop!" Daniel/Ronnie pleads. "Stop! Please, stop! Please! Don't hit me, please!"

"You quit your yellin'!" Josh/Marianne commands as he jerks Daniel/Ronnie up by the arm. "You'll get the neighbors watchin'!"

"Don't hit me, please, don't hit me!"

Josh/Marianne delivers a series of blows back and forth across Daniel/Ronnie's face.

Ronnie is in agony. He is not "fronting." No aspiring actor could put on a performance this convincing. The faraway look in his eyes, the coiled, tense body—Ronnie is back in Amarillo, reliving the events as they happened. He lifts his head off the floor and as loud as he can howls, *"Mom! Mom! Help me, Mom! Help me!"*

"We're going inside! I know someplace where you won't be screaming!" yells Josh, the aunt.

"Where are they going, Ronnie?" Soto asks. "Where?"

"Owwww! It's hot!" Daniel/Ronnie pleads, as if on cue. *"Don't put me in that water!"*

Ronnie lets out a terrible, heartbreaking scream. Even the fiberglass soundproofing cannot hold it.

And then, some malevolent, unseen but powerful force seems to take possession of Ronnie. He rolls away from Soto so fast, it is as if he is going down a steep hill. Soto lunges and gets an arm around him. Ronnie fights the arm off and keeps rolling. Soto leaps to his feet, takes a couple of quick steps, lands on Ronnie, and manages to contain him. Ronnie is sobbing so heavily, his body is convulsing. Sherry Whatley hurries over to help Soto.

"Look at it, Ronnie! Look at what is happening now," Whatley urges.

Whatley waits a moment for Ronnie's sobbing to subside, then nods to Tim, who opens the door. Mark, playing Ronnie's mother, walks into the room. Daniel/Ronnie runs up, falls to his knees, and wraps his arms around Mark/Marina's knees.

"Ronnie, what's the matter? What happened to your face? Those burns, where'd you get those red burns?" Mark/Marina asks.

"Aunt Marianne hit me, Mama! She hit me with a rope!" Daniel/Ronnie yells.

Mark/Marina turns to face Josh/Marianne.

"What happened to my son?"

"They were playing and got into a fight. I had to run out there and break it up," Josh/Marianne answers, dripping earnestness.

"How did Ronnie get all those marks on his face?"

"My baby was hitting him with a stick. That's what I'm saying. I had to run out there and get it away from him."

"Okay, all right then. Boys will fight, I guess. "

Suddenly, Daniel jumps to his feet and pushes Mark in the back, hard. This is not in the script and Mark wheels, surprised and perplexed. Daniel, his voice teary, is yelling at Mark. But not at Mark, his peer. He is screaming at the character Mark is playing.

"Why aren't you doing anything to stop it?" Daniel shouts. "You're his mother! You aren't doing anything to stop it! That's fucked-up!"

When a youth in Giddings uses the phrase "That's fucked-up!" or "That's messed up," he is pronouncing a kind of final judgment. Things are so far out of whack, there is no hope they will ever be right. In campus parlance, Daniel has "lost it," he has "gone off." This is supposed to happen to Ronnie—the whole role play has been constructed to turn it into a cathartic experience for him. It is not supposed to happen to Daniel, and this is precisely what makes these boys dangerous. It is impossible to predict what will trigger a violent outburst. That is also why every staff member has been schooled in restraint procedures to contain out-of-control youth. And why security officers continually patrol the campus in Chevy vans with a steel cage in the back, ready to respond within minutes, if not seconds.

Daniel sinks to the floor and starts to sob. Soto leaves Ronnie with Sherry Whatley and rushes across the room to kneel beside Daniel. Daniel lowers a shoulder and drives it into Soto, knocking him off balance. Soto recovers and moves in again and attempts to put an arm around Daniel. Daniel rips the arm off his back. And suddenly, the two are rolling across the room. Soto ends up on top of Daniel, holding him, containing him.

"Daniel, Daniel, chill out!" Soto pleads softly. "This is not about you! It's about Ronnie!"

"But, sir!" Daniel says, jerking the words out between sobs. "His mother should have done something!"

"I know, I know. But, please, help Ronnie through this! Hang in there. Don't let yourself go to your own stuff!"

Daniel calms down, crying softly and mumbling to himself. There is one scene left: the birthday party where Ronnie's mother abandoned him. Soto casts a quick glance at Whatley, who is kneeling beside Ronnie. Whatley nods. Ronnie is sobbing, his face buried in the gray carpet. He is still back in Amarillo. Daniel's episode has not registered with him.

Soto whispers something to Daniel. Daniel gets up and joins the other actors.

"Here's the house, Mommy," Daniel/Ronnie manages, although his voice is breaking. "See all the balloons by the door? This is where the party is! All my friends from my school are probably in there already!"

"You go in and have a good time, Ronnie," Mark/Marina replies. "Remember, Mommy loves you. And remember, take care of your little brother."

"You're going to pick me up, aren't you, Mommy?" Daniel/Ronnie says, his voice registering doubt.

"Sure, Ronnie. Now go have a good time."

Ronnie's sobs are echoing off the walls. The actors exchange quick whispers and change places to set up the next scene.

"Hi, Ronnie! I came to pick you up," announces Tran, who is playing Ronnie's grandmother.

"Mommy, where's Mommy? She said she'd be here!" Daniel/Ronnie wails.

"Your mother is gone, Ronnie. You'll be staying with us now. Don't worry. Me and Grandpa will take good care of you."

"No! No! I want my mother! I want my mother!" the real Ronnie shouts, and once again his body convulses in sobs.

Sherry Whatley nods to the actors, indicating that the role play is over. They slump against the walls, completely spent. Ronnie stays where he is, facedown in the middle of the room, sobbing into the carpet. Daniel is a light-skinned black; now, his face is so drained of color, he looks white. Mark and Johnnie are crying. Antonio is crouching in a corner, crying into his hands. Tran wanders into a corner and stands there, facing the wall. The other boys stare into the carpet.

Soto knee-walks over to Ronnie and quietly strokes his head. Moments pass and then he and Whatley exchange a nod and Soto gently helps Ronnie to his feet and walks him to a wall, where Ronnie collapses. The group waits while Ronnie composes himself. He finally stops crying but cannot lift his head to face the group. Whatley decides he is ready to listen and nods at Tim. Tim begins the feedback round that always follows a role play.

"Playing your cousin made me disappointed in my own mother," Tim reveals. "She should have put her foot down and stopped what was going on in my house. But she was powerless against my stepfather."

"Playing one of your cousins took me back to when I got hit," says Dwayne, a tall nineteen-year-old who committed a murder. "I never got love and comfort. Just ass whippings. Playing your cousin was hard for me. I did it to help you."

"I'm just like you," Antonio says. "I didn't have no one to love me. I didn't have no one to hug me till I got locked up. No one showed me no affection or concern until I got locked up."

"I don't like to see you hurt like that; I'm your roommate. It makes me feel sick inside," Johnnie tells Ronnie. "I don't know if I want my mother in my life and I don't know if your mother should be in your life. But I know we have a whole life ahead of us."

"I hate for those things to happen," Josh says, reflecting on his role as the aunt. "If I was to get out today, I couldn't deal with someone beating on children."

When every boy has his say, it is the therapists' turn.

"Hearing you cry because you are angry, hurt, lonely, those are the saddest sounds I can imagine," Frank Soto says softly. "The group can't replace your mother and all the things you missed. But we can take care of each other and give each other what we didn't have growing up. And the group will never do what your parents did: leave you by yourself.

"You did some good work, Ronnie," Soto concludes. "When you think about what happened in here today, ask yourself how you are going to make your life better. Think of how you can rebuild."

Sherry Whatley tells Ronnie she is glad he trusted the group enough to reveal so much. Trusting the group is an important start. "Trust is going to be a struggle for you, Ronnie. If you feel like you are being abandoned, you may go into a rage. You may even try to abuse a girlfriend, a spouse. You'll have to watch that. You'll have to work on that."

Whatley pauses for a moment before turning to Josh, who is sitting beside her. She is bothered by what Josh said about not being able to "deal with someone beating on children." It sounds to her like a justification for violence. Whatley's large, expressive brown eyes bore in on Josh.

"Josh, you are right: it hurts a lot to role-play someone who abuses children. But all of you have that in you. You've all hurt people; don't forget that. The hurt you feel for all the horrible things that have happened to you is the hurt your victims carry. They live with that pain. What you did to your victims, you brought about by your own hands. There can be no excuse for violence."

Josh nods, somber as if he were standing in front of a judge.

And then Whatley turns to Daniel.

"You are going to have to work hard to get control of your own stuff," Whatley tells Daniel. "You have to let go and be here for others. If Ronnie hadn't stayed focused, we'd have lost him, and when that happens, it is very hard to get him back."

"Mr. Soto told me to chill, but I just couldn't," Daniel replies apologetically.

With that, the group ends and the boys get to their feet. They meet in the middle of the room and exchange silent hugs. Then they walk to a corner to collect their black sateen jackets. No one has anything more to say, but that does not mean the discussion of Ronnie's role play has ended. Tomorrow, the boys will comb through it in core group. They will write about it in their journals and refer to it often in the months ahead. It is like the political process; it goes on and on, and it changes but never ends.

There is a rule of thumb at Giddings: If at the end of a group the therapists are exhausted and the youth are not, the therapists are carrying too much of the load. Today, the boys are completely drained, and so are the therapists. As the therapists march the boys back to Cottage 5-A, they have little to say, and they remain silent as they walk back across the campus to the social services building. There, they collapse into chairs in Sherry Whatley's office.

"Did you see how they were hugging each other?" Frank Soto asks rhetorically. "They've gotten to the 'pound puppy stage,' where they just revel in giving and getting affection. You'll see it with the kids you least imagined, tough, hard kids who all of a sudden are sitting next to each other with their arms around each other or a kid stroking another kid's hair. Somebody from the outside who walked in would probably think, Oh my gosh, they're all gay! It's not that. They don't know what it's like to feel love. They've never had that. The group helps them feel that. In the group, they learn how to give each other what they didn't have growing up."

Down in Cottage 5-A, the boys are eating lunch. Group went long, the cottage missed its turn in the lunch rotation, so one of the JCOs called the cafeteria and a security van arrived with the lunches, a carton of milk and a Styrofoam container for each boy that holds two small hamburgers, apple sauce, and potato salad. Ronnie sits alone at a table, staring down. He does not open his lunch.

"I just wanted to sleep," Ronnie said later. "I wanted to go to bed and sleep and sleep. I didn't want to think about anything. But the next day or two, I started feeling better. My peers helped me a lot. I got a lot of stuff out there. I wouldn't ever want to do it again, but I'm glad I did. It feels real good, getting that stuff out there."

5.

FOOTBALL BEHIND A FENCE

Hot, dry air blowing in from the west is mixing with humid, heavy air rolling up from the Gulf, turning Central Texas into a steam room. But as they step out of Cottage 5-A a few minutes before noon, Ronnie and Daniel are oblivious to the heat. They want to run and would, if running on campus was not forbidden. So they adjust the belts on their torn-up practice pants and express their freedom by swinging their gray helmets in an arc as they walk to the athletic field, where head coach Sandy Brown and assistant coach Lester Ward and a precious hour of football are waiting.

Ronnie and Daniel reach the track that surrounds the field and sprint to the end zone, where they line up with twenty-one other players and begin calisthenics. Time is short and there is so much to learn. "It's the Amazon out here!" Coach Ward yells as the players run wind sprints in the wet heat. "Work hard now and the referee will never see you tired! Never let a referee see you're tired!" Tall and powerfully built, Lester Ward still resembles the outside linebacker he was on the 1980 Baylor team that won the Southwest Conference championship. (The inside linebacker was the legendary Mike Singletary.) Quiet and devoutly Christian, Ward has been coaching and teaching physical education at the State School since the Dallas Cowboys cut him in the final round in training camp, twenty years ago. He says he is here because the Lord gave him a calling to come to the State School. "Football is a way a kid can open up and express himself in a positive way," Ward says. "I hate for these kids to lead squashed lives because they've never opened up and expressed what's inside them."

The players try to make eye contact with Ward as they run past, wanting him to see they are giving it all they have. Ward calls an end to the sprints and has the players form two lines. Pacing in front, Ward gets the call-and-response of the traditional black church going.

"I heard somebody messed up in class. If you mess up, do you get to come out here?" Ward asks.

"No, sir!" shouts the team.

"Do you get to play?"

"No, sir!"

"I don't want to hear about any of you showing negative."

"No, sir!"

"When you try to show negative, you start going downhill fast."

"Yes, sir!"

Ward stops in front of Tommy, a five-two, 135-pound wide receiver.

"I hear somebody messed up in the library."

"Yes, sir!" Tommy shouts.

"You had to get the last word in."

"Yes, sir!"

"You know you can't be doing that."

"Yes, sir!"

"If somebody says something about your mother during a game and you get angry and the referee throws you out, you hurt your team."

"Yes, sir!"

"Same in The Free. You get angry and say something and lose your job, you hurt your family."

"Yes, sir!"

"You know we gonna take care of this."

"Yes, sir!"

Moments like these are the reason the coach has stayed at the State School all these years. "I'm in a position here where I can put a kid above winning," explains Ward, who has soft brown eyes and the only beard on campus. Ward knows what he is talking about. Before playing on the last

team to win a football championship at Baylor, Ward was an all-star running back for the Temple Wildcats. Temple is a small Central Texas city
that fans in other football-crazy Texas towns point to when they want to
single out a community that has really lost its sanity over high school
football.

When a town's identity and the fortunes of its high school football
team are joined at the hip, as they are in Ward's hometown, the athletic
department runs the school and it is as important for the Wildcats to win
in Temple, Texas, as it is for the Packers in Green Bay, Wisconsin. Indeed,
the high school stadium in Temple resembles a scaled-down version of
Lambeau Field in Green Bay.

This is not to say that Ward and Sandy Brown do not care about winning. Both burn bright with competitive desire; Brown doesn't sleep the
night before a game, or the night after a loss. And they do win. In the
twenty-one years Sandy Brown has been head coach, the Giddings Indians have had only one losing season. What makes all the difference,
though, is the way they win. It turns out that a correctional institution, in
the purest sense, runs the best athletic program in Texas.

The $3,700-a-year football program is dedicated to an archaic princi-
ple: sports build character. When that goal diverges from winning, winning is sacrificed. If a boy is not progressing in treatment and not doing
well in school, a teacher or a staff member vetoes his request to play football. If a boy has had a behavior infraction or been referred to the security
unit in the last sixty days, he is not eligible to play. A boy who has not
served half his sentence cannot leave the campus to play football.

Josh, the young man in Capital Offenders, is a classic example. Josh
has the body and aggressiveness to turn the eye of a Division One football
coach. Big and strong, quick and fast, he was the Indians' star player last
year, a unanimous selection to the All-State team. Then he punched a boy
in the face in Capital Offenders, and it didn't matter that Brown and
Ward were planning to build this year's team around him. He was busted
from phase three down to phase zero in the resocialization program and
declared ineligible for football. Josh is now doing well in Capital Offenders, but he remains ineligible.

"When our bus leaves for a game, the best athletes are not on it,"

Coach Brown says. "I think we could win all our games if all the talented kids we've got here were eligible to play."

The Giddings State School plays in TAPPS, the Texas Association of Private and Parochial Schools, a conference made up mostly of small Christian academies. Football is a year-round sport in these schools, with weight training beginning the Monday after the last game. The nucleus of a team has been together since the Pop Warner League. Some kids have had private coaching; some attend Roger Staubach's football camps every summer.

Each season, Brown and Ward take a group of murderers, rapists, and armed robbers and turn them into football players. Their record would make them the toast of the Rotary in any Texas town, but Brown and Ward do not spend much time dwelling on wins or play-off appearances. Ask them what they are most proud of and they will tell you that in the twenty years they have been taking kids off campus to play football, not one player has tried to escape. They explain how on the field, boys who grew up learning to respond to violence with violence learn to break that deadly cycle. In two decades, not one Giddings Indian has ever gotten into a fight in a game. Not one Indian has ever been ejected for a personal foul or unsportsmanlike conduct.

Coach Ward says, "I can't remember a game where an opposing coach didn't come up afterwards and say, 'Coach, you got a real disciplined bunch of boys here. They play real clean.' To me, that's winning, right there."

"We have to play superclean," adds Coach Brown. "We're the criminals! If a fight breaks out, it's going to be our fault, no matter who started it."

When football practice began in August, Ward and Brown started where they always do, with fundamentals the average high school player masters in Pop Warner football: this is a three-point stance; the number the quarterback gives you in the huddle is the snap count; this is how you execute a block. "Make one big circle, arm to arm," Coach Brown told the team at an early practice. "Coach Ward is going to explain tackling to you. Listen up now: you don't want to end up in a wheelchair."

For Ronnie and Daniel, the season really began last spring, when they started talking about football in auto shop. "I'll go out if you'll go out," they told each other, and when practice started in August, they did. It was the first time either was on a football field. Now, Ronnie starts at right tackle on both offense and defense and is comfortable playing the position. He lines up next to Daniel, who is a tight end on offense and a defensive end when the other team has the ball.

Daniel threw himself into the one-hour practices and challenged a returning player for a starting position. He won it and has developed into a fearless pass rusher. The way Daniel sees it, redemption is at work on the football field, just as it is in the Capital Offenders bunker.

"The Lord blessed me with a lot of physical talent," Daniel says. "I messed up and never expressed it, so I'm constantly asking myself, 'What if?' Playing football gives me a chance to quit asking myself that question and get some of my life back. It's an opportunity to do something right."

How do you take gangbangers and teenage drug addicts who, in The Free, were too wasted to get out of bed in the morning, and turn them into a winning football team? "Easy," says Coach Brown, and points to Daniel as an example. Daniel came through the gate vowing no one could tell him what to do. Two years later on the football field, he all but begs the coaches to teach him how to be better.

"These kids are so eager, they're easy to teach," Brown says. "They're so starved for affection and attention, they'll run through walls for you."

The scrimmage at this practice underscores what Brown is saying. The players slam into one another and then quickly help one another to their feet and hurry back to their huddles, trying to squeeze as many plays into practice as possible. When Brown steps into the huddle to diagram a play, the players crowd together and listen eagerly.

Sandy Brown has five children, ages nine to nineteen. A jog he takes every morning keeps him lean and youthful-looking. The coach has a big mustache, speaks in a soft Texas drawl, and is unfailingly polite. But behind his good manners lurks a ferocious spirit. Brown still lives in Lexington, a small town eighteen miles north of Giddings, where he grew up mean and angry. "I used to punch a kid every day, just to see him cry," he recalls. Sandy was a star on both the high school football and basketball teams. Deep down, he knew, he just knew, if he went to the University of

Texas and tried out for the football team as a walk-on, he could play for the legendary Darrell Royal. When it came to desire, to putting his body on the line, he knew no one could match him.

But instead of trying out, Brown listened to the men who were telling him he was too small to play Division One football. He went to a community college but ran into academic trouble and did not play football. He went on to Texas A&M and dropped out twice. Along the way, he found an off-the-football-field target for his rage. Austin in the late sixties and early seventies was full of hippies, peaceniks, and kids who just liked wearing their hair long. When Brown came to town, it wasn't to hear Janis Joplin at Threadgill's or score a joint on Guadalupe. He came looking for fights. He managed to start more than a few, but not enough to satisfy him. One day Brown thought, Hey, if I grow my hair long, guys like me will think I'm a hippie and want to fight me! That way, I'll get more fights! Brown did let his hair grow and did indeed get his fights, but the fires burning inside only grew hotter and his rage spilled over into his relationships.

"I was seeing a girl and found out she was having an affair with a man in Austin," Brown recalls, his eyes burning as if this had happened three weeks, not three decades, ago. "I got a gun and went to kill the guy. I wanted to call him out, tell him what I was going to do, and shoot him in the gut so he'd die slow.

"I knew he lived in a house with a carport. I went up and down the streets all night, and I never did find that house with the carport.

"Years later, I had a boy playing for me named Kelly—he's an engineer now, by the way, doing really well, has a nice family. Kelly was in the State School for blowing his mother's head off with a twelve-gauge shotgun. One day after practice, I asked Kelly what he was feeling when he did it. He said, 'I was so angry, it was like I was watching someone else do it.'

"I knew exactly what he was saying! I'd been there myself, the night I was driving around trying to find the house with the carport. Kelly was me. These kids are me. I look at them and see Sandy Brown thirty-five years ago. Except, they did find the house with the carport."

Brown went back to Texas A&M, where he had an epiphany of sorts. If he could never play football again, he could coach football. That goal drove him to earn his degree and carried him to the State School, where he has taken hundreds of raw kids like Ronnie and Daniel and turned them into winning football players.

Is having once seethed with violence a prerequisite to working with violent teenage offenders? "No, not at all," Brown says with a slightly rueful smile. What is necessary, he explains, is an understanding that the youth are not the Other. It is being able to see your humanity reflected in them.

Brown tells a story about a small event that made a world of difference. A few months after he arrived at the State School, he marched a group of boys up to the Snack Shack—a once-a-week, behavior-dependent privilege. The lady behind the counter saw he was new and introduced herself.

"She said to me, 'You can change these kids with love and discipline. You can change them with just love, but it takes longer. But you can't change them with just discipline.' I've always, always remembered that."

Brown falls silent, recalling that moment. "Our medium is football," he continues. "Learning to block and tackle isn't going to change their lives. But coaches who take a personal interest in them might. Giving their all to something can help them change. Making a commitment and never giving up can help prepare them to be successful at whatever they do."

This far into the season, the Indians have not had much success. They are 1–2, an inauspicious beginning for a team that has not lost more than three games in a season in a decade. In their opener in San Antonio, the Indians played a Christian academy that ran a sophisticated passing attack. Covering the pass is always an Indians weak point. Brown and Ward simply do not have enough time to prepare defensive backs to cover receivers that run routes with the precision of ballet dancers. But the Indians did come away feeling good about themselves. Their offense put twenty-four points on the board and Jerrold, their terrific running back, scored three times.

For some reason, the State School team is always small. It is not unusual for the Indians to be outweighed by one hundred pounds per man on the line. But every season, the Indians have an exceptionally fast backfield. If a State School back can turn the corner on a sweep, it will be very difficult to catch him from behind. This was evident in the second game, when the Indians traveled to Holland, a small town north of Waco. Jerrold got around the corner on a sweep and went ninety yards to win the game in the final few seconds.

A week later, the Indians got another lesson in how tough high school football in Texas can be. The team traveled one hundred miles northeast to Iola to play the Bulldogs, a team that won a string of state AA championships in the 1990s. The Bulldogs crushed the State School, 42–0. But the Indians never stopped playing, blocking and tackling until the final whistle blew. This week, the team has lost its quarterback to a contraband infraction in the dorm (a JCO discovered letters from a girl in Cottage 3-A hidden in his clothes), but the Indians have a new quarterback, Kim, and they are crisp and determined in practice. Tomorrow, for the first and only time this year, they will play at home, against the Gainesville Tornadoes. It is their biggest game of the year. Gainesville is the only other TYC institution that fields a football team, and the game has been a grudge match since its inception.

"I always tell 'em, 'This game is for the "State" championship because it's between the only two "State" schools that play football,'" Sandy Brown says with a big grin.

Gainesville is five hours north, seven miles from the Oklahoma border. Because neither facility can handle large crowds, and because opponents do not want to play inside a correctional facility that cannot accommodate their fans, the only home games these two schools play are against each other. For this once-every-two-years event, youth in a horticulture program that prepares kids for jobs in landscaping have been hard at work on the field. Jerry Reeves, the school chaplain, has rigged up a small public address system and is working with boys who dream about being play-by-play announcers.

Practice ends and the players huddle on the fifty-yard line. Brown has Kim, the new quarterback who has been working feverishly to master the basic T-formation offense, kneel on one knee. "One-two-three, Indians, on the quarterback," Brown commands. "Everybody say one thing you like about him." Each player puts a hand on Kim's helmet and shoulder pads. "He comes out here and tries real hard!" "He's got heart!" "He's going for the team!" "One-two-three, Indians!"

The huddle breaks up and the players are heading for the gym when Ward barks, "Tommy!"

"Yes, sir!" the minuscule wide receiver shouts. He pivots, races over to Ward, and stands at attention, his helmet tucked under his arm.

"Let's have you do five," Ward says.

"Yes, sir!" Tommy replies, and eagerly, with no hint of resentment, runs five laps back and forth across the field, hands and feet touching the ground.

"We back the teachers one hundred percent," Ward says as he watches. "Tommy is a good kid, he just has to learn he can't always get in the last word, especially with an authority figure. If he does that in here where he's under constant scrutiny, he might do it to the traffic cop who pulls him over for a minor violation. That will make a bad situation worse."

Brown and Ward are in their small, dark office in a locker room under the stands in the gymnasium, going through a pregame checklist. A freshly laundered blue and gray game uniform hangs in front of every locker. Brown has called to make sure the team of referees he has hired are on their way. The horticulture crew are out on the field, finishing up a red, white, and blue flag at the fifty-yard line, their tribute to victims of the 9/11 attacks. Brown and Ward seem to be soothed by the voice of a pastor delivering a sermon at low volume on a boom box in a corner.

Outside in the brilliant sunlight, the Gainesville Tornadoes have arrived in a touring bus that is all windows, big and reeking of comfort, the type that retirees on a tour ride around in. Word spreads quickly about the bus, and staff are coming by to ogle and wonder why their team has to grind down highways in a yellow school bus with one of the coaches behind the wheel (Brown drives one way, Ward the other). A crew from Holden Productions in Dallas that is shooting a documentary about the football team for ESPN is setting up on both sidelines. The small bleachers will soon be packed with staff and high-phase boys and girls who have earned the right to attend the game.

There will be no dance after the game, but this is homecoming, none-theless. The players arrive in the locker room silent and focused, deter-mined to do well for the people who, at this point, are the most important in their lives: the JCOs, the caseworkers, the high-phase girls in the stands, working on syncopated hand movements to go with cheers.

When the Indians take the field, they break through a sign under a goalpost made by Cottage 7-A: GO INDIANS, SPEAR THE TORNADOES. On the sideline, the players keep jumping up and down, as if there is an elec-tric current under the field. The Indians kick off, and it is clear that play-ers on both sides came to hit. The sound of shoulder pads colliding at full speed echoes across the field, and bodies fly into the air. In the first play from scrimmage, Gainesville sweeps left and a wide receiver executes a perfect crack-back block on Daniel. For a split second, Daniel seems to levitate, his body parallel to the ground, before landing with a thud. He lies still and then has to be helped off the field, but three plays later, he runs back on.

The Gainesville quarterback keeps throwing quick outs to two re-ceivers who are at least six-four, much taller than the Indians' defensive backs, and he keeps the defense from keying on the pass by sending a rugged fullback into the line who tears through Ronnie's attempts to bring him down. The Tornadoes' quarterback fakes a handoff to his run-ning back, sweeps right, and falls into the end zone.

The Indians' defensive unit comes off the field, heads hanging. The players are bickering, accusing one another of missing assignments— "You had outside coverage on that play, not me!"

Brown and Ward have seen this happen time and time again. When the going gets tough, the tough break down. The Indians come from fami-lies where little if anything ever went right. They failed in school. They failed at crime—had they not, they wouldn't be locked up. Their gangs let them down; none of the homeys bothered to visit when they were in jail, awaiting trial. They have never learned to fight through adversity; no one ever cared enough to try to teach them how. So when an Indians player takes the field, no matter how pumped he is, somewhere deep down in-side, he is harboring a nasty secret. He expects something to go wrong, because something has always gone wrong. Which is, of course, exactly what losers do.

The coaches run a few yards onto the field to intercept the defensive unit. The calm, thoughtful manner Brown exhibits on campus every day is gone. The coach is angry.

"You're a team and you are going to play like a team!" he shouts. "You can't be pointing fingers at teammates! Go out there and you beat your man and do your best to help your teammate beat his man!"

"Football is simple, fellas," bellows Coach Ward. "You run hard, you hit hard. You stay focused. You don't let yourself get down. You don't let your teammates down!"

"Go out there and play like on every play, the game depends on you! Because it does!" Brown yells.

Jason is a sex offender who was on last year's team. He has turned twenty, too old to play high school football, so this year he is the team manager. Carrying a tray of water cups, Jason follows the coaches off the field. "No excuses!" he yells to no one in particular on the sidelines. "You can't say that no one ever cared about you! You can't say nobody cares if you succeed!"

The Tornadoes kick off and the Indians' offense roars to life. Ronnie and Daniel are knocking people down and Jerrold, the star running back, is gobbling up chunks of yardage. Kim, the new quarterback, is surprisingly cool. He even completes a wobbly pass to Daniel, who is immediately slammed to the turf by a big Tornadoes linebacker. The linebacker leaps up and beats his chest.

"Keep your bitch ass on the ground, right where your mama's is!" he screams at Daniel.

Daniel trots back to the huddle, as if he hadn't heard a word. The coaches exchange quick nods of approval. Gainesville has been talking "smack," or "downtalk," since the game began. Brown and Ward knew they would; every team does. The players on Christian academy teams are often the worst, throwing out taunts like, "Who did you kill? Your mother or your sister?" On the street, this kind of verbal assault demands an immediate response; let it go and you risk losing respect. That means getting labeled a pussy and becoming prey. For the coaches, football is a way to free the players from this deadly two-step dance.

The Indians score a touchdown. The Gainesville Tornadoes march right back down the field and score their second touchdown, and then the Indians take over the game. They are better coached, in better shape, and in Jerrold, they have the most talented athlete on the field. Jerrold is five-eight and 180 pounds of well-conditioned muscle. He is very fast—last spring at the state track meet, he ran a 10.5-second 100 meters, finishing second. But what makes Jerrold exceptional is an ability to slip tackles that cannot be taught. By the fourth quarter, Jerrold has scored twice and gained over two hundred yards.

In the game's closing moments, Kim drifts back and lofts a pass into the end zone that seems to have eyes. Two Tornadoes defensive backs jump as high as they can, but the ball slips over their fingertips and into the arms of Tommy, the five-two wide-out. Tommy comes racing out of the end zone, holding the ball above his head like the trophy it is. By NFL standards, his celebration is muted, but a referee throws a flag and hits the Indians with a fifteen-yard unsportsmanlike conduct penalty. Brown and Ward race onto the field and corral Tommy.

"We know you're happy. We know you weren't trying to show any-body up, but the ref didn't see it that way. You cost your team fifteen yards," Brown says.

"It's not just what you do. It's how people read what you do. Remember that," Ward adds.

Tommy nods and nods and nods, far too elated to speak. Two plays later, the game ends. The Indians win, 30–13. The players erupt in joy, throwing their helmets in the air and themselves on the ground.

"No celebrating, not while the other team is across the field!" Brown says sternly. "Line up, walk over, shake their hands. You want to celebrate after that, go down to our end zone."

The players do as they are told and then race to the end zone, where they keep thrusting their helmets in the air, whooping and hugging and exchanging high fives.

"It feels so good, sir! It just feels so good, miss!" Tommy says to every teacher and JCO who comes up to congratulate him. "I just wish my dad was here to see me catch that pass!"

"Welcome to tonight's play-off game between the Bay Area Broncos and the Gideon Indians!" says the public address announcer in a small high school stadium.

The mistake is understandable. The Indians are in League City, part of the steamy sprawl south of Houston, playing a Christian academy on their home field under a full moon. The Indians have rolled into the play-offs behind their bread-and-butter play, Jerrold sweeping left, Jerrold sweeping right, plays they run with a confidence that approaches arrogance. To make the play-offs, the Indians pulverized the Texas School for the Deaf in Austin, 66–6, a game that quickly became too painful to watch.

"Please bow your heads and join us in prayer," the PA announcer asks and lets a moment go by before saying, "Lord, we pray that Christlike conduct will be reflected on the field tonight." Sandy Brown is himself a born-again Christian and when the prayer ends, he says a silent prayer of his own. Then he gathers his team around him and suddenly becomes a football coach out to maximize his chances of winning.

"This team has to be apprehensive, they've never played us before," Brown says. "We're the criminals! In a street fight, the person that gets the hardest lick in first usually wins. Come out fighting! Explode! Get that momentum! Get them doubting!"

"Are you ready?" Coach Ward asks.

"*Yes, sir!*" roars the team.

"Are you gonna hit hard?"

"*Yes, sir!*"

"Are you gonna win?"

"*Yes, sir!*"

Several Indians are from the Houston area and some, like Kim, the quarterback, have family in the stands. This is Kim's final game. In five days, he will be released. Kim has been playing with the poise of a veteran and the coaches think he can take them all the way to the state championship game. And yet, they are philosophical about losing Kim. "Rather have him go this way than any other," Brown said before the game. "We'll work it out; we always do."

Kim takes the field with mixed feelings. After dreaming of his release date for two years, he now dreams of playing for a state championship. On the first series, the Indians' offense is tight, especially Kim. He is a split second late on handoffs and throws a pass ten feet over the head of a wide-open Daniel. The Indians turn the ball over on downs and as Kim walks off the field, Ritchie, an interior lineman, trots up to join him. At 185 pounds, Ritchie is the biggest player on the team and one of the co-captains. He drapes an arm around Kim's shoulders, says a few words, and uses his knuckles to rap on Kim's helmet.

This is more than just a co-captain lifting a quarterback after a shaky series. In The Free, Kim, who is black, belonged to a Houston gang affiliated with the Bloods. Ritchie, who is white, was jumped into a black gang, the Crips, sworn enemies of the Bloods. Had these two met on the street, they would have exchanged gunfire. In Giddings, they were placed in the same dorm. The two boys did what rival gang members always do when they find themselves living together—they watched each other from a distance, waiting to see who would make the first move. The JCOs were watching, too, and instead of "talking shit" to each other, the two boys sat in group after group, sorting through problems in the dorm. Slowly, they realized they liked each other. Playing football turned two young men who might have killed each other into fast friends.

The Indians' defense holds when Daniel slipstreams around a blocker to nail the quarterback. The Indians get the ball on their own thirty-yard line, and on the second play, Jerrold turns the corner on a sweep, breaks two tackles, runs over a third tackler, and goes seventy yards to score. The officials manning the first-down chains on the sidelines are Bay Area Broncos fans. "So damn fast!" one says, his voice full of gloom.

"If that young man's feet touched the ground, I didn't see it," the other official replies.

The Indians quickly score another touchdown. And then, some mysterious communication runs through the team and the players decide the game is in the bag. Kim strolls away from the bench to stand by the fence that separates the stands from the field and chat with an uncle. Ritchie ignores the game to face the stands and mime a conversation with his mother. On the field, the Bay Area Broncos do not think the game is over. They have a fine running back named Nick Bentley who attacks Ronnie's side of the line on play after play. If Ronnie doesn't bring him down, Bentley rumbles into the secondary for a big gain. Finally, he fights his way across the goal line. The Broncos kick off, an Indians receiver fumbles in the end zone, and Daniel manages to fall on the ball a split second before a Broncos lineman. Behind Bentley, the Broncos drive the ball down the field and are close to scoring when the half ends. It is 14–9, Indians, but the ecstatic Broncos fans who form two rows to slap their players' shoulder pads as they run to the locker room sense it is the Broncos' game to win, and so does Coach Brown.

"This is what I've got to say to you, fellas," Brown says in the visitors' locker room. "Congratulations. You've learned to play football. You've had a good season. But let me tell you, if you don't go out there and play like you are capable of playing, your season is over. You're through!"

"Who told you the game was over?" Coach Ward demands, his anger taking the players by surprise. "You wanted it the first three or four minutes, then you gave up. Do you still want it?"

"*Yes, sir!*" ricochets off the metal lockers.

"Does twenty-four want it more than you?" Number 24 is Nick Bentley, the runner slicing up the Indians' defense.

"*No, sir!*"

"Then let's go take it!"

On the Indians' first possession, Jerrold shakes off a tackler in the backfield, reverses field, and goes twenty-two yards for a touchdown. After that, the Broncos' defense wilts and Jerrold and the running-back corps break free for big gains on play after play. At the end of the third quarter when Jerrold scores on a beautiful sixty-yard run, the game is out of reach, 46–15. It ends, 46–21.

Jerrold is a handsome young athlete with a smile that lights up a room. The smile stays plastered across his face in the bus all the way back to Giddings. It grows even larger on the ritual "victory lap" around the campus at 1 A.M., when Jerrold and the players stick their heads out the bus windows and yell themselves hoarse, trying to wake up their peers. The smile stays put as Jerrold and the players turn in their uniforms and go through a contraband search in the security unit. The smile appears the first thing the next morning, when Jerrold wakes up and remembers the game.

Before he was locked up, Jerrold cannot remember a day when he smiled.

He grew up in Beaumont, a fatherless child. His mother was away all day, working several jobs to support nine children. Jerrold's two older brothers were in gangs and heavy into warfare, and not having a father either, they took it upon themselves to turn Jerrold into a man. At home, they punched the little boy, kicked him, and laughed when he cried. In the housing project, they pitted Jerrold against any boy willing to fight. If Jerrold lost, his brothers made him fight the kid again.

In school, Jerrold had a reading problem that left him behind his class and he quit going in fifth grade. No truant officer, no curious teacher, no one from social services came around to find out why. By the time his two older brothers went off to prison, one for attempted murder and armed robbery, the other for murder, Jerrold was as angry as an abused rott-weiler, cruising the project, looking for fights. He was ten years old.

"Fighting became important to me, know what I'm sayin'? Even if they weren't around, I felt I had to show my brothers I can take care of myself and won't let no one get over on me."

By age twelve, Jerrold was carrying a gun and dealing drugs. His spe-cialty was fry, marijuana soaked in embalming fluid. One summer day when he was fourteen, he needed to get across Beaumont to connect with another dealer and "rescore," i.e., buy more drugs. Nobody was around to give him a ride, so Jerrold stole a bike, made the connection, and then, magnanimously, gave the bike to his younger brother.

That afternoon, a cousin of the boy who owned the bicycle spotted Jerrold's little brother riding across the housing project. Angry, he con-fronted the little boy and grabbed the bike. Jerrold's teary-eyed little brother ran to their apartment to tell Jerrold what had happened. "I'll take care of it," Jerrold assured him.

Jerrold was too stoned on fry to fight later that day when he ran into the nineteen-year-old who had reclaimed the bicycle. The two exchanged words and pushes and then Jerrold took out a pistol and shot the young man six times. His victim survived, but barely. He now lives with a colostomy bag.

As Linda Reyes says, "They all come through the gate looking like psychopaths," and that certainly described Jerrold. He stayed sullen, uncommunicative, and quick to anger for two years. He entered Capital Offenders and for months hid behind his scowl. He couldn't stay awake. Tami Coy, one of the therapists, kept telling him, "Of all the people here, I trust you the least, Jerrold. I have no idea what's going on with you."

And then, Jerrold says, he "did a one-eighty. I'm not sure why. I just decided it was time I opened myself and just saw what happened, know what I'm saying?" Jerrold began staying alert and giving excellent feedback. He dug into his life story and every now and then, he even smiled.

"When we got to my crime story, we did the role reversal and I had to play my victim. I was scared, really, really scared," Jerrold recalls. "By me being so terrified, I saw the feelings my victim must have had and it made me imagine what he is going through today. I'm ashamed of myself. I tried to take a man's life over something petty. I wish he'd forgive me but I know he can't. It's something he's got to live with the rest of his life.

"I was a dangerous person. Keeping in mind how I messed up somebody's life will keep me from being dangerous again."

Joseph Campbell, author of *The Hero with a Thousand Faces* and a dozen other books that explore what it means to be human, boils down his advice for following the spiritual path into three words: "Follow your bliss." But what advice would Campbell have for Jerrold and thousands of other angry, lonely, drug-addled teenagers who have never experienced joy? How can they "follow their bliss" if they have never experienced, and therefore have no conception of, bliss?

Take Jerrold through his childhood. Ask him to remember a Christmas when he got a present and his face stays blank. Can he recall a trip to a park to go swimming? An amusement park where he spent all day on the rides? A day when he really had fun? A solemn Jerrold shakes his head no. The irony is, Jerrold never had fun until he was locked up, never felt joy until he played football for the Giddings Indians.

"I never experienced the things out there that I have here inside," Jerrold says. "The joy, the good times, the love from other teammates. It feels good to experience those things, even if you are locked up."

After pounding up I-35 for five hours in the yellow school bus, the Giddings Indians take the field at the huge Harvest Baptist Church complex in Watauga, north of Ft. Worth. The stands behind the Giddings bench are packed for the first time all year, even though this is the farthest the Indians have traveled from campus. Many players come from the Dallas–Ft. Worth metroplex, and their families are here. Girls clustered in the middle of the stands are stomping the aluminum planks and shouting, "Let's go, Indians!" They are residents of Willoughby House, a TYC halfway house in Ft. Worth, where many girls are sent when they leave Giddings. Early in the week, the head nurse in the State School infirmary called the halfway house and told the staff to make sure the girls got to the game.

As the Indians run out under the bright lights, Jerrold comes to a sudden stop. Two players run into him, but Jerrold doesn't notice. He is looking into the stands, craning his neck, silently asking himself, "Could it be? Could it be?"

It is! Jerrold breaks into his huge smile and races to the sidelines. "I didn't know if that was you or not! You sort of look like you!" he says shyly, shaking hands with a young man standing behind the rope that surrounds the field. This is the first time he has seen his older brother in more than a decade. After serving eleven years in a state prison, Jerrold's brother was released on Monday, only four days ago. Jerrold's pretty sister steps from behind her brother. Jerrold lights up and they hug, and then his little brother steps up for a hug. Suddenly, the smile vanishes and Jerrold turns serious.

"Where's Mom?" Jerrold asks, scanning the stands. "She called, we talked. Said she'd be here to see me play."

"She couldn't make it. The truck stop where she's waitressing wouldn't give her the night off," Jerrold's sister explains. "She was gonna call but she didn't want you getting upset."

Jerrold's shoulders slump. His sister sees this and quickly reaches into a pocket and waves a small, silver rectangle in front of him. "I got my cell phone! I'll call Mom, you'll talk to her after the game!"

Jerrold manages a grin and runs back to his teammates.

Tonight's opponents, the Calvary Academy Conquerors, are huge. The three interior linemen weigh 292 pounds, 294 pounds, and 295 pounds. The team from Ft. Worth is well coached and they have watched the Indians' game films. Their linebackers begin the game keying on Jerrold, but they cannot stop him. Cornered near the sideline, Jerrold spins, cuts back, and races through three arm tackles, going twenty-five yards for a touchdown.

The Conquerors methodically grind out a touchdown, marching eighty yards behind their huge line. When the Indians get the ball back, Joshua, a running back turned quarterback in the wake of Kim's departure, gets the offense clicking and the Indians come back with an eighty-yard drive of their own. Jerrold caps it, going into the end zone from fifteen yards out. At halftime, it is 16–11, Indians.

The Conquerors have rented the field and they disappear into a warm, well-lighted room where their coaches get busy, diagramming plays on a chalkboard. The Indians settle into the end zone, where a cold mist is rising from the grass. It may be the adjustments the Conquerors' coaches make; it may be that the Indians are stiff and cold and the Conquerors are warm and loose. Whatever it is, at the start of the second half, the Conquerors take over the game.

The Indians did not have much of a passing attack with Kim at quarterback. With Joshua, they have none. The Indians have nothing in their arsenal other than sending their backs on sweeps, and the Conquerors keep bottling those up. Time after time, the offense turns the ball over on downs. Meanwhile, the Conquerors' offense turns efficient and puts together two long drives for scores.

Midway through the fourth quarter, the game appears over. The Indians' interior linemen are exhausted, worn down by their huge opponents. And then, things turn strange; and then, a bit scary.

It is 25–16, Conquerors, when the Indians' offense comes alive, driving down the field to score. Joshua slips trying to run in the extra point and it is 25–22 with less than two minutes to go. The Indians have to score a touchdown to win—the team does not have a placekicker, or even a kicker who can convert extra points. All the Conquerors have to do is run out the clock. But on a routine dive-play into the line, a Conquerors back fumbles at his own forty-five and Tommy—five-two Tommy—playing free safety, recovers the ball. The Indians are ecstatic. And then, the team deflates. A flag is down. The referees are conferring.

The Giddings coaches think of themselves as guests in the TAPPS conference. They are respectful of officials and grateful to the coaches who voted to allow them into the league. But when a referee comes to the sidelines to explain that the flag was "inadvertent" and therefore the down does not count and will have to be played over, the coaches are enraged.

"That is ridiculous!" shouts Coach Ward, which for him is equivalent to screaming an expletive.

Coach Brown levels a finger at the referee. "We're gonna win!" he vows. "We're gonna win anyway!"

The down is replayed and the Indians' defense holds. To the great consternation of the Conquerors' coaching staff, their punter sends a high, end-over-end kick down the middle of the field, where Jerrold is waiting. Jerrold is even more dangerous in the open field than he is running the sweep. He knifes through tacklers and goes fifty yards down the field before being hauled down just inside the twenty-yard line. But wait: a flag is down! Again, the referees huddle.

Jerrold's brother and a group of Giddings fans have left the stands and are on the sidelines, pressing against the rope. The girls from the halfway house remain in the stands but they are very quiet, sensing trouble. Parents, brothers, uncles, and mothers, people who have been in brawls, have been in prison, are glaring at the referees. The JCOs who are along to provide security duck under the rope and get between the fans and the referees. One of the JCOs walks up the sideline until she is parallel to the forty-five-yard line, where the referees are huddled. "You have to do right for the kids!" she yells. "Don't teach them this! They're only kids!"

Finally, the head referee leaves the huddle and announces that the flag was thrown in error. The play stands. The Giddings fans erupt in joy. People who don't know one another's names wrap their arms around one another and jump up and down in unison.

The Indians send Jerrold around end, but the dazzling running back is spent and the Conquerors force him out of bounds for no gain. The Indians try a pass play. The execution is slow, the pass is wobbly, the Conquerors' defensive backs knock it down. On fourth down, the Indians try a pass to Daniel, running a slant into the end zone. A Conquerors defensive back tips the ball away.

The Conquerors are wild with relief, throwing their helmets in the air. Their fans are pouring out of the stands and moving toward the field. The game is theirs. Coach Brown has run down the field to console his players. But wait: there's a flag!

The Indians' coaches spent the week teaching their undersize linemen how to get low and cut the legs out from under their massive opponents. The linemen have been doing that all night and at the end of the game, one of the Conquerors' Goliaths was sick of it. After the whistle blew, he said good-bye to his smaller, quicker opponent with an elbow that sliced across the eyes. A referee threw the flag.

The penalty gives the Indians a first and ten at the Conquerors' nine-yard line with twenty-four seconds left. The Indians sweep right, but Jerrold is forced out of bounds for no gain. Ward quickly diagrams a pass play. Tommy will go to one corner of the end zone to decoy; the pass will go to Daniel in the other corner. The pass is on target, floating to Daniel when Tommy races in front, bringing Conquerors defenders with him. Four players go into the air at the same time and somehow, Tommy, the smallest, comes down with the ball. A referee throws both hands in the air. Touchdown!

Butch Held, the mild-mannered State School superintendent, runs to the center of the field and pounds his knees in joy and disbelief. The Indians' coaches are jumping about and waving their arms in the air. JCOs are crying on one another's shoulders. Jerrold's siblings are embracing. The halfway-house girls are making a terrific racket in the bleachers. But

Tommy, the hero, remembering the penalty he got after his touchdown catch against the Gainesville Tornadoes, quietly hands the ball to a referee and then takes off up the field, jumping for joy.

"I caught that ball, sir! I caught that ball for a touchdown!" Tommy keeps saying on the field after the game, where Giddings fans are milling about, not wanting to leave. Jerrold is talking to his mother on his sister's cell phone. Players hug, separate to look at one another, and then hug again.

"All year, I been doing that, sir!" Tommy tells Butch Held. "If they throw it to me, I catch it! All year long, sir!"

More to himself than to Butch Held, Tommy says, "I wish my father was here to see me catch that pass, sir."

Tommy's father is serving life in a Texas state penitentiary. Tommy has been writing him letters for years, but has never received a reply.

Football boils down to execution. Execution trumps talent; talent that executes wins championships. The Indians are talented; they have great heart and have had a remarkable season. But a team that practices an hour a day is not going to execute at a level that will win a state championship in Texas.

On the following Friday, the Indians again travel north, this time to Waco to play another Christian academy, the Pantego Panthers. The winner will advance to the TAPPS state championship game. The Indians are never in the game. The Pantego passing attack is baffling and the Indians never do figure it out. The Pantego defense shuts down the Indians' running game. Jerrold is a factor but only on defense, where he makes tackle after tackle. Pantego wins, 40–0.

When it is over, Coach Brown gathers his team in the center of the field. His players are in tears.

"If it hurts to lose, that just shows you are a winner," Brown says. "I'm extremely proud of all of you. You've had a great season."

The defeat hurts, but losing is probably the least of it. When the players pick themselves up and stand for a final team picture, they reach out for one another, draping an arm around a teammate's shoulders or plac-

ing a hand on the back of someone's head. This season has been the most
fun these boys have ever had. This is the first time they have experienced
success. Their teammates are the first true friends they have made. And
now, it is over. Tomorrow, they will go back to living sixteen-hour days
under the bell jar, with no football for relief. That hurts, real bad.

Sandy Brown is in pain, too. He loves football, and he loved this team
as much as any he has ever coached. But Brown has found a way to console himself. Every year at the end of the season, he gets up early and
makes pecan pies from scratch. Every staff member who volunteered time
to help the football team gets a freshly baked pie.

This year, the coach bakes and personally delivers sixty-eight pecan
pies.

6.

"I FELT POWERFUL
WITH THE GUN"

Ten weeks have gone by since Ronnie finished telling his life story. Four boys have now completed their crime stories, and today Ronnie will begin his. He dreads this part of Capital Offenders. All the boys do; none wants to examine the pain they have inflicted. In fact, a crime story can be a litmus test that reveals a true sociopath. Veteran psychologists have vivid memories of a Dallas youth who was as remote and cold as an arctic night. He was convicted of two murders and the FBI had investigated him as a possible serial killer (the youngest such suspect ever). He passed his days on campus utterly detached, never showing a trace of emotion until the moment he began his crime story. And then he came to life, reveling in the sadistic details. The psychologists halted the narrative and the young man was transferred to prison, where he is serving two life terms.

Ronnie sits in his chair and keeps bending at the waist, rocking gently to a rhythm only he hears. His left hand is wrapped in an almond-colored elastic bandage. Ronnie is going through laser surgery to have the tattoos on his hands removed, a procedure an Austin-based group of plastic surgeons offers for free to Giddings students. On the street, a gang tattoo can make a boy a target, both for rival gangs and for members of his former crew, who consider him a traitor. No gang tattoos means no suspicious looks or difficult questions when a boy applies for a job.

It is cold outside and the boys' black sateen jackets are stacked in one corner. The jackets are standard TYC wear for every boy and girl on campus, except the football players. They wear blue letter jackets with gray sleeves. Daniel's is on top of the heap, Ronnie's is right below it. Embroidered on the front of both jackets in red script are the words FIRST TEAM, ALL STATE, a remarkable achievement for boys in Texas playing their first year of varsity football.

Ronnie's All-State status is no indicator of how well he will tell his crime story. Toughness on the field and the courage needed to face a violent past can be two very different things. That is the way it was with the best player the Giddings Indians ever produced, a six-two, 220-pound slab of muscle named Luther, who washed out of Capital Offenders twice.

When Luther was in the State School, it was easy to pick him out, even marching in formation. His body flowed, as if his hips were oiled, and the other boys were stiff and rusty. Luther ran a 10.4-second 100 meters and cut like a lightning bolt, but preferred blasting over linebackers to zigging around them. Opposing coaches came up to Lester Ward and Sandy Brown after games to tell them Luther was the best high school running back they had ever seen.

"Coach, do you think Luther could have anchored the backfield at the University of Texas?" Lester Ward was asked after Luther's last season. Ward is careful in his judgments and thought for a moment. Then he said, "Yes, sir, I believe he could."

"Could he take the Longhorns to a major bowl?"

"Luther had that in him," Ward replied.

That was all Luther had in him. Luther was in and out of every program Giddings has to offer, and for him, they were a waste of time. Luther is the reason we need prisons.

"Luther was a psychopath," says Corinne Alvarez-Sanders, who failed him twice in Capital Offenders, and she does not easily give up on a kid. "There was nothing inside Luther but ashes."

Luther's past resembled the lives of many of his peers in the State School. His mother was a prostitute; the only evidence of his father's presence was his birth. He bounced from one aunt to another, one step ahead of the social workers until eventually they lost track of him. At age four, Luther was playing on the front porch while an older brother paced back and forth, keeping a wary eye on the street. But he must not have been paying close enough attention, because a car passed, shots were fired, and Luther's brother fell dead, raining blood on Luther's toys.

Ten years later, Luther was a crack cocaine dealer operating out of the .357 Crips gang. One night in a motel, he robbed a dealer who belonged to a rival gang. Luther was sure the guy had no idea who he was, but at 2 A.M. that night, he heard sounds on his front porch and peeked through a blind to see the dealer out there, holding a pistol close to his leg. Luther went out through a back window.

The rival dealer jumped in a black Mustang waiting at the curb. The Mustang was closing in as Luther ran past a convenience store just as a twenty-one-year-old man was getting into a beat-up Ford Escort piled high with newspapers. The young man was studying graphic design at a community college and delivering papers at night. Luther pulled his nine-millimeter and made the student drive to a housing project where his "auntie" lived. It was the only place he could think to go. The Mustang followed close behind. Luther described what happened next in chilling detail.

"We got there and when I told the driver to stop I was thinking, 'This guy might be getting ready to pull one of those hero moves and follow me in,' so I shot him in the leg. I was gonna shoot him again, but I looked in his eyes and he was like begging for his life, so I didn't.

"The Mustang heard the shot. I got out of the car and it was turning around real fast. I ran up to my auntie's and told her what happened. She said we had to call nine-one-one. They got there too late. My victim bled to death in his car."

Luther failed Capital Offenders twice because he had no empathy for his victim. Luther had no empathy, period. The leader of the Crips in the State School, devious and malevolent, Luther reveled in setting up fights, watching from a distance, and then claiming he had nothing to do with anything. If Luther had a determinate sentence, he would not have lasted two years in the State School.

Luther was, instead, "old law," or a Type A violent offender. As "old law" implies, Type A was on the books long before the determinate-sentencing laws were written in 1987, and expanded in 1995 to cover twenty-two crimes. The law is rarely used today, although every now and then, a Type A sentence emerges in a plea bargain. On the day a Type A offender turns twenty-one, unless he has done something really stupid like hit a staff member, he must be released. The Giddings staff loathes this sentence because there is no way to equate progress in treatment, academics, and behavior in custody, with a parole.

Luther arrived on campus at age fourteen with a two-year minimum sentence. Giddings officials kept him there until his twenty-first birthday, and from sixteen on, when he thought he should have been released, Luther lived in a perpetual state of rage. Just weeks before he turned twenty-one, a visitor asked Luther what he planned to do when he got out. He had given the matter some thought.

"I hear they wearin' lots of gold," Luther replied, a glint in his eye. "I'm gonna want some, and I ain't gonna be able to afford it workin' jobs I'll be able to get, like flippin' burgers. I hear they fightin' you for their gold these days. Somebody tries to fight me, they makin' a mistake."

The staff heaved a collective sigh of relief when they learned that soon after he walked through the gate, Luther was arrested in a stolen car. A judge gave him a long prison sentence. The staff knew Luther was going to prison; they were afraid he was going to kill someone to get there.

"Some people are born with a limited capacity for emotional attachment," says Ann Kelley. "Combine that with an abusive upbringing and you can get a psychopath. Psychopaths are at high risk to reoffend. If you can't put yourself in another person's shoes, if you can't call upon any internal experience to imagine what another person's experience is, you will keep on hurting people."

Luther lacked more than empathy. He had no capacity to imagine a future for himself, something he shares with most of the youth who leave the State School for prison. Luther could have traded the blue Crips wear for an NCAA Division One football uniform, but no matter how many linebackers he ran over or defensive backs he outran, Luther could not envision himself playing college football.

"I used to tell him, 'Luther, get in there in Capital Offenders and deal with the things you need to deal with and get out of here!' " Sandy Brown recalls. " 'You'll go to a junior college, you'll play a season and transfer to a Division One school.' Over and over, I told him that. He couldn't see it. He just couldn't visualize it.

"Luther was at home on a football field," Brown concludes. "It was easier for Luther to face an opponent than the issues in his life. Capital Offenders is a lot harder than playing football."

When Ronnie begins his crime story, he resembles Luther. He appears to have little capacity for self-exploration and no ability to store wisdom. The alert, forthright youth who told his life story has disappeared, replaced by a sullen, monosyllabic, hard-eyed young man. The therapists begin by asking Ronnie to describe his earliest crimes. His answers are abrupt, truncated. "Stealing stuff." "Acting out in school." "Beating on my brother." When therapists and peers try to draw him out, Ronnie replies with a shrug here, a grimace there.

The boys know Ronnie is scared and hiding behind indifference; most of them have done the same thing. They are not about to let him secret himself behind a face that is vacant of all expression. Therapists and peers who were gentle and supportive when Ronnie was telling his life story, teasing out insights, trying to make him realize the harm he suffered was not his fault, now turn aggressive. Ronnie needs to understand his crime story isn't about him; it is about what he did to others.

"I told what I done, why ain't you?" asks Antonio, the tattooed gang warrior who just completed his crime story. "How you gonna take responsibility for things you done if you don't put it out there?"

"Are you going to sit there and make us work to pull it out of you?" challenges Mark. This is somewhat ironic, for Mark had great difficulty getting through his life story. Over three sessions, he struggled to get a narrative going and explore events in detail. The therapists wonder if he will be able to complete a crime story.

Ronnie ignores attempts to draw him out and continues to list his crimes—"I jumped a kid after school in fourth grade"—with one description more listless than the next. And then, instinctively, the boys home in on Kenny, Ronnie's little brother. Ronnie is carrying a load of guilt about Kenny. He tried to kill his little brother, and doesn't understand why.

"I used to chase him around the house with knives, threatening to kill him," Ronnie volunteers, leaning forward, finally engaging in a memory. "I'd do it just to do it. It was fun to see him scared, running away from me. It felt good to have control over that situation. I liked it."

Daniel, the group's self-appointed historian, likes to recall events that others may have forgotten and relate them to what is happening now. It is both effective and a way for Daniel to demonstrate how intelligent he is.

"That time you found your stepfather's gun and went looking for your brother: Were you just going to scare him then?"

"I felt powerful with the gun," Ronnie replies, his eyes widening. "I decided to scare my little brother. He was in his room, playing Nintendo. I put the gun to the side of his head and said, 'I'm going to kill you now.' I wasn't serious but he freaked out. 'Please don't kill me, Ronnie! I love you, Ronnie!' "

"He didn't know if you were serious or not. You had a serious face on, right?" Antonio asks.

Ronnie nods.

"He was crying, he was scared. Him crying increased the power rush," Josh insists.

Ronnie nods and says, "I cocked the gun and said, 'I'm going to kill you, motherfucker.' I pulled the trigger. Nothing came out.

"I thought, Fuck it, I'll use it on myself. I cocked the gun again and put it to my head. Just then, my stepdad came in. He took the gun away from me and aimed it at the ceiling. It fired. The second time, I had pulled the hammer all the way back. A bullet had come into the chamber."

From Ronnie's point of view, death metal bands and the Hollywood genre Quentin Tarantino has mastered are only playing with concepts. Ronnie and other boys in the circle aren't playing with anything. They are true nihilists. Before they came to the State School, they had determined they would die young. That didn't worry them; it was simply the way things were. Ronnie shrugs, sits back in his chair, and answers the next question before it can be asked.

"I felt, Fuck it. That's how I felt. I almost killed myself, but I didn't care. It would have been okay."

The boys are staring at the floor or are looking up, anything to keep from looking at Ronnie. It is as if everyone wants the soundproofing to absorb the sadness, the stupidity.

"Why would it have been okay?" Sherry Whatley asks quietly.

"I was always feeling hurt. Nobody cares about me. Why should I care about myself?"

A boy here, a boy there nods in assent, silently saying, "Yes, I've felt that way, too."

"How old were you when you found the gun? Eleven?" Jackie Urbach asks. Ronnie nods. "Where'd you learn to point it at somebody's head and say, 'I'm going to kill you?' "

Ronnie shrugs. "Seen people do it in movies. Saw it done on TV."

Tipper Gore and Frank Zappa and their debate over censorship on Capitol Hill have come and gone, but arguments over the effects of violence in rock lyrics, in films, and on television go on and on. The V-chip is here, rap CDs carry a warning about lewd or violent lyrics, but have they made any difference? Sex and violence continue to be as prevalent as saturated fat in the American pop culture diet.

After years of listening to violent young offenders like Ronnie link the media to violence, frontline State School staffers have developed their own take on violent images. The graphic, almost obsessive portrayal of bloodshed does not cause violence, any more than nihilistic lyrics in heavy metal music breed suicide. But the media has an effect. Ann Kelley sums it up this way: "Does the media cause violence? No. Does it play a role in violence? Absolutely!"

Kelley is referring to the concept of modeling, one of the primary ways human beings learn. It is amazing how often in group a youth will refer to *The Cosby Show,* offhandedly saying something like Daniel did one morning: "I liked to watch reruns of *The Cosby Show.* That's how I knew the way a family is supposed to be."

The Cosby Show is an archetype for a generation, just as *Ozzie and Harriet, Leave It to Beaver,* and *The Donna Reed Show* were to earlier generations. Children who grow up in homes that reflect these archetypes, who grow up safe surrounded by loving caretakers, may see lots of violence on TV and find it riveting. But as they watch, there is something inside telling them, "These things happen but I'd never do them. This is *not* the way things are supposed to be."

When a youth like Ronnie sees violence in a film or on television, he may respond differently than a youth raised in a nurturing home. He grew up around adults who threw children out windows, beat up women, dealt cocaine, and stashed loaded weapons in the closet. When Ronnie sees some psychopath hold a gun to the head of a character in a movie and say, "I'm going to kill you, motherfucker!" he may not regard it as aberrant behavior, so far removed from the norm it qualifies as entertainment. He may see it as a reflection of the way things really are.

"Violence in the media is a confirming experience for children who have experienced violence and abuse at home," says Linda Reyes. "They get violence at home, they get in fights at school, they get violence on television and in the movies. Where do they get a nonconfirming experience?"

The day after Ronnie put a gun to his brother's head and then turned it on himself, he skipped school. He was sitting on the couch watching television when he heard his stepfather's Firebird pull up. Figuring Jimmie was still angry about the gun, Ronnie ran to his room. Sure enough, Jimmie appeared in his doorway, grinning his crooked grin. Ronnie wondered if he could make it through the window, or if he should go limp when Jimmie started hitting him and then suddenly bolt for the door.

"You know what? You are one crazy little motherfucker," Jimmie said. "First, you find my stash and take my gun. Next thing you do, you turn it on your damn little brother. Goddamn, Ronnie. Billy the Kid ain't got nothin' on you!"

Ronnie stared at his stepfather, waiting.

"Come on out here, I wanna show you something," Jimmie said and turned and walked away.

Ronnie followed him into the living room, terrified he was walking into a trap. Jimmie dropped onto the couch; Ronnie took the chair across the room. He was not allowed on the couch when Jimmie had it.

"Sit over here by me," Jimmie said. "You so damn inquisitive, I'll show you something."

Ronnie edged over to the couch, ready to bolt if Jimmie tried to grab him. From the pocket inside his Levi's jacket, Jimmie produced a baggie stuffed with marijuana buds. He ripped a paper from a Zig-Zag pack on the table and as he crumbled a bud over it, Jimmie said he knew Ronnie had been scrounging around, smoking roaches. This time, Ronnie was going to smoke a real joint.

Jimmie and Ronnie smoked that joint and washed it down with Budweisers. Jimmie rolled the second joint one-handed as Ronnie watched, amazed. They ate a box of cheese crackers and a pack of Oreos. When Marina came home, Ronnie was sound asleep on the couch and Jimmie was rolling another joint. Marina glared at him and stomped down the hall to their bedroom.

That was the pivotal afternoon in Ronnie's life.

"After I almost killed myself with the gun, I kind of bonded with my stepdad," Ronnie tells the group. "We drank, smoked weed, did drugs. The only kind of affection I was getting was getting high with him."

For Jimmie, Ronnie was a pawn in the nasty little war he was fighting with Marina. For Ronnie, Jimmie was a great way to pay his mother back for years of neglect. Ironically, by becoming Jimmie's doping and drinking buddy, Ronnie was forcing his mother, at long last, to begin acting like a mother.

"My mom took me aside," Ronnie tells the group. "She said, 'I don't want you doing drugs. I don't want you doing things with Jimmie. Promise me you won't.' I told her I would stop, but I didn't. She lied to me. She promised she would take care of me. I was supposed to be her baby."

The afternoon he first shared a joint with Jimmie, Ronnie was eleven. By age thirteen, he had become his stepfather in miniature.

His mother managed to get him out of bed and off to school most mornings, but once Ronnie was there, he got into a fight almost as often as he got to class. Adults who swung by Jimmie's house to score dope sometimes had their children in tow. When these kids spotted Ronnie in school, it was, "Hey, man, can you sell me . . . ?" and "Hey, man, can you get me . . . ?" Ronnie eventually developed a nice side business for his stepfather.

When school ended each day, Jimmie was usually down the block, waiting in the idling Firebird. Ronnie hopped in and they made the rounds, stopping by a bar where Jimmie had "a meet," or going by Jimmie's brother's house. Jimmie and his brother were partners in the drug business. His two sons, Ronnie's stepcousins, were only a few years older than Ronnie but were already seasoned gangbangers, dopers, and thieves.

Jimmie and his brother sent Ronnie's stepcousins on trips to El Paso to buy "product"—cocaine, marijuana, pharmaceutical speed—that had been smuggled over the border. They financed these dope runs by sending the cousins and a few of their trusted gang buddies out to burglarize homes. They fenced what the teenagers stole and then sent someone off to El Paso. The business was lucrative, there was a market for every ounce they brought back, but Jimmie and his brother ran a sloppy operation. Everyone involved did so much coke and smoked so much weed, they kept coming up short of both money and product. The brothers' solution was simple: send the young hoodlums out to rob more houses. That was fine with Ronnie's cousins; break-ins were what they liked doing best.

It took a while for the cousins to get used to Ronnie being included, but eventually, they did. They signaled acceptance by tagging him with a nickname—"White Man"—because he was half white. "I liked the life, I was drawn to it," Ronnie tells the group. "I remember once when I first started smoking with them, I coughed. My cousin didn't down me for it. He said, 'You get a better high when you cough.' That felt good."

Jimmie let Ronnie in on a big secret: he had girlfriends, lots of them. Their daily rambles almost always included a stop at a girlfriend's apartment. The women and the settings were different, but the routine was always the same. Jimmie got a hello kiss, Ronnie a hug. They sat down and made themselves comfortable while the girlfriend pulled beers and Dr Peppers out of the refrigerator. Jimmie chopped cocaine into lines, he and the girlfriend did a few, and then Jimmie fired up a joint. Jimmie and the girlfriend started kissing, their hands exploring each other. One pulled the other off the couch and they disappeared into the bedroom, leaving Ronnie with the TV.

"My stepfather would leave half a joint for me, and that made me feel accepted," Ronnie recalls. "I knew what they were doing in there. That's how I learned to take advantage of females."

"Take advantage?" Urbach asks.

Ronnie looks as surprised as if she has just asked him to explain the facts of life.

"You've got drugs. You get them high. You have sex," Ronnie replies. "I learned that from my stepdad."

While Ronnie was running with Jimmie, Marina was doing what she could to bring a bit of sanity to the house. By her own admission, Marina was addicted to crack cocaine. Jimmie had taught her how to cook it, and she made small batches for herself, but somehow managed to cut back until she was using only enough to get through work at the nursing home. She quit drinking alcohol and ran off Jimmie's friends, losers who had been hanging around forever. She insisted that Jimmie stop dealing drugs out of the house. Jimmie and Ronnie responded by treating her as a pain in the ass. Ronnie took messages from Jimmie's girlfriends and passed them on when his mother wasn't around.

"It was like, Fuck her. She wasn't there for me. She had her life then, I've got my life now," Ronnie says, looking around the group, seeking understanding. "I did get mad at my stepdad once, when I saw him hitting my mom. I gave myself all kinds of excuses—'She shouldn't be doin' so much bitchin'—but it still bothered me. I didn't do anything to him, though. I didn't want to mess up what me and my stepdad had."

One afternoon, Ronnie and Tyler, the stepcousin Jimmie had pitted him against during the family reunion, were starting on a joint when Kenny arrived home from school. He took one look at Ronnie and said, "I'm telling Mom."

Ronnie ran to the kitchen, grabbed a butcher knife, and returned, pointing the blade at his brother. His cousin did not move a muscle.

"You're going to tell Mom? I'm going to kill your ass first!"

"Ronnie, no!" Kenny screamed.

"I chased him around the house two or three times and then out into the yard," Ronnie says in his monotone. "He was screaming and crying and running and that pumped me up. If I'd have caught him, I'd have stabbed him. The only thing that saved him was, he ran down the street to a friend's house.

"He told my mom about it," Ronnie continues. "She was shocked I'd chased him with a knife and didn't know what to do. I told her I was just playin'. I made out like it was all a big joke, like it wasn't serious. I was laughing about it. She didn't like that I did it, but she believed me. In reality, I wanted to kill him."

"Talk about thinking errors," Sherry Whatley muses aloud. "Your mom is worried about you using marijuana. She's not thinking about you killing her youngest son."

"Why your mom would take that as a joke is beyond me," Frank Soto adds. "You chased him with a weapon."

Therapists pay particular attention to the kind of weapon a boy uses. A boy who uses an automatic nine-millimeter intends to inflict mayhem. A boy who uses a knife is trying to make a point. The closer a perpetrator gets to a victim, the more personal the crime.

"You wanted that closeness with a knife," Jackie Urbach tells Ronnie. "You wanted him to know it was you."

Ronnie nods slowly and the group is silent until Johnnie, who is sitting next to Ronnie, shifts in his chair to face him.

"When I hear the things you did, I get a cold, sick feeling in my stomach," Johnnie says. "I didn't have no little brother to take it out on, so I did it to my grandparents. I hate the things we did to the people who loved us. I hate the person I was. I'm glad I can see the person I was and can change. I don't want to hurt anybody anymore."

Josh waits while the group absorbs Johnnie's declaration, then slowly, methodically, confronts Ronnie.

"After you saw Mr. Strings holding his stomach, you had fantasies about using a knife on your aunt," Josh says, recalling Ronnie's life story. "But you never stabbed your aunt. You took a knife to your brother. You turned out to be like your aunt. Exactly who you didn't want to be."

"I was your little brother," Antonio says softly. "Shit. My brothers chased me around with bats, they threw pans at me. I'd call my mom at work and she'd be just like your mother—'You can't be doing that, you need to be brothers.' I wanted her to say, 'I'll take care of it,' but she never did.

"My two brothers always beating me up, my dad coming home drunk, pushing on people, beating us up, making us fight, my sister telling everybody to stop. It was confusing for me. Shit, I'm just a fucking kid, I didn't know what the fuck to do. I'd run to my room and I'd be crying and my brothers and even my sister would be laughing at me. I'd yell something and my dad would come in and make me face the corner. I had to kneel on uncooked rice for about an hour. It hurt. It hurt. My knees, it left dents in them. I'd be crying.

"I wasn't nothing but a kid. I didn't know what to do with all that. I got older and let it out any way I could, by shooting people."

Tran has been paying close attention, staring intently at each speaker. Now, he leans forward and looks at Ronnie.

"After you chased your brother with the knife, what happened to him?" Tran asks.

"He started staying with his friends. He didn't want to be at the house when I was there."

"When children go to school abused, it's their parents doing it," Josh says. "But with your brother, it was you. Your brother had to grow up scared. You had him growing up in agony."

Ronnie is contorting in his chair, his face twisting in pain. To the therapists, this is promising, almost a relief. They know that in order to change, to redeem himself, Ronnie needs to see what his vengeful entitlement—"I was hurt, so I could hurt my brother"—did to Kenny. If he grasps that, he will cease to see Kenny as a receptacle for his rage and Kenny will become, in Martin Buber's great term, "a Thou," a human being with feelings, thoughts, sanctity. A young man, no matter how violent his past, who can look at a person and see "a Thou" is not likely to willfully inflict pain ever again.

Ronnie continues his saga of doping and dealing drugs with his stepfather and reaches the night that his mother came home from work early to find Jimmie in their bed with one of his girlfriends. In what seemed like a matter of seconds, the woman was dressed and Jimmie was walking her out to her car. He came back in, shot Ronnie a look, and raised his eyebrows. Ronnie nodded toward the patio. Jimmie went out and found Marina standing by a pile of bricks. The bricks had been there for years, waiting for Jimmie to brick-in the patio. Marina picked up a brick and threw it at Jimmie. It missed.

"Ha-ha-ah-ha-ha," Jimmie taunted.

Ronnie was standing by the sliding glass door, watching the fun.

"Ha-ha, Mom, you missed!" he jeered.

Marina picked up another brick and threw it at her son. It fell short of his feet. Ronnie and his stepfather thought that was hilarious.

"You fuckers! I hate you both!" Marina screamed.

"Oh, boo-hoo-hoo," Jimmie mocked.

Ronnie pretended to cry, too, and he sounded just like his mother and that cracked up Jimmie. Marina screamed a long string of obscenities and when she finally ran out of steam, Ronnie said, "Ma, why don't you just shut the fuck up?"

"Fuck you all! I'm leaving!" Marina shouted, and ran past Ronnie into the house. Ronnie went after her and jerked his mother's long black hair, snapping Marina's head back. Jimmie slapped his knees in delight. And that sent Marina over the edge.

"She ran through the house, screaming and tearing down ceiling fans," Ronnie remembers. "Then she put her fist through a window. She cut her arm. It was a really deep cut; I could see this little vein wiggling. We took her to the hospital and she stayed two days. They said she'd had a nervous breakdown. I didn't visit her. I just kept doing the same things I was doing with Jimmie."

Years later when Marina recalled that night, she remembered it the way her son had.

"I did have a nervous breakdown," Marina said. "Only, I didn't know it. You don't know it when you are on crack. I ran my hand through a glass window, blood was spurting everywhere, and I took off running down the street like a crazy woman. They put me in the hospital and that's when I decided to leave Jimmie. I was going to kill him or he was going to kill me. I went back to get the boys, but Ronnie wouldn't go."

The way Ronnie tells it to the group, the afternoon his mother walked in with her arm all bandaged, he and Jimmie were on the couch, smoking a joint.

"She said, 'I'm leaving.' My stepfather said, 'Okay, get the fuck out. But I'm keeping Ronnie.' Keeping me gave him power over my mother. And by then, I was a good moneymaker."

Marina left and with the help of a brother got herself an apartment near the nursing home. She made one last attempt to wrest her son away from her second husband. When she remembers that day, there is a kind of lightness in her voice, as if she is amused by her own futility.

"I went to the police station and got a piece of paper," Marina recalled. "That's all it was, really, just a piece of paper. I went back to the house and showed Ronnie the paper. 'This gives me permission to take you,' I said. He yanked the paper out of my hand and threw it across the room. I slapped him. I said, 'Ronnie, I'm not doing this to be ugly. You're going to get locked up. I know what that's like. I been locked up.' He said, 'Mom, all you do is bitch, bitch, bitch.' I had to slap him again. He was thirteen. I told him he was gonna be locked up by fifteen. He went down to his room and cried, and I left."

To celebrate getting rid of Marina, Jimmie started partying, meaning nonstop consumption of drugs and alcohol, punctuated by sex. Ronnie's two cousins moved in and Jimmie and his brother operated their drug business out of the house full-time. When they had product to sell, Ronnie tied a rope around a fence post and customers and "females," as Ronnie habitually calls women, showed up at all hours. Gangbangers hung out, getting high with the cousins, bragging about homes they had broken into, things they had stolen, and planning their next hit.

It was okay if Ronnie did drugs with them, but the stepcousins never took him along when they went out on a job, and this made him feel left out. One day, he saw his chance: he noticed a door was unlocked at school. He told the stepcousins about it and they decided to hit the school—and take Ronnie along. Ronnie was thrilled.

"It was my chance to get involved," Ronnie recalls. "I did it for acceptance."

"Were you scared the first time you went in?" asks Tim, the cat burglar.

Ronnie shakes his head no.

"When I had that fight with my cousin, I wasn't scared," he says. "Not being scared, that became my reputation. I didn't let myself be scared."

Criminals who operate as lone wolves—the talented safecracker, the psychopathic serial killer—are few and far between. Ronnie and the other boys in the group are common criminals, common in the sense that they are products of context. The same forces that work to civilize—the need for acceptance, the need to establish and maintain a reputation, the desire to follow in the footsteps of an older role model—led them into antisocial behavior.

On a football field or in a corporate conference room where tough decisions have to be made, a reputation for being fearless can be a good thing. Having that same reputation in a gang can get you killed. It promotes risk taking and one-dimensional thinking, which becomes set in stone when a boy picks up a street name. Gang names like "O.G." (Original Gangster), "Loco," and "Trigger" not only identify behavior, they define individuals. Once a kid gets a nickname like Loco, he has to live up to his rep by being more loco than anyone else.

Above all, Ronnie valued the acceptance of his stepfather, his stepcousins, and their gangbanger associates. The rest of the world mattered little. Its inhabitants were nothing but fodder for the small circle of thieves.

After Ronnie led the bandits into his school, he got what he wanted, full acceptance in the crime club. Every time they went out to rob a house, Ronnie went along.

"We'd pick rich houses, big houses where we knew there would be good stuff. We'd try to make sure nobody was home," Ronnie tells the group. "We'd steal jewelry, TVs, VCRs."

"How many burglaries did you end up doing?" asks Tim, who did quite a few himself.

"Lots."

"How many victims did you have?" Tim continues.

"Quite a few," answers Ronnie.

"More than ten?" Tim inquires.

"More in the hundreds, probably," Ronnie says.

"How come you can't be more specific?" Jackie Urbach challenges.

"I never thought I'd have to think about it. I thought I was going to be killed," Ronnie says.

"Did you ever see pictures of the people who lived in those houses?" Frank Soto asks.

"There was pictures, sure, but I didn't take the time to look at them. I was there to get what I wanted."

"Did you ever think of the sentimental value that a ring or a necklace might have? Did you ever think that people worked a long time for those TVs and VCRs?" Sherry Whatley asks.

"We looked at them as rich people," Ronnie says. "They had insurance. They'd get it back."

"A lot of people got hurt by your actions," Whatley says. "You breeched their safety."

"It didn't bother me," Ronnie replies. "I had the life I wanted. I felt free."

A freedom akin to what the barbarian must have felt, galloping into a village, sword drawn, eyes gleaming.

"What'd you do with the money you got for fencing all that stuff?" Frank Soto asks.

"Turned it over to my stepdad," Ronnie says.

"Jimmie took your mother away from you. Then, he takes your childhood from you," Frank Soto observes. "Jimmie tears up people's lives."

Ronnie and Tran are vigorously nodding their agreement.

"Jimmie is just like my uncle," Tran tells Ronnie.

Tran's story, like Ronnie's and some of the other boys', traces the classic arc from abuse to handing out abuse. His uncle, a street hoodlum in Dalat, Vietnam, started beating Tran when the boy was five. Tran survived by becoming his uncle's servant, hurrying to get his coffee ready in the morning and having a cold drink waiting when his uncle came home in the afternoon heat. His uncle liked having a servant and turned Tran into his pet, a "Mini-Me" hoodlum. His uncle's friends were amused when he downed shots of whiskey in a café and then passed out.

"My uncle likes his friends seeing me look up to him," Tran said when he narrated his life story. "He likes me trying to be a little gangster. I act just like my uncle, the way he walks, the way he drinks. He's fighting people, he's robbing people on the street. He gets drunk, yells at people, kicks people. I'm getting more violent. I kick people, too."

When the world comes into focus for boys like Tran and Ronnie, it is black and white. They are weak and lonely and have no one to protect them. Tran's uncle and Ronnie's stepfather are strong. They have money, drugs, and women and they hand out abuse. To an abused boy, life is very simple: be weak and die, or become strong and survive. So Tran transformed himself into his uncle and eventually became a better criminal than his uncle ever had been, leading the largest Asian gang in the Dallas area. And Ronnie did his best to become his stepfather. In a black-and-white world, there is no alternative.

"A violent kid sees victimizing as strength," says Larry Reue. "If he is weak and a nobody and has no self-esteem, people will run over him, because that is what people do. So he says, 'I'm not going to take it anymore!' and integrates the person he hates most into his personality. The only strong role model he has is the monster. He becomes the monster."

"But," Reue adds, pausing for emphasis, "there's an ambivalence about this. Part of him still hates the monster. That ambivalence is the opening for therapy."

Listening to Ronnie and Tran tell their stories, you begin to realize how much the German philosophers Arthur Schopenhauer ("Everything is Will and the manifestation of Will") and Friedrich Nietzsche ("To change 'it was' into 'thus I willed it'—that alone shall I call redemption") understood about the human spirit. Next to the need to survive, a human being needs to form connections. If no loving figure is around, he will bond with his abuser and seek power, control, and recognition in ways he learns from his oppressor. Healthy human beings also seek power, control, and recognition. The difference is, being loved and nurtured and in turn being able to love sends those forces in directions that build families and community and careers, which contribute to the greater good.

When love is not there to temper these forces and they mix with anger, God help us.

7.

GLAD THEY WERE HOME

One reason why so many kids like Ronnie come to the State School "poly-addicted" is that crime, like drugs, is a search for a high. Aiming a gun at someone's head is a rush—there is no faster way to power and control. Planning and pulling off a convenience store robbery or a drive-by shooting is a sustained high. But like a drug high, a crime rush wears off fast, and so in a search for bigger highs, the criminal takes greater risks.

That's the way it was with Ronnie's gang of burglars. When he joined them, their modus operandi was to make sure no one was home before they broke in. That evolved into hoping that one night, someone would be home. Surprising a couple in their sleep, threatening their lives, forcing them to turn over money and jewels they might have hidden, what a rush; what power and control!

One night, someone was home.

It started when narcotics officers arrested a gang member Jimmie sent to El Paso to buy cocaine. The crew sat around smoking fry and talking about hitting a house that night so they could fence the stuff and get someone on the road to El Paso the next day. At 2 A.M., Ronnie and his two stepcousins were casing cul-de-sacs in a wealthy neighborhood where the homes were so large, they looked bloated. They picked out a place and used a rock to smash a window in the rear. Narrating the story, Ronnie refers to his victims by their first names, Joseph and Martha, something the State School insists young felons do. It helps to personalize the victims, turn them into human beings.

When the seventy-one-year-old Joseph came out of the bedroom to investigate noises, Ronnie hit him high and a stepcousin hit him low. They dragged him into the master bedroom and threw him on the floor, then yanked sixty-nine-year-old Martha out of bed and pushed her down next to her husband. Joseph suddenly had trouble breathing and clutched his heart. Martha screamed about his having a heart condition and how he would die if he didn't get his pills. One of the stepcousins ran into the bathroom and opened the medicine cabinet. Martha described the capsules and the stepcousin came back with the medicine and a glass of water. Joseph took a pill and the robbers helped the elderly couple off the floor and back into bed. One of the crew stayed with the couple while the other two ransacked the house and carted valuables out to the car.

Ronnie decided that anyone who lived in a place this nice had to have a safe and went to the kitchen for a knife. "I thought, Fuck it, man, where's the safe?" Ronnie tells the group. "I picked Joseph up by the arm and said, 'Motherfucker, you better tell where the safe is or I'll cut off your fingers.'" Joseph said they didn't have a safe, but did have $7,000 in a checking account. The robbers held a conference. Ronnie and one of the stepcousins would kidnap the elderly couple and take Joseph to the bank in the morning. The other stepcousin would drive the car with the loot back to Jimmie's, get a few hours of sleep, and head to El Paso with the money.

Ronnie and his stepcousin loaded Joseph and Martha into their car and took them to a Holiday Inn, where they waited for the bank to open. Joseph and Martha sat on the bed, holding each other and crying while the robbers smoked fry and popped pills. When Ronnie told Joseph it was time to go, the couple held each other so tight, the robbers had to pry them apart. Martha begged to go along, but the stepcousin said, "Hell no, you're staying with me in case anything goes wrong."

On the way to the bank, Ronnie noticed a yellow light on the dash, warning the car was about to run out of gas. He pulled into a gas mart and got out. Ronnie had been smoking all that fry and popping all those pills;

it was amazing that he could drive. When he stepped out of the car, the heat and light of the Texas morning hit him and he got dizzy and put both hands on a gas pump to steady himself. Ronnie heard a click and looked through the car window. Joseph had hit the door locks and was moving with the agility of a much younger man. Now he was behind the wheel, starting the engine. He literally burned rubber out of the gas station.

Had Joseph not escaped, Ronnie would have killed him.

It takes Ronnie two hours to describe his committing offense. When he finishes, the boys gather in the small hallway outside the group room while Ronnie sits alone in a corner, his head in his hands. Ten minutes go by before Sherry Whatley, who will be processing, comes in and whispers something in Ronnie's ear. He gets up and moves to the center of the room, where two chairs are waiting. The group file in and Antonio, who is playing Ronnie's stepcousin, walks up to Ronnie.

"Hey, White Man. Let's smoke a J," Antonio says.

"Jimmie's got some shit over here on the table," Ronnie says.

Seconds ago, Ronnie was ashen in terror. Now, he is comfortable, miming smoking a joint with Antonio. Johnnie, playing Ronnie's little brother, enters the room and stops to remove an imaginary backpack. He sniffs the air and sees Ronnie and the stepcousin.

"You guys are smoking a joint! I'm telling Mom!" Johnnie announces.

Ronnie runs to a corner and picks up a blackboard eraser, a prop that represents a knife. Holding it beside his head, he approaches Johnnie, who backs away from him.

"I love you, Ronnie! You're my big brother! Please don't stab me! Please don't kill me!" Johnnie pleads.

Ronnie lunges at Johnnie, who takes off running. To Ronnie, this is real. The regression is complete. Ronnie really thinks Johnnie is his brother, and he really does want to kill him. He gets Johnnie by the sweat-shirt. Johnnie glances back, catches the look in Ronnie's eye, and twists out of Ronnie's grasp. He darts to a corner and turns his back to the wall, ready to move in any direction. Frank Soto intercepts Ronnie, wrestles him to the floor, and gets him in a restraint hold. Ronnie keeps fighting. Several boys move in to help Soto keep Ronnie pinned down. Whatley waits a moment, then motions Johnnie over.

"Why do you want to hurt me?" Johnnie asks, standing over Ronnie. "I love you, man. I love you like no one ever loved you."

The rage leaves Ronnie like air escaping from a balloon.

"Fuck, man!" Ronnie sobs. "Fuck, man, I fucked up! I fucked up again!"

Soto and the boys release Ronnie and he pounds the floor with his fists.

"I fucked up!" he keeps saying over and over again. "I fucked up!"

"You were going to stab him, weren't you?" Sherry Whatley asks.

"I was," Ronnie agrees, and buries his head in his arms.

The therapists let the tears pour into the gray carpet. They motion the boys over to a corner and whisper further directions. Because Ronnie is too distraught to continue to play himself, Daniel takes over the role. Whatley goes to Ronnie and helps him back to the chair across the room. Ronnie is crying very hard while the boys are arranging chairs, preparing for the next scene. Ronnie trembles and wipes his eyes and will not look up when Whatley asks him. She steps behind him and gently lifts his head. Someone turns the rheostat and the room grows very dim. Someone else slaps the fiberglass soundproofing, signifying a window being broken. Ronnie bolts upright in his chair.

Jackie Urbach, playing Martha, is lying on the floor next to Josh, who is playing Joseph. Quick as feral cats, three boys are prowling the room, opening and closing imaginary dresser drawers.

Urbach wakes up and shakes Josh.

"Joseph, somebody is out there!" Urbach whispers.

"Let me go see," Josh says, fumbling for his glasses.

Josh gets up and demonstrates an uncanny ability to simulate the gait of an old man, locking his knees and shuffling across the room.

"Look at him! Look at him!" Whatley says in Ronnie's ear. "He's an old man!"

Ronnie tries to get out of the chair. Whatley presses down on his shoulders and keeps him there as Daniel, playing Ronnie, crouching behind a chair, springs at Josh and hits him around the shoulders just as Antonio tackles him around the knees. Josh screams as he falls to the floor.

"What's happening, Ronnie? What are they doing to him?" Whatley shouts in Ronnie's ear.

"Oh, don't hurt me, you young boys, don't hurt me!" Josh moans. "Me and my wife never hurt nobody! Take anything you want, just don't hurt us!"

Josh is crying real tears.

"Shut the fuck up!" Daniel commands, and Josh shudders in terror.

"Shut up, motherfucker!" echoes Antonio.

Tim yanks Jackie Urbach out of bed and pushes her down next to Josh. Ronnie begins howling like a coyote on the Texas plains.

"Look! Look what you did!" Whatley says, ignoring Ronnie's wailing. "Look at it! Look what you did!"

"Get what's here!" Antonio yells.

Tim hovers over Josh and Urbach while Antonio and Daniel run through the group room, overturning chairs, throwing them against the wall. The effect is uncanny; it really feels like a home is being ransacked.

Ronnie lurches out of his chair and falls face-first on the carpet. He lies there until Whatley helps him to his knees. When he looks up at Josh and Urbach, tears are streaming down his face.

Daniel has the blackboard eraser in one hand. He jerks Josh off the ground and holds it under his chin.

"Motherfucker, anyone who lives in a house this big has got to have a safe. Where the fuck is it?" Daniel demands.

"We don't have a safe, all's we got is some money in a checking account!" Josh says, his voice breaking.

At this point the role play begins to feel like an exorcism. If you didn't know better, you would swear demons were leaving Ronnie and swirling around him. He knee-walks to Josh, who is lying crumpled on the floor. He throws himself on top of Josh and works his arms around him.

"I'm sorry! I'm sorry!" Ronnie keeps saying as his tears soak Josh's T-shirt.

The feelings Ronnie is expressing now must have been there the night he invaded Joseph and Martha's home. He ignored them then to maintain his reputation for fearlessness. He buried them under drugs, and the rush of doing a robbery and threatening the lives of an elderly couple. Ronnie, it seems, has an innate sense of right and wrong. It must be innate, because he did not acquire it growing up. If it is there in Ronnie, then most criminals must possess it. They work hard to keep that voice muted, and there is no better place to do that than in prison. That is what makes penitentiaries such a fraud.

Ronnie holds on to Josh and sobs, "I'm sorry!" over and over again. But being sorry now isn't enough for the therapists.

"You weren't sorry then!" Whatley shouts, hovering over Ronnie. "You wanted his money, his jewelry!"

"I don't want to do it no more! I don't want to do it no more!" Ronnie sobs. "I'm sorry! I'm sorry!"

"You weren't sorry then! You wanted to find the safe!" Whatley shouts.

"I fucked up! I was fucked-up!" Ronnie howls.

"Fucked-up on drugs is no excuse!" Frank Soto yells. "You didn't care! You just cared about getting dope!"

"I fucked up, man, I fucked up!" Ronnie wails.

The actors and therapists step back, leaving Ronnie to cry on the floor for another extended period. Finally, Frank Soto nods and two boys help Ronnie off the floor. On his feet, he appears transformed into an old man. His arms hang limp, as if they are very heavy, and the boys steady him as he shuffles back to his chair. Time and again, youth going through role play end up doing "the Capital Offenders' Shuffle." It is as if they are walking away from a head-on collision.

Ronnie is staring straight ahead, waiting for the next act. This is the role-play reversal, where Ronnie will play Joseph, his victim. Jackie Urbach, playing Martha, sits down next to him. Urbach is quiet for a moment, then suddenly squeezes Ronnie's arm and says, "Joseph! I heard something! I think somebody is out there!"

Ronnie jumps up and takes a few steps before Daniel and Antonio jump him.

"Please don't hurt me, please don't hurt me," Ronnie pleads, and he sounds like a scared old man.

Daniel releases his grasp and Ronnie sinks to the floor. His chest heaves, as if he is struggling for air. "I can't breathe, I can't breathe!" Ronnie cries.

"Go! Go! The bathroom! The medicine cabinet! White capsules with a red band in a brown bottle!" Urbach yells.

Ronnie twists on the floor as Antonio rushes to an imaginary medicine cabinet and returns to mime handing Ronnie a pill and a glass of water. Ronnie falls limp to the floor.

Again, the boys run around the room, slapping the backs of chairs. Daniel thrusts the blackboard eraser up under Ronnie's chin. "Where's the safe at? Where's the motherfucking safe at?" Daniel demands.

Ronnie seems to remember exactly what Joseph said.

"Don't hurt me, young man. There's no safe! The wife and I have a checking account, the balance is around seven thousand dollars. I'll tell you which bank, I'll take you there, I'll see that you get it, just let us be for a moment."

When it is over, the group files out into the hallway. The last one through the door turns off the lights.

Ronnie lies on the floor, crying and twisting in private agony. Five long minutes elapse before the boys file back in. Two of them lift Ronnie off the floor and lead him to a wall. There is a long silence and then Josh begins the feedback. He is still in character, speaking as Joseph.

"Sick children broke into my house and threatened me and my wife with knives," Josh says. "You had no regard for me and my wife. I almost had a heart attack. That's fucked-up. I pray to God to help you."

"How did you feel, playing Joseph?" Sherry Whatley asks, trying gently to bring Josh back to being Josh. He answers as Joseph.

"Terrified! I almost died of terror! Young children knock me down. They hold me and my wife hostage for seven hours. Imagine what it's like after that. Me and my wife don't want to sleep in our own house anymore. Burglar bars are not enough to keep these bad-assed kids out these days."

"Josh?" Whatley asks.

"It ain't easy, being in one of these," Josh replies, slowly shaking his head.

Whatley watches Josh for a moment. Satisfied he is coming out of his character and will be all right, she moves on to Antonio.

"What if those heart pills weren't there?" Antonio asks. "You could have been charged with murder. It's a blessing to have you here at the State School."

"When you pulled that knife on your little brother, it made me feel sick," Tim says when it is his turn. "I've done that. Knowing the things I did is painful. I knew you were hurting and I wanted to comfort you but I knew I couldn't. I knew you had to feel that. But I want you to know, I love you. Really. It's not fake love."

Ronnie is sitting next to Tim. He crawls closer and Tim puts an arm around him. Dwayne has his arm around Josh, and Antonio is holding Johnnie and stroking his head.

"Nobody cared about me, I didn't care about anybody," Ronnie says, his voice barely audible. "Then. Not now. Now, I see it. I feel it."

When each boy has had his say, it is the therapists' turn.

"I hope you can see your patterns," Sherry Whatley tells Ronnie. "You didn't get love from your mother. You got angry inside and started hurting your brother. You never had a family. You didn't have a dad and so you chose your stepfather. You didn't have a family so you joined a gang and said, This is my real family. I hope you remember what happened with that family. From here on out, Ronnie, you are going to have to be your own parent. I hope you can do it."

A boy does not go into a role play and, like Saul becoming Paul on the road to Damascus, come out transformed. The people who designed role plays believe in process, not epiphanies. Role plays can produce great insights, but insight, as Ann Kelley is fond of pointing out, is not enough. Jackie Urbach sums that up when she ends the group.

"Don't use your pasts as the reason for who you are today," Urbach says. "Let this program be the start for who you will become. You're going to get out. If you carry what you've learned here with you, if you keep it alive inside you, it will be there when you need it. You won't remember the details of the role play we just did. But you will remember what a robbery does to people, and what it does to you. And you'll choose not to do it."

———

Saturday and Sunday are visiting days, but on this Wednesday afternoon, there is a long line waiting to go through the gate. The visitors move up the long sidewalk to the chapel, where the high school is holding a commencement ceremony. Parents and grandparents, brothers and sisters file into the chapel. Someone plays "Pomp and Circumstance" on a piano and forty students march slowly in. Those who will be receiving a high school diploma are wearing blue gowns with gold trim; those who have earned a GED have on sky blue robes with gray trim.

The crowd gathered in the chapel look like patrons in a photo taken in a blues bar in Houston circa the 1960s, when Lightnin' Hopkins and Johnny Copeland were playing. Some of the women have on dresses that do not fit particularly well; some of the men have rheumy eyes and are missing teeth. Some are holding handkerchiefs and dabbing their eyes. They did not think their son, or their granddaughter, would live to reach age seventeen, let alone be up there on the stage in a cap and gown, receiving a degree.

Ronnie is in the third row, in the middle of the GED honorees. His mother, Marina, is near the back, dressed in a dark brown pants suit. She and her new boyfriend, an auto mechanic, have traveled seven hours to get here, and the whole time, she was thinking about how lucky Ronnie was to be in the State School, and how good she felt about playing a role in that.

Moments after Joseph peeled out of the gas mart, Ronnie called the Holiday Inn to alert his stepcousin, but the room didn't answer. He made his way back to Jimmie, who called him a fucking fool and told him to get the hell out. The cops were on his tail; what was he thinking, leading them right to Jimmie? Ronnie took off and made it to his mother's apartment, where he told Marina he had stolen a car and the cops were after him. He took a shower and fell asleep on the couch. He woke up to find Marina hugging him and crying.

"That's you, isn't it?" she said, pointing to the television. A local news reporter was doing a stand-up in front of the Holiday Inn, where Ronnie's stepcousin had been captured in the parking lot.

After briefly flirting with putting her son on a bus back to Oklahoma, Marina convinced Ronnie to let her drive him to the police station. A few months later, a judge gave Ronnie's two stepcousins fifty-year sentences in state prison. Because he voluntarily surrendered, the same judge sent Ronnie to the TYC with a twenty-five-year determinate sentence.

"I saw the police handcuff him. Just seeing that, I turned away from drugs," Marina recalls, years later. "When the police led him away, I turned away from drugs and haven't used since. They say you can't stop crack just like that, but I did."

When the graduation ceremony concludes, there are cookies and punch. Students scurry about, grabbing a caseworker or JCO or psychologist and ushering him or her across the room to meet parents and take a picture. The parents shake hands and smile, but many are visibly uncomfortable. They know that the staff know a great deal about them, and they can't help but wonder if beneath the smiles, they are being judged.

"When kids come to Giddings, their parents often shower them with gifts," Frank Soto observes as he watches the introductions. Since the only piece of clothing the TYC allows students to select are shoes, parents will sometimes buy their children the most expensive basketball shoes on the market. Or they will put $100 in a boy's account and tell him to treat himself and his friends to cookies and candy when his dorm is allowed to visit the Snack Shack at the end of the week.

"The kids are such pound puppies," Soto continues, shaking his head in wonder. "They are so forgiving, any attention they get, they'll accept. It's, 'Wow, maybe Mom has changed!' Sometimes, Mom really has changed. Sometimes, it's just guilt. Sometimes, she is substituting material things for love. And sometimes, it's subtle bribery."

If subtle bribery does occur, it is usually when a boy is preparing to tell his life story in Capital Offenders. "Some parents get very uncomfortable," Soto says. "They think, Maybe if I send my kid a pair of Air Jordans, he won't tell what really happened."

The students whose parents have attended graduation are fortunate to have family members who care about them and are still involved in their lives. About half of all State School students do not return home when they are paroled. Their families have been shattered; a father is in prison, a mother is drug-addicted, an uncle is an active criminal. Sometimes, a boy or girl has too high a profile in a gang-infested neighborhood to go back home. But whether a boy finds himself back in his old room or sharing a bedroom in a halfway house is not as important as whether or not he has come to terms with his past; in particular, with his parents.

"One of the most important things that can happen in Capital Offenders is for a kid to see his parents as they really are," Frank Soto says. "Then they can begin to understand those feelings that are there, deep down inside. If they don't get to those feelings, those feelings are going to get to them. They will come out, and they will use them against a wife, or someone else."

A few hours after graduation ends, Ronnie gets a chance to explain his feelings to his mother. Marina and her boyfriend go to the Ramada Inn across the street from the State School to take a nap, then she returns for a family session with Dr. Sherry Whatley and Maxine Cooper, Ronnie's caseworker. Ronnie is about to complete Capital Offenders and the plan is for him to return home when he is paroled. Cooper and another caseworker, Loretta Triesch, encouraged Ronnie to establish contact with his mother when he arrived in the State School almost four years earlier. Ronnie started by writing letters. This led to phone calls and finally Marina coming to the State School to visit. She arrives in Whatley's office and moments later Ronnie appears in the doorway, holding the coveted pass that allows him to walk across campus unescorted. Marina leaps out of the big chair to hug him, even though she has just seen him.

"Did you tell them about Kenny?" Ronnie says before he even sits down. He is bursting with pride.

Kenny and two friends robbed a convenience store, not far from the apartment where he and Marina were living. Kenny got probation and was doing well until he began smoking marijuana heavily. Worried that she would lose him, Marina called Ronnie to ask advice. He told her to call Kenny's probation officer and have him do a spot drug test. When Kenny came up dirty, Ronnie told his mother to ask the probation officer to send him to a boot camp.

Marina followed her older son's advice and Kenny ended up spending six months in a TYC boot camp. He came back healthy and filled with pride and has been doing well in high school for over a year.

"He's doing so great!" Marina says with a big smile. "He goes to school and works out every day."

Sherry Whatley fills Marina in on what happened in Capital Offend-ers and, going through Ronnie's file, pauses when she reaches the letter Ronnie wrote to Joseph and Martha, his victims. Every youth serving time in the State School has to write one of these letters. Ronnie tells Joseph and Martha that he thinks of them every day and knows they can never accept an apology, but he wants them to know how sorry he is for what he did. "It makes me feel nasty inside because you were living out your days in peace and security and I took that away from you. I have grandparents I love dearly and wouldn't want anything to happen to them. I have made changes and want you to know I will never harm anyone again." The TYC has a form letter it sends to victims, saying that a youth has written a letter of apology and asking if they are willing to receive it. Martha and Joseph were, and there is a letter from them in Ronnie's file, saying they are proud of him for facing what he did.

Whatley turns the meeting over to Maxine Cooper, who takes Marina through Ronnie's "success plan," the State School's name for parole. Cooper explains that leaving the State School is not like graduating from college and entering the job market. The stakes are much higher than that. That's why she and Ronnie started this process months ago, begin-ning with developing realistic goals. Ronnie kept saying he just wanted to play football. Cooper told him that although he had a great year, he was not going to college to play ball and would never play for the Dallas Cow-boys. She knows what she is talking about. Her husband, Earl, was an All-American running back at Rice who played tight end for the San Francisco 49ers and is remembered for catching Joe Montana's first touch-down pass in the 49ers' first Super Bowl victory in 1982.

Cooper kept asking Ronnie the same questions: Where do you want to live? What kind of work do you want to do? What kind of relationship do you want with your mother? Your father? You went through the chemi-cal dependency program; you know you will be in a situation where peo-ple are getting high; what will you do?

You were in a gang. You were quick to anger. What happens if you are in a mall and a gang member gets in your face? How will you handle that?

You developed tremendous appetites for drugs and sex. What will you do for excitement now? You can't get high on crime and drugs and stay in

The Free. How will you find fun in a world where you have to work and pay the bills?

"A success plan prepares kids for life without us," Cooper explains to Marina. "It's a package to carry the things they have learned through the gate. It's not just words on paper. Ronnie's *life* is at stake. If he doesn't follow his plan, he could end up hurt, dead, or in prison."

Nodding gravely, Marina says she has talked to administrators at the nursing home and they have promised to have a job waiting for Ronnie. If that doesn't work out, she is active in a church, and friends there have offered to help Ronnie, too.

Ronnie waits for an opening and when he sees it, he says, "Mom, I need you to know: you were a terrible mom. You never put me and Kenny first. Do you know what happened when you left us alone with our aunt when we first came to Amarillo? You know what drugs did to you; do you know what your doing drugs did to me and Kenny? Do you know you really hurt me, Mom? And Kenny? And how much I hurt Kenny, too."

Marina's eyes snap with anger and she grasps the arms of her chair and pushes herself back. It is as if she is replaying the scene in the kitchen in her sister's apartment in Amarillo, years earlier.

"You need to take care of your own damn business," she snaps at Ronnie. "My life is my business!"

"Mom, your life is my business," Ronnie says patiently. "I was there. I was hurt. Remember that night you first took me out with you? Remember Mr. Strings? You didn't come over to get me that night, Mom. I was hiding in the fireplace and you didn't come over and pick me up and make sure I was all right. Do you know how that made me feel, Mom? Think about it. I was only five years old."

Marina picks up something in Ronnie's tone. He isn't attacking her; he isn't threatening her. He is trying to make her understand. She starts to cry, and her defensiveness vanishes with her tears. She spends most of the next hour listening to Ronnie explain what it was like to have her as a mother. Marina keeps saying she was lost in drugs and had no idea things were this bad. She keeps promising to be a good mother when Ronnie gets out on parole. The session ends with mother and son crying in each other's arms.

"Parents aren't usually that amenable," Cooper observed afterward. "Marina has dependency issues. It seems like she's transmitting her dependency issues to her son. Because of that, I think, she'll be able to learn from her son. He's become the adult; the mother is more like the child. Ronnie is going to go out there and hold the family together."

Three weeks after Ronnie got his GED, Capital Offenders ended. With illnesses, time off for mandatory staff seminars, and the difficulty students experienced telling life and crime stories, it took nine months to complete the group. One afternoon, Ronnie and Daniel came back to Cottage 5-A after an auto-tech class in the vocational building. They smelled like brake fluid and were going through the sleeping area on their way to the showers. Something seemed different and they stopped and looked around. Mark's bed had been stripped and his PA, personal area, a small closet with adjoining shelves, was empty. Ronnie and Daniel looked at each other and shook their heads, sad but not surprised, and vindicated, too. Mark was not a good group member. Now he was gone, on his way to prison.

Mark murdered his sixteen-year-old girlfriend and was going to spend the next forty years in prison. In Capital Offenders, he was the most taciturn, least active member of the group, spending most days marooned on an island of his own. He limped through a life story filled with horror— the grandfather who used a belt buckle to beat him, the uncle who repeatedly raped him. He was unable to complete his crime story, even though therapists kept giving him chances to start over at the beginning.

Strict policy guidelines must be met before a youth is transferred to prison. Mark appeared before the Special Services Committee twice. The first time, he was warned about failing to make progress in high school and in Capital Offenders. If he did not show he wanted to change, the committee would consider him a high risk to reoffend and recommend he be transferred to prison. Mark didn't change and the second time he appeared, the committee voted unanimously to make that recommendation.

The recommendation went to Butch Held, the superintendent, who concurred. Mark's "packet," as the paperwork is called, then went to the TYC main office in Austin, where staff members who review prison transfers signed off on the decision. Only then did a van arrive to carry Mark away to prison.

When a determinate-sentence offender enters the prison system, he joins teenage inmates who have been tried as adults and sent directly to prison. With each passing year, fewer youth are tried in criminal courts and sentenced to prison in Texas. Still, decisions on how to charge a youthful defender are made at the local level, and can be highly arbitrary.

A prosecutor in a small West Texas county may seek a life sentence in a rape case; a prosecutor trying a similar rape case in Travis County, where Austin is located, may ask for a determinate sentence with a three-year minimum. Sometimes, a prosecutor's decision can appear to be influenced by who the victim was. That appears to be the case with Napoleon Beazley. Beazley would seem to have been an ideal candidate for the Giddings State School. He committed a hideous crime, but so have many youth incarcerated there.

Beazley was seventeen the night he and two friends carjacked a 1987 Mercedes and executed the driver, John Luttig. Luttig's wife, Bobbie, escaped by playing dead. Beazley was president of his senior class and the starting running back on the Grapeland High School football team. He graduated thirteenth in a class of sixty. At his trial, evidence surfaced that he was also a cocaine dealer. The trial attracted great attention because John Luttig was the father of J. Michael Luttig, a judge who sits on the Fourth U.S. Circuit Court of Appeals in Virginia. Judge Luttig attended Beazley's trial and made impassioned pleas for the death penalty.

Beazley's two crime partners testified against him and were given life sentences. Beazley was sentenced to death. It took eight years for the appeals to wind through the legal system, and in that time, Beazley adopted a stoic stance that never changed. "I don't blame my family, I don't blame my friends, I don't blame society, I can't blame a federal judge. I don't blame anybody else for being here but me," he said at one hearing.

But voices around the world were raised, blaming America for sanctioning capital punishment for youth under age eighteen, and Texas for moving forward to carry it out. Letters demanding that Beazley's sentence be commuted to life in prison poured into the Texas Board of Pardons and Paroles in Austin. One of the most powerful came from Cindy Maria Garner, the district attorney in Beazley's home county. Garner wrote that although she had "been a strong advocate for the death penalty my entire life and have made decisions regarding the death penalty during my tenure . . . I would not have sought the death penalty had this case been filed in Houston County." Garner said she had known Beazley and his family for over ten years. She noted that Beazley had no prior record and "did not exhibit behavior indicating he would be a continuing threat to society. I am further concerned that the decision to seek the death penalty in this case was based, in part, on the fact that the victim's son was a federal judge."

In May 2002, Beazley was put to death by lethal injection in Huntsville. He was twenty-five. In his final statement, he said, "I'm disappointed that a system that is supposed to protect and uphold what is just and right can be so much like me when I made my shameful mistake."

Since the death penalty was reinstated in 1977, seventeen youths under age eighteen have been executed in America. Nine of the seventeen executions, or 53 percent, have occurred in Texas. Another twenty-eight who committed capital crimes before they turned eighteen are on death row, awaiting execution.

Mark had a chance that Napoleon Beazley didn't get. He did not or could not take advantage of it. That is why when a boy is transferred from the State School to the Texas Department of Criminal Justice, TDCJ personnel consider him a double loser.

The Texas Department of Criminal Justice houses male teenage prisoners in the Clemens Unit, 125 miles south of Giddings, near Brazoria. Clemens is a few miles from where the Brazos River empties into the Gulf, close to the San Bernard National Wildlife Refuge, where the American alligator lurks. In its way, Clemens is every bit as frightening as the giant reptile. There are no nice green lawns and shady oak trees and limestone-facade buildings in Clemens. Razor wire glints in the sunlight, hot winds kick up white dust on the dreary grounds, heavy bars cover the windows, obscuring the sunlight. It is very humid this close to the Gulf, but there is no air-conditioning in Clemens. There is no air-conditioning in any cell block in a Texas prison. When a fight breaks out, no one breaks it up and calls a behavior group to sort things out. Guards mace the entire cell block and move in when the mist clears. There is no treatment in Clemens. Inmates in white jumpsuits tend row crops in the fields, watched by armed guards on horseback.

Young men who have been transferred to Clemens often write letters back to Giddings, telling staff members about "shankings" (knifings) and referring to themselves as "stupid" or "hardheaded." Knowing what they do now, the writers wish they could come back to Giddings and start over. In a way, some of them do. Inmates in the Clemens Unit have started their own behavior groups. The group leaders most often are from Giddings, because they have the most experience in groups.

It costs slightly over $100 a day, or close to $40,000 a year, to house a youth in the Giddings State School. Ronnie's rehabilitation will therefore cost taxpayers in Texas around $160,000.

It costs $44 a day to house an inmate in TDCJ prison, or $15,664 a year. If Mark serves his full forty-year sentence—and tough sentencing guidelines make it probable that he will—Texas taxpayers will spend more than $626,000 in today's dollars to keep him behind bars.

Part Two

THE GIRLS

8.

"IS THAT MAN THERE?"

It's always a small event when a column of boys passes a column of girls marching back and forth across campus. Heads move back an inch or two, eyes slide to the side as the columns pass. Boys and girls eat at separate times, attend classes in separate wings of the high school, and mix only in the chapel. The boys never get to ask the questions they spend so much time wondering about. How much sex has a girl had? Was she in a gang? What kind of drugs did she use? What kind of crimes did she commit? What are the girls' groups like? What do their dorms look like? Do they shower together?

The boys' questions essentially boil down to one: Is life inside the fence the same for girls as it is for us? The answer is no. The girls are different.

The ratio of boys to girls at the State School usually runs 325 to 65, and if anything, anger, alienation, and criminality run deeper in the females than in the males. Differences between the sexes begin with the head and the heart.

"With boys, antisocial behavior is cognitive," says Tom Talbott, a veteran girls' caseworker. "Boys go about creating an image: 'I'm bad, I'm in a gang.' Girls come from their emotions. They've been hurt, bad. They are going to take it out on anyone they can."

On paper, boys can appear more ruthless. Johnnie's description of his committing offense in the boys' group, for instance, was all the more chilling because it was not especially unique. Johnnie was the classic wannabe, a small, insecure kid who would do anything to get himself jumped into a gang, including using his grandfather's car to ferry shooters to two drive-bys in one night. In the second, the shooters fired into a yard party, killing a twenty-year-old college student who had no gang affiliation.

"They were pumped up, they were glorifying it, they were yelling," Johnnie recalled, painting the scene in the car immediately after the bullets were fired. "One of them said, 'I seen that motherfucker hit the ground!' The other said, 'Yeah, the motherfucker hit the ground!' I downplayed the seriousness of it in my mind and didn't say anything because I wanted to be accepted."

Two young thugs gloating over an indiscriminate killing while the wannabe behind the wheel thinks he has finally earned his way into the gang—that's depraved. And yet, the depersonalization, the lack of humanity that makes the crime so hideous, can be a tool therapists use to get into a boy's head and help him find his humanity, as they did with Ronnie.

Johnnie was a rarity, one of very few boys going through Capital Offenders who had never been physically or sexually abused. Johnnie's problem was his mother's abandonment. Although the TYC has never run statistics on abuse rates among boys in Capital Offenders, veteran therapists put the figure at 95 percent or higher. With boys, the abuse often has a definite beginning and an abrupt end, as Ronnie's did. Or the abuse may have happened just once. With Daniel, it was a single episode of sexual abuse.

The twenty-two girls housed in Cottage 1-A, where Capital Offenders veterans live with girls going through the program now, did not shoot someone dead because he was wearing blue and they were down for red; none of them killed a clerk in a convenience store because he laughed when she demanded he empty the cash drawer. Most of these girls committed "relationship crimes." Some were in their early teens when they hooked up with a felon—usually a parolee in his early twenties—and went on a crime spree. Others attacked members of their immediate families, often after years of abuse.

Among the girls, the rate of sexual and physical assault anecdotally is 100 percent. Larry Reue ran girls' groups for ten years, and in all that time he can think of only one young woman who had not been abused. She was from an upper-middle-class home in Houston and was as estranged from her family as the two boys who committed the Columbine High School murders. She spent years in her room, silently furious that she wasn't as smart as her older sister, and that her parents paid little or no attention to her while showering praise on the sister. And then, she took revenge, binding and gagging her parents, ransacking the house, and taking off with a boyfriend who she thought had killed them.

Among the girls, abuse, particularly sexual abuse, starts very young—sometimes when the girls are toddlers—and goes on for years. A girl who night after night is molested or raped by a father, a stepfather, an uncle, or Mom's latest boyfriend detaches from herself. She ends up having out-of-body experiences. It's as if she is hovering over the bed, watching it happen.

Being detached from themselves is one of the things that makes girls dangerous. "If it ever comes down to you and me, it's going to be, 'You lose. Sorry,' " says Tami Coy, director of the girls' program. But there is much more to working with girls than just helping them connect with feelings they have spent years suppressing. When a boy opens up, it is usually in a group, and he can usually keep his feelings in check until the next group. When girls connect with their feelings, they stay connected, all the time.

"With boys, what you typically get is a conduct disorder," Coy observes. "With girls, you get conduct disorders, plus a whole load of emotional issues. They become very needy. Girls are more volatile than boys. They get set off very quickly—you never know what can cause it, it might be the littlest thing—and when they go off, they don't show any restraint."

"Girls," Coy concludes, "require more work than the boys."

Coy reads the file of every girl who comes through the gate, and over the years, she has detected a pattern that also helps explain why girls seem more hardened than boys. Girls tend to get more chances—because they are girls.

"Girls are not more brutal than boys. Their crimes are more shocking because a girl did it. It's always, 'Oh my God, I can't believe a girl did that!' " Coy says. "A prosecutor or a judge sees a girl crying and thinks, Oh my gosh, that could be my daughter! That's probably why the girls we get have lots and lots of priors, and why girls are much more underprosecuted than the boys. You look at a committing offense and see what a girl actually did, it's often astonishing. She pled to aggravated assault. What she actually did was attempted murder."

Coy has been at the State School fifteen years, since she volunteered while going through Texas A&M. An Aggie through and through, Coy goes back to College Station every chance she gets to watch a football game, and on a Friday morning, the day before a game, Coy is wearing Aggie colors—blood red and gray—as she sits in a behavior group in the living area of Cottage 1-A. The large circle includes Ann Kelley; two psychologists who are running the girls Capital Offenders group, Mike Hilgers and Jeri Pamp; a JCO; a caseworker; and the twenty-two girls in residence. Confrontations have occurred, tears have been shed. The girls have used up all the Kleenex and now a roll of toilet paper is traveling around the circle.

The girls are dressed in regulation gray sweatshirts, forest green prison pants with elastic waists, and running shoes. They are all Giddings veterans, although two are in orange jumpsuits, signifying they recently did something to get busted down to phase zero, rock bottom in the resocialization hierarchy. The room feels less like a correctional institution than the common area in a college dorm. The lighting is fluorescent, the cement-block walls are painted a white semigloss, the floor is gray linoleum, buffed spotless. The tables are round (if a fight breaks out, there are no edges to slam into), and in one corner, wood-frame couches covered with pale purple cushions face a TV.

This group was called because the girls are threatening to beat up Jani, a short, compact girl with dark hair and hauntingly beautiful black eyes. Jani is one of seven girls in the current Capital Offenders group. COG is designed to be the therapeutic equivalent of the Three Musketeers. A member makes a solemn commitment to the group not to discuss revelations outside the group room, no matter what. Jani has been doing whatever she can to sabotage bonds that are forged by intimate revelations.

Over the last three sessions in Capital Offenders, Cristina, an articulate Latina barely five feet tall, has told her life story. When Cristina was very young, her mother delighted in pretending she did not understand what her daughter was trying to tell her. She waited until the little girl was purple with rage, then asked why Cristina never said she loved her. Cristina screamed, "I don't love you! I hate you! I hate you!" That always made her mother laugh. She thought Cristina was cute when she lost her temper.

At age six, Cristina discovered that to be close to her mother, she had to drink with her. She spent many nights riding around the West Texas plains, her mother and a boyfriend in the front seat, she sipping a cold beer in back next to the ice chest. The next morning, she was often too hungover to go to kindergarten.

When Cristina was eight, on an average day she drank three or four beers, smoked two marijuana joints, and sometimes inhaled a little gasoline with her older brother. In her early teens, Cristina's consumption expanded to crack cocaine, especially after being raped at age thirteen. She talked about that terrible event for the first time in Capital Offenders. Through tears punctuated by a quick, hearty laugh, Cristina completed the narrative, and felt good about it. Jani portrayed her mother in the role play and Cristina felt good about that, too. Until she discovered Jani was mocking her, just as her mother once did.

Jani gleefully revealed Cristina's secrets to anyone who listened, imitating the way Cristina told her life story and the way she had played Cristina's mother. That is why the girls are outraged, why they want to beat Jani up, and why they have been in a behavior group for three hours.

Cristina is doubled up in her chair, trying to turn herself into a clam. Her forearms are resting on her thighs; her face is buried in her hands. A girl on one side has an arm around her; a girl on the other is stroking her head. Jani sits across the circle, smirking. The girls look at Jani, and at Cristina, and stay angry.

"Jani, why are you doing this to Cristina and your group?" Ann Kelley asks.

"I like to play," Jani replies airily. "I like to see people's reactions, to see people cry. I like that."

"Do you like people not liking you?" a girl asks.

"Yeah, I like that," Jani replies.

"I don't buy that, Jani," Jeri Pamp says, her soft voice turning firm. "You want attention."

"I don't care about myself and I don't care about the group," Jani says, dismissing Pamp. "Doing the group is an easy way out. And when I get out, I'll reoffend. Start the paperwork. Send me to the pen. I'm tired of this."

"You don't want to stay here where you're safe?" asks Elena, one of the Capital Offenders girls, genuinely surprised. "In prison, you think they will care? They'll turn their heads when they see you beaten."

Before coming down to the cottage, Hilgers, Pamp, and Kelley spent an hour discussing Jani. Going through her case file, Ann Kelley read aloud the results of a personality test that asks a respondent to turn "stem words" into a sentence. After words like "I hate," Jani wrote, "what happened when I was little." To "Sometimes I cry," Jani responded with, "because the people I love hurt me." Asked to draw a family picture, she depicted her mother yelling, "You better leave!"

The three psychologists recognize that Jani is exhibiting aspects of a borderline personality, someone so empty inside, she will never stop crying, *See me! See me! See me!* But the psychologists do not want to kick her out of the group. That would replicate what happened at home—Jani was twelve when her mother kicked her out for good. If they remove her, Jani will tell herself, "See, I am no good. I knew it." Her cycle of destructive, attention-seeking behavior will spin on, ruining her life and harming others, as it did a shopper whose arm Jani slashed with a knife while jacking her car in a mall parking lot.

"I'm going to push you away before you can push me away," Jani announces. "I feel I'm not worth any of this. Not worth any friends, or the group. I feel like I'm going to die a battered woman."

That is how every girl in this room feels, much of the time. But they don't make attention-getting statements like "Send me to the pen." If Jani keeps creating dramas where she plays the leading lady, she will suck the energy out of the cottage and the Capital Offenders group. The therapists will be forced to do triage; there are twenty-one other girls in the room who need attention as much as Jani.

"Cristina, what about you? Where are you?" Kelley asks.

When she looks up, Cristina is dry-eyed. Back home in the barrio in El Paso, Cristina carried a knife and used it a dozen different times. Three years in the State School have taught her to verbalize anger rather than express it with a weapon.

"My eighteen years of anger to my mom are coming up," she says. "I want to get up and throw it on Jani, but I won't. I want to cry, but I won't. I will later. Right now, I don't want to give her that satisfaction."

Jani mocks this with a big smile.

"Stop smiling!" one of the veteran girls snaps. "You think this is funny?"

"I do think it is funny," Jani replies. "I make myself laugh to see other people's reactions."

Across the circle, a small blonde with heavy acne wearing an orange jumpsuit asks Tami Coy for permission to use the restroom. Cheryl grew up in a gated subdivision on a golf course and progressed from severe conflicts with her parents to fights in school and problems with drugs and alcohol. She ran with teenage drug dealers and participated in the kidnapping and torture of a boy the dealers were certain had ripped off their stash. Cheryl and three others spent twenty-four hours torturing the boy, hitting him across the face and the back with an electrical cord, shoving a gun barrel in his mouth and ordering him to "Suck on this like a bitch."

When Cheryl comes out of the bathroom, she walks around the outside of the circle. As she is passing, Jani glances up and smirks. Cheryl suddenly lunges at Jani and grabs her hair.

"You whore! You fucking whore!" Cheryl screams.

Cheryl yanks Jani off her chair and they crash to the floor. Cheryl lands on top but Jani spins and suddenly she is on top, punching Cheryl in the face. Cheryl screams and swings wildly; Jani screams and lands blow after blow. Mike Hilgers, Ann Kelley, and the JCO jump in to separate the two while Pamp races to the center of the circle to head off a phalanx of girls led by Elena, whom Pamp knows is a fighter. She wraps her arms around

Elena. Two girls duck underneath their arms and they form a circle and hold each other and cry while, a few feet away, the fight continues. It takes three adults to wrest Cheryl away from Jani, and she stands against a wall panting, watching as the fight continues.

Staff members have varying opinions on how girls differ from boys. But on one point, frontline staff all agree: boys and girls fight differently.

With boys, it is usually a fistfight in the "back area" next to the showers and sinks, a location difficult for a busy JCO to oversee, especially if he is distracted by a well-planned diversion. When a boy gets knocked down and stays down, it is as if a boxing referee has counted him out. The fight ends and the combatants and spectators scatter, hoping the JCO won't figure out what just happened.

A girls' fight is a no-holds-barred mêlée, with biting, eye scratching, and hair pulling. And when a girl hits the ground, the fight doesn't end. Terrible things happen when someone pins a girl on her back. That is why on the floor, Jani's strength seems to have multiplied fourfold. Screaming "Get off me! Get the fuck off me!" Jani keeps bucking the two-hundred-plus-pound JCO into the air. When Ann Kelley tries to secure Jani's head, Jani uses it as a battering ram to keep Kelley at bay. Hilgers manages to get his arms around Jani's ankles and is holding on for dear life when four large men wearing black combat boots, black combat pants, and black T-shirts labeled SECURITY burst into the room. Two of them get Jani in handcuffs and lift her off the ground, but she kicks and struggles all the way to the steel cage in the white van parked just outside the door. *Boom! Boom! Boom!* The sound of Jani throwing herself against the cage comes echoing into the cottage. Meanwhile, Cheryl is docile as two officers escort her out the door and into a second van.

The circle slowly reassembles; the girls gradually compose themselves. When everyone is back in the chairs, Jeri Pamp says, "For a lot of us, that was like being back home, wasn't it? That's why we're so upset, isn't it?"

Girls exchange surprised, "How did she know?" looks. Pamp comes from an alcoholic family and lost a brother she dearly loved to the disease.

———

The next day, Jani appeared at a formal hearing in the security unit. Had she requested one, an attorney would have represented her. A hearing officer placed her on a thirty-day behavior management plan, meaning that for the next month, Jani will eat, sleep, and go to school in the security unit. When she emerges, she will be in an orange jumpsuit and will be moved to a pretreatment cottage, where she will start all over.

If the adult prison system represents John Wayne going for his gun, the TYC is Shane, Roy Rogers, or Gene Autry teaching a kid who has been bucked off a horse to get back in the saddle. Nothing did more to instill that ethic in the Texas Youth Commission than the landmark lawsuit *Morales* v. *Turman.*

The lawsuit began in El Paso early in the 1970s, when fifteen-year-old Alicia Morales ran away from home. Alicia was the oldest of eight children and the only one working to support the family. She turned every penny over to her alcoholic father, who in turn gave her $5 a week spending money. When Alicia asked her father to increase her allowance, he beat her and she ran away. Her father filed papers and took his daughter to court, where a judge declared Alicia incorrigible and committed her to the TYC.

The judge who sentenced Alicia Morales and dozens of other Texas judges who sent hundreds of other youth to TYC institutions either ignored or was not aware of *In re Gault,* a 1967 U.S. Supreme Court decision that grew out of an Arizona case. In *Gault,* the Supreme Court ruled that juveniles are entitled to the same due process protections that adults are given under the U.S. Constitution.

Steve Bercu was very familiar with *Gault.* A young attorney working for the El Paso Legal Assistance Society, Bercu had filed a writ of habeas corpus in state court on behalf of twelve girls who had committed "status offenses" (offenses only minors can commit, like running away) and were sentenced to the TYC. Bercu went to the TYC facility in Gainesville to interview Morales. The Gainesville superintendent agreed to allow Bercu to interview her, but only in the presence of staff members. Bercu refused, arguing that after *Gault,* juveniles had the right to the same attorney-client privileges that adults did. The Gainesville superintendent called an assistant attorney general to ask for an opinion. The assistant AG told the superintendent not to let Bercu interview the girl in private.

Bercu and his backers from the Youth Law Center in San Francisco filed a suit in federal court, *Morales* v. *Turman,* Turman being James Turman, the director of the TYC. Bercu chose to file the suit in the U.S. District Court for the Eastern District of Texas because the presiding judge, William Wayne Justice, was one of the most intelligent and fearless figures on the federal bench. The judge ordered the TYC to open its institutions to investigators, and teams of college students spent weeks interviewing youth in Gainesville and other facilities. What they found was appalling.

"The horrors came out during the trial," recalls Neil Nichols, the TYC general counsel. "Staff was macing kids until their faces peeled. They were running them blindfolded into walls. They were putting kids in isolation for three or four months with nothing but chamber pots. I'd been reading the trial transcripts and when I went up to Gainesville to see for myself, I expected to find monsters.

"I didn't see a single evil person. I saw people who loved kids to death. And yet, they were the same people who were doing these horrible things. That's what happens when you don't have programs and standards. That's what happens when people in a closed setting have too much power."

Conditions were appalling across the TYC with the exception of one institution, a school for girls in Brownwood. State legislators asked why the Brownwood facility was so much better than the other TYC institutions. The answer they received was Ron Jackson, the superintendent. With *Morales* getting national media attention, the legislature quickly appointed Jackson to head the TYC. Jackson came with a mandate to provide treatment for every juvenile it held in custody.

"Ron was an orphan, raised in an orphanage in Corsicana and adopted by the warden," says Neil Nichols, the second person Jackson hired. "Ron knew institutions from the inside. He established the treatment culture in the TYC. When he retired in 1994, he was the longest-tenured agency head in Texas."

Large institutions, especially those run by the state, have a way of forgetting their purpose and evolving into bureaucracies whose primary purpose is providing secure jobs for employees. Asked how he kept this from happening, Jackson, with a Texan's brevity, replied, "You do what's best for the kids. You keep focused on that." His emphasis on treatment earned him the enmity of more than a few juvenile court judges, who thought there should be a greater balance between treatment and punishment in the TYC. None was more prominent than Hal Gaither, a juvenile court judge in Dallas.

"Ron Jackson never accepted the fact he was in corrections. Ron Jackson was a social worker," Gaither said.

Gaither is not antitreatment. Early in the 1990s, he wanted to reward boys who were doing well in the Dallas detention center, and came up with the idea of taking them to a Texas Rangers baseball game and having them meet the players during batting practice. He arranged a meeting with George W. Bush, then part owner of the Texas Rangers, to see if this was possible.

"I figured the meeting would take fifteen minutes at the most," Gaither recalled. "Bush said, sure, the Rangers would be glad to help, and gave me the name of someone to call. I was getting up to leave when he said, 'Wait a minute. I want you to teach me the juvenile justice system. I want to run for governor and I want to be the best governor this state ever had.' I said, 'Well, it's not simple. It'll take a while.'

"After that, we met every Friday morning. I know he was running what I was telling him by others. He ended up making the reform of the juvenile justice system one of the cornerstones of his campaign. And when he was elected, he did exactly what he said he was going to do. I respect that."

During his campaign, Bush attacked the TYC for being "soft on teenage predators," as so many other candidates across the country were doing in the 1990s. He charged that the TYC was "broken." That riled Ron Jackson.

"George Bush was not deeply versed in the juvenile justice system and he had no feel for juvenile justice issues. He did what was politically effective," said Jackson, who retired when Bush became governor in 1994.

Steve Robinson, a huge, approachable man, took over the TYC reins and absorbed the Bush attacks. Every time Robinson went up to the capitol, one legislator after another informed him that "the TYC is broken."

Robinson, it turned out, had a flair for marketing.

"I'd tell them, 'The TYC is not broken. It's just broke,' " Robinson recalled.

The message got across: if Texas wanted to have a youth commission that held kids accountable and delivered treatment to larger numbers of youth, the legislature was going to have to increase its size. With the backing of the governor, the TYC acquired and built facilities and almost doubled its size in four years. Frontline staff, the JCOs, got long-overdue pay raises.

At Governor Bush's urging, the TYC instituted regulations requiring that boys have their hair buzz-cut; boys and girls were to march when they moved from place to place within an institution, to address staff with "yes, sir" and "no, miss," and to wear standardized clothing. The TYC also hired "apprehension specialists" to track down youth who violate their parole. The changes the Bush administration brought to the TYC were for the most part cosmetic and ultimately did nothing to disturb the treatment culture that was firmly entrenched when Ron Jackson retired.

"The TYC needed to get bigger. We were having to spit out general offenders in six months because we didn't have enough beds to keep them," says Larry Reue, the veteran psychologist. "And it was nice when kids started coming out of the Marlin Assessment Center saying 'yes, sir.' Kids were a little further along the road when they arrived."

The following Tuesday, six Capital Offenders girls are back in the bunker with an empty chair in the circle. Mike Hilgers walks over and picks it up. "This is heavy, this is symbolic," he says as he places it on the stack in the corner. The girls watch without comment, then go back to talking about boyfriends—Cristina and Tommy, the little wide receiver on the football team; Keisha and Kim, the quarterback.

Mixing the sexes creates nightmares for the State School staff. The TYC does it because specialized treatment programs are concentrated in Giddings; girls need these programs as much as the boys, and Texas does not have the money to build a separate treatment facility just for them. Because the sexes mingle only in the chapel and the meds line in the infirmary, more kids are probably pursuing the spiritual path, and more may be on psychotropic medication than there ordinarily would be, because of what staff members call "the secondary gain."

Despite the restrictions, relationships pop up all over campus. A fair number of staff members think this is not such a bad thing, despite prohibitions against passing letters or talking in the hallways in school. The kids will have to deal with the opposite sex when they get out; why shouldn't they develop a few skills while they are confined?

Some of the Capital Offenders girls think TYC romances are like the green prison pants, to be discarded just before going through the gate. Others believe relationships will work in The Free because they have, after all, been confined together, and who on the outside understands what it is like to be locked up in Giddings?

Either way, a boyfriend is an opportunity for a girl to plan, or test-plan, a future; to enliven a regimented day with a jolt of excitement when she sees *him* marching across campus; and to beat the system by passing contraband, as Kim recently did, when he told Keisha to study page 34 in her math book. Sure enough, there was a letter. Staff uncovered it during a dorm search over the weekend, and Keisha, a tall black girl with a quick wit, is wondering why her caseworker is so bent out of shape about it. They put boys and girls together, don't they? What do they expect?

"Oh well." Keisha sighs.

In The Free, "oh well" means no big deal, as in, "Oh well, sorry we couldn't connect for lunch." In confinement, the phrase denotes a resignation that can be deadly. "Oh well, I did a crime. Oh well, I got caught. Oh well, I am locked up. Oh well."

"So, it's an 'oh well,' " Hilgers says, challenging Keisha. When Keisha doesn't return his look, Hilgers puts the brakes on talking about boys. "Soooooo," Hilgers says quietly, "what do y'all think about Jani being removed?"

"It's sad," says Nicole, her big grin at odds with her words. Nicole is a tall strawberry blonde with freckles and dancing eyes who has a habit of blurting out whatever she thinks, like a precocious four-year-old. "I'm trying not to smile but I can't help it," she admits.

The other girls are smiling, too.

"Will Jani be in the next Capital Offenders?" Nicole inquires.

"I don't know; it depends on how she manages herself," Jeri Pamp replies. "Not everyone makes it to the promised land."

Hilgers scans the group, stopping at Elena. Then he asks the question that is the prelude to a life story.

"Elena, how are you feeling?"

Short and stocky, Elena oils her short brown hair and combs it straight back, like a rockabilly singer. Easily the most kinetic group member, she is forever popping out of her chair to rotate her head and twist her arms and shoulders until her back cracks. Then she retucks her sweatshirt into her pants and drops back into her chair. Elena's face is round; she has beautiful gray eyes and a smile that grows so wide, it can appear diabolic. But now, she is slumped in her chair, staring at her feet. Elena doesn't want to tell her life story.

"I got feelings I don't want to deal with," Elena says when Hilgers asks why.

When Elena came into the TYC, psychologists in the assessment center labeled her "defiant in orange," a reference to her jumpsuit. She refused to participate in anything—she'd scream, "I don't give a fuck," when a staff member confronted her. She denied she had ever been sexually abused, although the evidence was clear she had been. Elena hid her crime behind false humor, laughing off her assault as if it were a farce. And yet she cried herself to sleep almost every night and, every so often, banged her head against a wall.

In two years Elena made enough progress to enter Capital Offenders, where she has been an alert and perceptive contributor, delivering insights in the clipped speech of a street-smart Latina. But when something goes wrong in her family—her family is very large, and things often go very wrong—Elena is overcome with hopelessness. In the past, she has acted upon those feelings, once swallowing 120 Tylenol capsules, another time using a blanket to try to hang herself in a detention center. Now, she withdraws into herself.

"Maybe it would be good if you experience those feelings and at the same time stay in control," Hilgers suggests. "We're okay with you being angry if you stay in control."

"I don't like being close to people," Elena replies.

Hilgers and Pamp are a team, as fused as referees in the National Basketball Association, who confer using their eyes and lightning-quick hand signals. A glance tells Pamp that Hilgers has an idea that might draw Elena out. Okay, Hilgers says, since Elena doesn't want to tell her life story, let's have the group tell it for her. The girls think that's great.

She's one of twelve children. No, thirteen.

She's had six dads. No, it's six brothers and four dads. No, it's seven brothers.

They're all in jail. Not jail, prison.

The big smile appears and Elena bolts upright. All she needed was a push.

"Twelve brothers and sisters, six by the same father!" she exclaims. "One dad, three stepdads. My really, really, really dad, he's just my sperm dad. My best stepdad, Leo, had a big old belly, we called him Buddha, he practically raised us. Buddha was fun. He gave us money if our ears were cold. We'd put our ears in the freezer and run back to him."

In most of the girls' families, an adult or an older sibling is an active criminal. Elena's family is not only larger than the other girls', it is more chaotic. If her brothers and sisters, her stepfathers, aunts, and uncles, had been less impulsive, the family might have been prosecuted under RICO, the Racketeer Influenced and Corrupt Organizations Act. They ended up behind bars anyway, but they went one at a time. So many of Elena's siblings have been locked up, gotten out, and been locked up again, Lucy, their mother, has trouble remembering the charges.

"Let's see," Lucy says, setting herself to the task during an interview in San Antonio. "Tomas, he's my oldest, he went in for dealing. He got out but he just got locked up again. They said he was driving a stolen car.

"Rogelio. What was Rogelio's little reason for being locked up? I think it was selling drugs.

"Leticia. She's locked up. I can't remember if it's a state or federal prison. She's in a gang.

"Benny. Let's see. I should have it right here in front of me. I just got a letter. He's in a federal prison camp. I don't know the charges but he's got a three-year sentence.

"Carmen's locked up, I really don't know where. I've got them all over. But she's coming home in six months, I know that.

"Aurelio's locked up again. He's in that prison near Houston, I forget its name. It was a gang thing. I've lost my kids to drugs and gangs.

"A part of you dies when you hear a child has been arrested," Lucy concludes, giving up on recounting her children's criminal dossiers. "It's scary when they go away. I always wonder, Are they going to be okay? Is someone going to hurt them? My heart's been broken into a million pieces. I've got one child left, Sarah, my baby, and I always told myself I'd keep her. She got pregnant with her first boyfriend at thirteen and had the baby at fourteen. Sarah started going off to meet people and wouldn't come home. They put her in an alternative school but she got into a fight with a black girl on the bus and they took her away from me. When I found out she was in juvenile hall I thought, Here we go again. . . ."

Thirteen children, thirteen rap sheets. But Lucy has tried, at least intermittently, to be a mother to her children, and is still trying. "I want to build a better life so I can be here for them when they get out," she says. "Welfare never got me nowhere, I've always worked. I've cleaned houses, done laundry, waitressed, tended bar, worked as a nursing assistant in an old folks' home, and now I'm a clerk in a Diamond Shamrock gas station.

"I want to accomplish something, for me," Lucy vows. "I've taken the GED three times and I'm going to take it again until I pass. I want a paper that shows I'm not dumb. I want to take that paper and use it to get into real estate classes. I'm looking forward to doing that."

Lucy appears twenty years older than her actual age, forty-three. Her eyes have lost their luster, her hair its sheen; her upper arms are flaccid, her middle has grown thick. It is hard to detect any trace of the graceful girl she was at thirteen, the long-legged beauty with waist-length hair and even white teeth. When Lucy was in eighth grade, something happened that knocked her legs out from under her. She never has regained her footing. Her daughter is aware of this, and zeros in on it early in her narrative.

"At thirteen, my mom was raped, that's how she got pregnant with my oldest brother," Elena says. "He was twenty-one and he proposed. My mother said no, but my grandmother said yes. He abused my mom. She'd run back to my grandmother's house and my grandmother would kick her out. She'd go back home and take beatings. She'd be cooking and cleaning and he'd come home from work and kick everybody out. He'd be in there for hours and hours and they'd be outside, crying. He'd let them inside and then he'd make her have sex with him.

"When she'd hit us, she'd just black out and go blank and she'd hit us and hit us and hit us. There were marks on us, bruises and everything. I think she was taking her anger out on us. I didn't take it like that then. But looking back on it now, I do."

Lucy is quick to confirm that she indeed was raped and beaten by the man who fathered six of her children, before he went off to prison. It's her life and she wants the facts known, ugly or not. "I was so desperate, I tried suicide. His mother was on medications for epileptic seizures and depression and I took all her pills. They found me and I had my stomach pumped and after that, I said, 'Lord, even you don't want me.' Rogelio, my second son, came along when I was sixteen. I dove in front of a car after he was born; they took me to the hospital with a broken leg and back injuries.

"Once I tried with a gun, but a friend took it away from me. Oh! There was the time I tried to use the cops. I went into a depression and they put me in the hospital. When I got out, I called the police station and said I was going to kill myself. They asked me how. I said, 'I'm going to use your gun.' "

This last event occurred in the wake of Leo, or Buddha's, departure. He and Lucy were together eight years and in that time, she did not attempt to harm herself. That does not mean things were placid at home. Lucy was working full-time and Leo was working for the San Antonio Parks Department, building benches, picnic tables, and gazebos. Her children roamed the streets pretty much as they pleased. And yet, they were a family.

"Leo treated me right and he treated the kids right. He was exactly what the kids were searching for," Lucy remembers. "We were renting a pretty neat little home and we were all very fond of him."

Leo and Lucy did not have a child together—Lucy says he went to the doctor once and was told he had a low sperm count. But the kind, fun-loving Buddha was Elena's dad from ages two through nine, and her early childhood memories are not that different from those of a child who grows up in a poor but intact family—except for the stealing.

"Stealing ran in my family," Elena tells the group. "I don't know if my mom told my older brothers to do it, but the older kids took care of the younger ones and they'd go out and come back with stuff. Mostly we stole because we never had any money, except only for food. The first time I did it, I was scared. I was five years old and I stole a purse. After that I took guns and G.I. Joes—I was a tomboy, I didn't like Barbies. I dug a hole in the back and buried them. They were mine. I used to steal my mother's Tupperware bowls and hide them in the garage. They were pretty, I liked looking at them.

"I wasn't scared, wasn't paranoid, I got a thrill out of stealing. I'd race out of a store if I got caught. By ten, I was addicted to it. I was stealing most of my clothes."

Elena is the product of a relationship Lucy had with a man shortly before she met Buddha. Lucy didn't know he was married and had three children; he didn't mention it until she told him she was pregnant. "Then he said he had to leave me and go back to his own family," Lucy recalls. "He'd come back once in a while, but all he talked about was his problems with Gracie, his wife. Two or three days after Elena was born, I knocked on his door and when he opened it, I said, 'Excuse me. You have a daughter.' He went on with his life and his family and when we ran into him in the street, he wouldn't come up to us. He never helped financially."

Elena remembers her seventh birthday because her mother led her into her bedroom, sat her down on the bed, and picked up the telephone. Her mother said something in Spanish, which Elena does not speak, and handed her the phone. A male voice on the other end mumbled something and hung up. Elena handed the phone to her mother.

"My mother started cussing and called right back," Elena tells the group. "They were arguing; she gave me the phone and I said hello and he hung up again. My mother went away, but she had a piece of paper with the number written on it. I waited for a few minutes and then I called back. A woman answered the phone. I said, 'Is that man there?' That's what I said. 'Is that man there?' The woman said, 'Who's this?' I told her my name. She said, 'Your dad's not here, stop calling! He don't want you!'

"I didn't call again. I had Buddha, my stepfather. I just wanted to know who he was."

Sadly, Elena did not have Buddha much longer. "My mom and my stepdad started having problems," Elena recalls. "My mom started going away from us. She'd go out drinking with my aunts and come home drunk. I mean, really drunk." One Saturday night, Lucy and her sisters came home to find that Buddha had packed his things and left. "He and I had our differences, and we split up," is all Lucy will say about it.

Lucy had trouble making the rent and the family kept moving. At one apartment complex, she paid the family next door to watch her kids when she went off to work. It was a mistake and it alienated her daughter. Elena tells this part in the same matter-of-fact way she has been narrating the rest of her story, although now her voice is rich with feeling.

"The next door neighbors sold marijuana and did spray," Elena says, using the street term to describe inhaling fumes from a can of spray paint. "They were dirty, really, really dirty, and they always had drugs and were always spraying. My mom gave them money to watch us; they wouldn't do it. I was eight or nine and I'd have to watch their babies and my own little sisters. My mom would give them money for food. They wouldn't spend it on us.

"I'd tell my mom about all this. I'd tell her and tell her and tell her that they were always selling and always sprayin'. I told her they didn't even take care of their own kids, they're not going to take care of us. She'd be, 'You're lying. You're lying.' She'd ask them and they'd say, 'We never did that,' and she believed them, not me. I hated my mom for that. She didn't listen to me, her own daughter. I'd just withdraw from her, I wouldn't even talk to her or nothing, I'd just be by myself listening to the radio. I guess that's why I didn't tell her anything. Like, when I got molested, I didn't tell my mom because I thought she wouldn't believe me."

"So, how do you feel about your mom?" Pamp asks.

"I don't know. I love my mom, I got feelings toward her. But then again, I'm confused. I'm mad at her and I hate her. I have homicidal feelings toward her for doing what she did with all those men. When I tried to tell her about it, she'd be, 'There you go again.' I'd say, 'Forget it, Mom.' "

" 'All those men?' " Cristina asks, peering across the circle at Elena.

"The men would stay there, they'd fuck her, let her cook, and then they'd leave," Elena replies, her voice rising. "It was one of my stepfathers that molested me. When I got here I wrote my mom about it and she wrote back, 'I didn't think it was him. I thought it was somebody else.' She said, 'I'm sorry,' and she stopped writing. She just left it like that. I love my mom, but I'm mad at her for not being there for me."

"But it seems like you took your anger out on other people," Hilgers observes. "Why was your mom untouchable?"

"I always felt like my mom has her own problems, she has enough on her mind," Elena explains. "This is when my brothers started really, really gangbanging and she was always going to court for my sisters. And she was a single parent, too."

"But couldn't you have told her how angry at her you were?" Hilgers asks.

Elena turns her gray eyes on Hilgers. When the group began, the girls all objected to working with a male therapist, none more strongly than Elena. They have since grown comfortable with him, and the male issue has not come up, until now.

"Sir, when you hear stuff about us being molested, what do you feel?" Elena asks.

Hilgers chooses his words carefully. "I'm overwhelmed. Not because I'm a man. Because I'm a human being."

"Most of us have been through sexual abuse; half of us hate men," Elena presses. "How does it make you feel that men are out there, doing this to little girls?"

"I'm very aware I'm the only man in here," Hilgers replies. "I try to monitor myself. I try not to talk in a loud, man's voice. I've got a desire to comfort, hug; being a man, I'm careful about that."

Elena thinks about that for a moment and apparently decides to accept it. She doesn't say anything to Hilgers or even nod in his direction; she just goes on with her narrative.

Elena's older brothers graduated from shoplifting to stealing cars and joining gangs. Now, Lucy was scrambling to move her family from place to place because her home had become a drive-by target. "My brothers would be gone for days but they'd always be coming home and telling Mom, 'We're going to stay here tonight,' " Elena recalls. "And then the rivals would be doing drive-bys at my mom's house. This is when my mom left me and my little sisters with my older sister Carmen in a one-bedroom apartment. My dad Buddha wasn't there and Carmen was supposed to take care of us, but she'd lock the door and run away. She was getting into gangs. She'd come back two or three days later, all beat up. The gang was jumping her in. My mom didn't do anything to her. Carmen got pregnant, but she had a miscarriage.

"My sister Carmen and I were close and I was mad. I didn't like her getting all beaten up; I was scared for her. So this one time when she ran, I went with her. She was thirteen or fourteen, I was ten or eleven. We went to a gang party. Everyone was drinking Mickey's [Mickey's Big Mouths], and I started drinking, too. Carmen got mad, she took the beer away from me. I said, 'You do it. Why can't I?' The guys said, 'She's down. Let's see what she's all about.' The guys took bets on how many Mickey's I could drink. That was the first time I drank beer."

With all these problems with gangs and the courts and working one and sometimes two jobs to get the rent together and keep food on the table, Lucy felt she deserved one night of fun a week, so every Saturday, no matter what, she went drinking with two of her sisters. Her sisters could afford to take Lucy out on the town. They were Surenos, full-time gang members who dealt drugs and carried guns. The Saturday nights ended on a playful note, at first.

"My mom and my aunts would come home drunk, and when they got drunk, it was *their time,* the kids didn't have any say," Elena recalls. "They'd come home at two A.M. and hit us with pillows to wake us up. It was fun, but then my mom started lining us up in the hallway. If the house was clean, we could go back to bed. If it was dirty, she'd hit us. She'd spank us six or seven times and take us by the ears and throw us across the room. And then we had to clean the house. We started wearing extra clothes to bed, like three or four pairs of pajamas. She'd be hitting us and we'd act like we were crying, but we'd be looking at each other and laughing."

It was during one of these middle-of-the-night rages that Lucy tried to stage a police-assisted suicide.

"My mom went to the kitchen and started smashing glasses on the floor," Elena recalls. "Then she started breaking pictures. She was yelling, 'I hate this place! I wanna die! Fuck the kids!' Then she called nine-one-one and said she was going to kill herself. The cops came and they were going to handcuff her, but she grabbed a gun from one of the cops and shot it in the air. They really got pissed off! They threw her to the floor and took her away."

Lucy spent almost two years in the Bexar County Jail and her three sisters divided her eight children among them. Elena and a younger sister went to live with Sonia, one of the two gang-affiliated aunts.

"She'd treat her kids nice and do us wrong," Elena recalls. "We slept in the tub, me and my little sister Esther. We ate baloney sandwiches and leftovers and we had to eat on the stairs, she wouldn't let us eat at the table with her family. She made me stand on bottle caps, faceup. Esther was just a baby and my aunt burned her with hot water. She and her boyfriend would throw her back and forth across the room, play catch with her like she was a football. All this time, we had no idea where Mom was."

Elena jumps up to do her back cracking and plops back down in her chair. She is telling her story with great energy, smiling as she searches the circle for reactions. But there is no sadness, no hint of pain or anger, in anything she says.

"Do you spend a lot of time thinking about your life?" Hilgers asks.

"The fun stuff. I block all the other stuff out," Elena replies easily.

"It's like she's telling about other people's lives, not her own," Michelle observes, and the other girls nod in agreement.

Girls quickly become adept at exploring feelings. For them, feelings are like a river. They wade in and let the current carry them along. For boys, feelings are more like a swimming hole. They dive in, climb out, and stand on the bank, thinking about their next dive.

"We did something wrong, we got beat. That's the way I looked at it," Elena tells Michelle.

"You said yourself, your mom was taking it out on you," Michelle points out.

"That's now, that's looking back on it," Elena counters.

Next to Jani, Michelle was the girl the group disliked most when Capital Offenders began ten weeks ago. There is a cold fury in Michelle she kept hidden behind a prickly, scowling, prissy facade. When she told her life story, the group saw behind the mask. Michelle had a stepfather who began raping, beating, and threatening to kill her when she was four years old. She crawled into her mother's bed for protection and her stepfather raped her there—while her mother pretended to be asleep. On Saturdays when her mother took classes at a community college and her stepfather looked after Michelle and her little brother (Mom was a hairdresser studying to be a psychologist, ironically), Michelle's stepfather took the kids to a video store, where he picked up a week's worth of X-rated titles, and then to an abandoned church where, in a room filled with red light, he joined a group that worshiped Satan.

It took Michelle three sessions to relate her life story, and when she finished, there was a stillness in the group room that approached the reverent. Jeri Pamp finally broke it, quietly observing that when anyone asked how Michelle was feeling, she replied "irritated" or "pissed." But, Pamp observed, "it doesn't look irritated or pissed to me. It looks like hurt. It looks like a lot of sadness."

"Anger is going to be there till I die. I don't want my past to get the best of me," Michelle said in her breathy voice.

"Michelle, it's anger that keeps the past alive for you," Pamp pointed out. "You don't have to battle it for the rest of your life. Maybe if you understand the sadness, some of the rage will go away. Can you let yourself feel the sorrow?"

Michelle sat very still and then began sobbing, huge, eloquent sobs that filled the room like music from a pipe organ. The girls were crying with her. And then, Michelle's sobs dropped an octave and her body convulsed. It was unbearable, like watching a mother mourn the loss of a child. When the catharsis ended and Michelle regained her composure, Rachael pronounced a kind of benediction. Rachael is a quiet black girl from Corpus Christi who sat in group unconsciously rolling a Kleenex into a perfect joint, a task she performed countless times for her father, a small-time dealer.

"Those were tears of survival," Rachael said.

Michelle has not been the same since. The young woman with pale white skin and light blue eyes who kept herself apart, sitting alone in a corner during breaks, is now the center of the group. She is a terrific little therapist, alert and kind, and at the same time insistent, as she is now with Elena.

"You had to be feeling something when all this stuff was happening; tell us," Michelle demands.

Elena thinks about that for a moment, then says, "I thought no one listened to me. That's when I started feeling hurt and anger and getting suicidal feelings."

"Wasn't there no one you could talk to?" Michelle asks.

Elena takes another moment, then replies, "I was very determined in school; I was a silent person who would do my work. My favorite teacher, Miss Gonzales in fourth grade, she saw through me, she saw I was hurting. She would always ask, What is wrong? What is wrong? I would never tell her, I'd just start crying. She'd take me upstairs and we'd sit by a window and I'd never talk, I'd just cry. But Miss Gonzales, she was there for me.

"It got to a point where I'd sit and think and think and think: Why is my life so messed up? Why are my brothers in gangs? Why does my sister run away and hang out with gangs and come home all beat up? Where's my mom? Why don't I have a father anymore? Stuff like that. I'd get frustrated and bang my head against the wall. I was constantly banging my head. I always felt like I was the outcast. It got to the point where I didn't want to be anymore."

Lucy got out of jail late in the spring the year Miss Gonzales was Elena's teacher. She found an apartment in a flimsy complex on the other side of San Antonio and Elena never saw her favorite teacher again. Her life might have followed a different trajectory had her relationship with Miss Gonzales continued. So many agencies looking for volunteers use the slogan "One person can make a difference," it has become something of a cliché. But it is true, nonetheless. It happened with Francisca, one of

Elena's three aunts. Elena can't mention Francisca's name without calling her "my prosocial aunt."

Like her sisters, Francisca dropped out of high school, but unlike the other two, she did not join a gang. She worked in a Burger King and dreamed of becoming a nurse. She enrolled in a continuation high school and signed up for chemistry, but after the first class she knocked on the instructor's door and told her she was dropping out. She hadn't understood a thing the instructor was talking about, she couldn't read the text, she was too dumb to ever be a nurse. The instructor refused to let Francisca quit. She tutored her that whole semester and Francisca ended up getting an A. When the class ended, the instructor said, Okay, the next thing you're going to do is take the SAT. What's the SAT? Francisca asked.

She scored in the 1400s, and with her chemistry instructor—now her mentor—hovering over her shoulder, Francisca applied for scholarships and eventually won a grant that paid for four years of college. Francisca is an ICU nurse in a hospital in San Antonio and has two children of her own. She took in two of Elena's brothers when Lucy went to jail and ended up raising them. These days, when someone in Elena's extended family comes out of prison, he or she almost always gets paroled to this "prosocial" aunt. With her support, several have learned a trade and have left the criminal life behind and are raising families.

So, why did Francisca turn into a caregiver and her other sisters into gangbangers? There is no simple explanation, but having a vision of a better life and bonding with a role model who can help make that vision a reality appears to be absolutely critical.

"The factor that seems to be consistent is, the sibling who comes to terms with a tough childhood and turns into a caregiver has almost always found someone to bond with," Linda Reyes said. "Somewhere, somehow, she found a role model. The sister who ends up in prison did not."

The social services system exists, in large part, to connect children like Elena with positive role models by placing them with foster parents who really care, or in programs that really work, like Head Start. Social workers appeared at Elena's house after her mother tried to use a police officer's revolver to blow her brains out. They took the children to a shelter and then drove them to their new homes with three different aunts. But after that, the social workers disappeared. No one ran a records check and discovered two of the aunts had long criminal records. If they did, they ignored what they found.

Elena, like the other girls in this group, has been both sexually and physically abused. Elena and the other girls came to school with fresh bruises. Michelle, for example, wore long-sleeved shirts on even the hottest days to cover them. These girls' teachers either failed to notice or overlooked the bruises; or they accepted flimsy excuses. If a teacher did refer a child to the school nurse, and the nurse sent the girl to a doctor, the doctor failed to refer her case to Child Protective Services. Or, if a doctor did make a referral, social workers failed to do an investigation. Or, if they did do an investigation, no one acted on the findings. The bottom line: no one intervened.

The social services safety net in Texas is not torn apart. But in Texas, as in the other forty-nine states, the net has a very loose weave.

9.

MEETING KATY

The first time Ric and Judy Nesbit visited the Giddings State School, they arrived in a van that carried a dozen shattered, angry parents. Their anger went so deep, and was so richly deserved, most of them could relate only to those who shared it. That is why they had joined the North Texas chapter of the Parents of Murdered Children.

Anyone intrepid enough to ask the moms and dads in the van what life had been like since they lost a son or daughter would have received the same answer: It's been hell.

But what did "hell" mean? It meant the parents had discovered the killers who'd destroyed their children had kept on murdering.

Friends and some family members, loving and supportive at first, had left by now, or were making themselves scarce. They had come to the funeral and cried and hugged, then had gone home to their own families, where, thank God, things were safe. Many were acting as if grief were contagious, like a virus. Some stayed away because they were afraid—or had no idea how—to enter such a devastated inner landscape. Others, well-intentioned though they might be, turned out to be empathic idiots: the brother who said, You've had a few weeks off. It's time to start getting over it. The mother of a daughter's best friend who cut off contact just when it mattered most because, The situation in that house is just too much for a twelve-year-old!

Many of the parents had lost, or were in the process of losing, their spouses. In grief this profound, little irritations that were always dismissed—"That's just him"; "She's like that, always has been, always will be"—became magnified, and unbearable. A wife needed to talk; her husband had no patience with words. A dad wanted to travel, to try to leave the memories behind, at least for a while; his wife shuddered every time she turned the key and left the house on an errand. Couples who once looked into each other's eyes and saw love, now saw horror and wreckage. They stopped looking.

The parents in the van were no longer demanding that God give them back their children. They knew that would not happen. But they did demand that society, through the criminal justice system, deliver retribution, and with it, some sort of catharsis. Now, one of many sad and terrible things these people shared was a feeling of being re-victimized by the system.

For some, the worst came in court when a police officer took the stand and described the crime scene in minute, gruesome detail. No one had bothered to tell the parents this was coming; no one had attempted to prepare them. For others, it was the afternoon the alleged killer was led into the courtroom and paused to let a bailiff unhook his handcuffs. He looked up and the parents made eye contact. They had been waiting for this moment, fully expecting the killer to crumble. Instead, he gave them a scowl that said, Man, this don't mean shit to me.

The parents were college-educated, taught to trust rational thinking. But reason had turned out to be a puny tool, no match for the everlasting nightmare they were living. No matter how much they learned about the murderers, no matter how often they dissected every bit of information that surfaced about the killing, no matter how hard they searched, the answer to that monumental one-word question "Why?" refused to appear.

Most now accepted that it never would. They would never comprehend how anyone could assume the right to kill their son, murder their daughter. But the search for "Why?" did lead them to the bottom of their loss, and the bottom was this: along with their children's lives, the killers took their children's privacy, their dignity. These wounds went the deepest, perhaps because they were so visual.

As Ric and Judy Nesbit rode along, pictures of their daughter, Katy, flashed through their minds, as they did wherever they went, whatever they were doing. Ric's favorite picture was Katy's first. It always amazed him because Katy was only an hour old and there she was, looking around for something to do. Image followed image and always ended with Katy's last photograph, a picture made by the medical examiner: Katy on a steel slab, naked, bloody, and alone, in the city morgue.

And now this.

This was an outrage!

Someone from the Texas Youth Commission had called Parents of Murdered Children to inform the group that in the course of a specialized treatment program called Capital Offenders, therapists were showing crime-scene pictures and autopsy reports to violent teenage offenders. Treatment specialists had been doing this for years before someone from the TYC central office decided it was a good idea to ask the victims of violence what they thought about it. The parents were furious. Therapists were showing their children's autopsy pictures to the kinds of kids who murdered them? The TYC could not have come up with a more insidious way to continue to victimize their children and tear away at whatever healing the parents might have accomplished.

The parents in the van were on their way to Giddings to confront the staff that was using the crime-scene photographs. They were going to set these people straight.

When the parents got their first look at the TYC's premier facility, the emotional tinder in the van went up in flames. They were expecting a prison, a hulking, gray, ugly prison, with cell doors clanging and armed guards barking at stoop-shouldered inmates.

This is it?

This is where they put the murderers?

"The worst of the worst"?

It looks like a prep school!

It looks like a summer camp!

As the visitors were issued passes in the gatehouse, they noticed the guards were unarmed. They asked about this and were told there were no guns on campus. Only four security officers are authorized to carry pepper spray. They walked up the long sidewalk leading to the administration building, taking in the freshly mown grass and lovely oaks in silence, until they passed a group of students tending a flower garden. Then one of the mothers—a woman whose daughter was murdered by two high school friends—gave voice to the outrage every parent was feeling: We are putting flowers on our children's graves while their killers are planting flowers! How can we ever get justice if this is where they send murderers?

Ric and Judy Nesbit are an attractive couple in their late forties. Judy is petite, with soft brown eyes and brown hair that flows down her back. Judy had a wonderful sense of humor and a droll way with a story before Katy was murdered. Ric wears his salt-and-pepper hair long in back and short in front, has caramel brown eyes and a barrel chest, evidence of the athlete who set a national record in the breaststroke in high school and won seven NCAA championships in college. Ric is very direct, even by the standards set by the straight-talkin' Texas stereotype. Now, however, he did not to say a word, or even nod in agreement. On the trip down, Ric had privately dubbed the group the "Kill 'em Committee," and he considered himself and Judy charter members.

Katy's murder had left Ric raging at God; at a society that made it easy for teenage murderers to get guns; at a legal system that gave him no sense of closure. He and Judy were seeking retribution, obeying a human instinct that was already ancient at the creation of the Code of Hammurabi.

The parents entered the school library, sat down at a long table, and watched the treatment staff file in and take seats across from them. After the introductions, Dr. Corinne Alvarez-Sanders opened the meeting by saying that as the parents had no doubt noticed, the Giddings State School is pretty, but it is pretty only on the outside. Prison is just the opposite of the Giddings State School. Outside, it looks ominous. Inside, it is easy. We hold these kids accountable in the strictest possible way, sixteen hours a day.

We are not using your children's pictures, Alvarez-Sanders continued. We show a victim's autopsy picture to the youth who committed the murder. Making them face what they've done is one way we hold them accountable. Most violent kids have been subjected to so much violence, they have shut down their feelings. We put kids in a room and make them examine their pasts. We turn up the emotional heat and make them connect with their feelings. When they open up and start to feel, they connect with their anger and the sadness it masks. Slowly, they begin to see how they used that anger to justify hurting others. They experience someone else's pain. They develop empathy.

At that point, one of the mothers slammed the table with the palm of her hand. Are we still in Texas? Or did we somehow make a wrong turn and end up in California? All this touchy-feely stuff, what difference does it make? If a criminal says, "I'm sorry," so what? The criminal is still a criminal; the people he hurt are still hurting, the people he killed are dead and in the ground.

That broke the dam. Like floodwaters, the parents' anger came bursting forth.

The lady at the gate called them "students." Is that what you call them, "students"? We call them criminals!

What did these kids do to deserve such a beautiful, comfortable place, besides kill somebody?

You think these kids have a right to a life? Our kids, they're the ones who had a right to live!

How can you work with these kids? How can you care? They didn't care about our kids!

Once a criminal, always a criminal! Any fifteen-year-old who can point a gun at someone and pull the trigger is a born killer!

All the treatment staff could do was listen. And as they listened, the parents began to tell their stories. They needed the therapists to know what it felt like to hear a knock on the door in the middle of the night and wake up to see a blue light flashing through the windows. What it felt like to wait for months while defense attorneys swarmed over the evidence like fire ants, searching for legal loopholes that might spring clients they knew were guilty. To finally have the trial begin, to finally get a conviction, and then to discover that many of the killers had ended up here. This whole place was an insult to the victims of violence.

The stories continued for almost two hours. Psychologists who dealt with unbelievable abuse and unspeakable acts of violence every day were openly weeping. They could not explain why the parents' children did not get a second chance and the young criminals in the State School did.

They could not explain why life can be so brutally unfair. Finally, there was a lull and someone suggested they take a break.

Ric Nesbit was sitting at the point of contact between the two groups, at one end of the table next to a psychologist. The psychologist leaned toward him. Ric, he said, you realize these kids are going to get out someday, don't you? Do you want us to do everything we can to help them change while they are still young and capable of change? Or would you rather we didn't treat them?

Nesbit looked at the psychologist for a long moment and slowly began to nod his head. Ric was thinking of Sammy, his little brother. Sammy was smart and handsome, a great athlete. And Sammy was an addict. Sammy burned out everyone in the family, except for Ric, who became his caretaker. Sammy went to prison three times; each time, he emerged angrier and meaner. Sammy ended up dead in a cheap motel in Houston with a needle in his arm.

Would Sammy be clean and sober and alive today if he had gotten treatment behind bars? Maybe not. But it would have been worth a try.

Ric went into therapy after Sammy died. He believed he had failed because he could not keep his brother alive and wanted to discover what he had done wrong. The sessions led to Ric abandoning a successful career in commercial real estate and taking a large pay cut to become a certified drug and alcohol treatment counselor in a Ft. Worth high school. He was able to reach some of the kids he worked with. During the break, he wondered how these therapists were able to reach some of the violent kids they worked with.

When the meeting reconvened, the psychologists explained their work in detail and the parents gradually realized they had more in common with the people across the table than perhaps any group outside themselves. These people knew violence; they understood what it does. The parents began sharing insights.

The psychologists were so moved by the parents' stories, they had turned introspective. Ann Kelley, for example, was questioning her decision to work with violent young offenders. She had gotten into psychology to help people help themselves. So why wasn't she out there, working with the victims of violence? Kelley realized she probably used the word "victim" as often as a stockbroker says "funds," or a carpenter "wood." But as she listened to the parents tell their stories, she realized the kids' victims were not as real, to them or to her, as the people sitting across the table. If there was some way to take an abstraction—"victim"—and turn it into a living, breathing person . . .

Kelley decided to take a chance.

"We have a responsibility to victims. You've helped us focus on that today, and we're really grateful you came all the way down here to do that," she said. "We could fulfill that responsibility better if some of you would consider using what you've been through in a way that could be very valuable. Would any of you consider coming back to tell your stories to students going through the Capital Offenders group?"

Alvarez-Sanders was waiting for this.

"What we're doing here works. It really does," she said, leaning across the table. "We've done follow up studies and measured outcomes. There's no way the legislature would fund what we're doing if we couldn't show them statistics that show we're effective. We'd love to have you join us. We'd love it if we could work together."

Ric Nesbit was willing to give it a try.

Nesbit did not show it, but he was terrified. What if the young criminals were so hardened, they'd meet his story with apathy, or worse, mock his pain? That would turn him into even more of an emotional cripple. He decided to take the risk. Maybe, finally, there might be a way to salvage some small meaning from Katy's meaningless death.

Ric and Judy Nesbit are in Ann Kelley's office, holding Styrofoam cups of incredibly bad office coffee. The office is crowded—Mike Hilgers and Jeri Pamp, the psychologists from the girls' group; a TYC official from Austin in charge of the victim impact program; the supervisor who oversees the program on the Giddings campus—and it is early, seven-thirty in the morning. But there is much goodwill in the room and the atmosphere is buoyant. Ric and Judy have been coming to Giddings two or three times a year for almost five years, and staff members like Kelley are always delighted to see them. To Kelley, the Nesbits are more than old friends. They give her strength. Ric and Judy show how courageous people can be.

Ric and Judy are here to present a victim impact panel. The girls' Capital Offenders group has just finished its round of life stories. Victim impact falls between the end of life stories and the beginning of crime stories. It is the demarcation that shifts the focus from what was done to a youth, to what a youth has done. Pamp and Hilgers brief the Nesbits, describing the girls and their committing offenses; the way they told their life stories; the progress, or lack of progress, they are making in treatment. Ric and Judy listen intently, interrupting now and then with a question. They have become very good at this. When they get in the group room, they will quickly match names and faces with criminal records.

As they leave the building for the Capital Offenders bunker, it is obvious that Ric and Judy are, literally, the walking wounded. Judy walks with a pronounced limp, an ever-present reminder of the terrifying night in 1992 when two intoxicated teenagers in a stolen vehicle ran an intersection and slammed into her car, putting Judy in the intensive care unit for three days.

Walking beside his wife, Ric limps up when she limps down. In August 1991, he set a breaststroke world record for master swimmers. A year later, a terrible car crash ended his competitive swimming. Like the tide, memories of those terrible nights have receded. Memories of a far darker night, August 26, 1995, the night their sixteen-year-old daughter, Katy, was murdered, have not ebbed.

"I never thought of myself as a victim," Judy tells Pamp and Hilgers. "I don't like being called a victim, but that is who I will always be: 'that woman whose daughter was murdered.' When it was just us, the Parents of Murdered Children, people could look at us and think, Freaks. But now there's a lot of us. The parents who lost children in the September eleventh attacks are parents of murdered children. I doubt they think of themselves that way, but they are."

When the Nesbits enter the group room, the Capital Offenders girls are sitting in two rows, facing a television and a table where a large posterboard covered with snapshots stands behind a display of girls' shoes. The display begins with a little pair of ballet slippers and ends with white running shoes, stained with blood.

The Capital Offenders girls are rigid in their seats and formal when Hilgers and Pamp introduce them. Ric and Judy settle into their chairs, and Ric leans forward, his caramel brown eyes moving from girl to girl.

"Ask any question that comes to mind," Ric says. "You are not going to hurt our feelings or create any feelings that aren't already there."

Ric begins with his family history. Two grandparents died of sclerosis of the liver; his mother was an alcoholic. He tells the girls about Sammy, his little brother who went to prison three times. The first was for possession of marijuana seeds back in the late 1960s, when drug laws in Texas were among the most repressive in the country. The second was for shooting a drug-dealing partner, crippling him for life. The third was for a parole violation. Three days after his final release, he was dead of a drug overdose.

"Sammy was a bad person, a really bad person. He was my little brother. I loved him," Ric says. "I tell you this because I want you to know I've seen the criminal justice system from the other side, through a family member."

Judy and Ric begin to tell the girls about their twenty-eight-year marriage and as they do, they pass around pictures of their daughters, Katy and Sara. The girls study the pictures very carefully. "I was thirty-five when I had Katy," Judy says. "I waited for a man I was certain would be a good father. We planned her. We wanted her."

Ric and Judy show the girls pictures of Christmases and birthdays and camping trips and talk easily about their two daughters. At sixteen, raven-haired Katy was intriguing and beautiful. Her room was a shelter for homeless cats and wounded birds. She collected stacks of magazines and then, on impulse, stayed up all night cutting out pictures and pasting them on a wall, creating a big collage. Six months later when she was tired of the collage and magazines were stacked halfway to the ceiling, she did another one.

Katy was an A student, but her restless spirit, her willingness to experiment, and an openness to risk led her to drugs. She quit going to school and finally ended up in rehab. Every weekend, Judy and Ric drove to the rehab center for family therapy sessions.

"There was lots of healing. Katy was doing great," Judy says. "She went back to high school, she got good grades and caught up with her class."

In July 1995, Ric took Sara, Katy, and Katy's best friend, Anna, on a camping trip high in the Rocky Mountains in Colorado. "A great time, a great, great time," Ric says fondly. "I'm so glad we did it."

Three weeks later, they were back in Ft. Worth and summer was ending. The Labor Day weekend was just ahead and Sara and Katy were getting ready for school. On a Saturday morning, Anna came over to tell Katy there was a party that night. Katy spent the afternoon getting ready, spilling the hot-pink nail polish she was applying on the floor of the back porch.

"Don't worry! I'll have her back by midnight!" Anna called cheerily as the girls went out the door.

Anna was like a third daughter to the Nesbits. To Katy, she was like a big sister, enforcing the protocol Katy had committed to when she left rehab: no drugs, no alcohol, home and in bed at a decent hour.

That night, Katy did not follow the program. She stayed at the party until around one-thirty and left with Sean, Anna's boyfriend, in Michael McEachern's Bronco, a vehicle famous for its window-rattling, eardrum-blasting sound system. They dropped Sean off at home and on the way to Katy's house decided they were hungry and pulled into the order-from-your-car line at a Whataburger.

"Little did they know that a fifteen-year-old employee who was off the clock and his eighteen-year-old friend were using the place to plan their next carjacking," Ric says. "They saw the Bronco crawling up the line and heard the sound system throbbing and decided they wanted that one. The eighteen-year-old knew Michael; they played basketball together in the park. The eighteen-year-old said, 'Hey, man, can we get a ride?' Michael said sure. Katy opened the door and let them in.

"The eighteen-year-old sat behind her, the fifteen-year-old behind Michael. The fifteen-year-old pulled a thirty-eight automatic and put it to Michael's head. He'd been showing the gun for weeks to anyone who would look at it. He'd run shells through it so often, there were no markings on the casings. We know from the eighteen-year-old's confession that Michael tried to reason with them. They said, No, if we let you go, you'll tell. We have to kill you. They drove for half an hour, trying to reason with them. When they got to a desolate part of town where there are no lights, out on the Trinity River bottom, the fifteen-year-old decided it was time. They got out of the car. Standing three or four feet away, the fifteen-year-old shot Michael in the forehead. The sound was really loud and there was a flash of light from the gun. He shot again and hit Michael in the chest. He aimed at Katy and the gun jammed. The fifteen-year-old went crazy and Katy froze. He was screaming, 'Kill the fucking bitch,' at the eighteen-year-old. The eighteen-year-old ejects a couple of shells, raises the gun, and points it at Katy's face. She was looking him in the eyes and he said he couldn't pull the trigger while she was looking at him. She broke eye contact, he fired and hit her below the ear. The shot severed her spine, she fell like a rag doll. She died instantly.

"A couple taking a shortcut home passed by and saw a Bronco with its lights on but did not see the bodies. The husband wanted to get out and see what was happening; his wife was frightened and stopped him. They raced up to Bell Helicopter and alerted a security guard, who called the police."

At six-twenty on Sunday morning, the Nesbits were awakened by a hysterical call from Anna. Anna managed to tell Ric that Michael McEachern and a female companion had been murdered. She had to talk to Katy, right now. Ric heard a click, indicating Anna had an incoming call. She hung up but called back seconds later. Anna had just talked to Michael McEachern's mother. The girl who was with Michael was named Christine Jones.

Some invisible force, more powerful than anything Ric had ever experienced, slammed him against a wall. Christine Jones was the name on a fake ID Katy carried when she was drinking and doing drugs. She had told her parents she had destroyed the ID; Ric and Judy had believed her. Ric stayed suspended in some place beyond time, and then he lost it.

"I was screaming, yelling," Ric tells the girls. "We went up the stairs to her bedroom; Katy wasn't there. We raced to Michael's home; it was only a few blocks away. We got out and were stopped by a plainclothes cop. We told him why we were there. He said, 'You're mistaken, we've got a Christine Jones.' We described the bright pink nail polish she had on and we described her jeans. The officer said, 'I think maybe there's been a mistake. I'd like you to go to the medical examiner's office and identify the body.' He drove us downtown and he took us to a little room with a window, like a window in the room where they put babies when they are first born. It was our baby. Katy was lying under a sheet with her head showing. Our lives have not been the same since."

The Capital Offender girls have dissolved in tears and are blotting their eyes with Kleenex and blowing their noses. Ric and Judy watch for a while before Ric says, "I'd like for you to meet Katy." The lights dim. Hilgers turns on the TV and the words "What Murder Leaves Behind" appear on the screen. The girls lean forward in their chairs, fascinated, horrified. A sound track Ric has compiled from Katy's favorite songs begins to play. Home videos made and preserved by loving parents appear on the screen: there's Katy, a darling little girl at a gymnastics meet; Katy and Sara sharing presents under a big Christmas tree; Katy in a ballet class; Katy in a school play; Sara at Katy's birthday party.

Suddenly, the amateur videos are shattered by the grave, polished voice of a TV newscaster. The girls lurch back in their chairs. The television anchor reports the bodies of two teenagers were found this morning near Bell Helicopter. Clips from news stories show the story of the murders as it unfolds. There are scenes from the funerals. There are grieving eulogies and shots of friends holding each other and sobbing as a hearse pulls away.

When the lights come up, Ric is holding the picture of Katy taken moments after she was born. The newborn is looking around, trying to figure out what is happening. "That being Katy's first picture, I never thought this would be her last," Ric says. He holds up a picture of Katy's bloodied body on a gurney. The girls look and look away. They dab their eyes with Kleenex and look again.

"In a way, they killed three people that night," Judy says, picking up the narrative. "Sean, Anna's boyfriend, the boy they dropped off before they went to the Whataburger, was severely traumatized by what happened. He went into a tailspin and never came out. Sean became a terrible heroin addict. Sean died from an overdose.

"In that one night, Anna lost her best friend, Katy, and her boyfriend, Sean. Anna had a breakdown and spent a month in a hospital. She's okay now; she's doing fine."

Judy folds her hands and looks down. When she continues, her voice is very small, and yet it fills the room.

"When we came home from the medical examiner's, Sara said, 'Was it her?' And we said, 'Yes, it was her.' Sara said, 'Is it okay if we pretend she is away at camp? I missed her so much when she was away at camp.' Sara was twelve when her innocence was taken away, and that just makes me rage. She won't talk about it, she won't go to counseling, she won't go to family gatherings. Ric has two daughters from an earlier marriage and she sees how close her two older half sisters are and that causes her so much hurt. That's gone for Sara. She doesn't have an older sister to take care of her."

The room falls still and stays that way. Finally, Michelle, in her wispy voice, asks, "What happened to the boys who shot Katy and Michael?"

Teenagers can execute two people in cold blood, but they are still teenagers, as naïve about crime as they are the rest of life.

"A kid was out washing his car that Sunday morning," Ric replies, and for the first time, his voice sounds tired. "The fifteen-year-old passed by and said, 'Hey, did you hear they found a Bronco abandoned?' The kid said he hadn't, and the fifteen-year-old said, 'Well, I don't know nothing about it, but I'll install a stereo in your car for two hundred and sixty dollars.' The kid went into his house and talked to his mother. They agreed he had to tell someone and he called the police. The police found CDs and the changer in the fifteen-year-old's house. The amplifier was in the eighteen-year-old's garage."

"The trials were every bit as traumatic as the funeral," Judy says. "When someone is ripped out of your life, a numbness settles in and that shock protects you. By the time the first trial took place fourteen months later, the numbness was gone. The eighteen-year-old confessed; the fifteen-year-old never has. I'm sure his mother still thinks he is innocent. The DA elected to try both boys in the adult system. Both were sentenced to forty-year-to-life terms in the penitentiary. They didn't get the opportunity to reexamine their thought processes and have a chance for a better life. Their lives are basically over."

"You have that opportunity," Ric says. "So tell us: What's it like to have us here?"

Whatever composure the girls have left vanishes when Ric looks at each of them. He pauses and nods at Nicole. She uses her sweatshirt sleeve to wipe her eyes and then bursts into tears.

"It hurts!" Nicole wails. "I robbed a store, I pointed a gun at somebody. I could have pulled the trigger! I could have took somebody's life!"

Nicole stops, then realizes she has more to say. "You do this to help us, but it hurts you!"

"It plays in our heads, all day, every day," Ric says softly. "Playing the video or showing you Katy's shoes doesn't make it hurt more. Katy isn't here to say, 'Hi, I'm Katy!' But you got to meet her. So, today is a good day."

"She was innocent!" Rachael says between sobs.

"Are you?" Ric asks.

"No! I have a lot of guilt! I stabbed a boy. I almost killed him!"

"Can you use that guilt to make sure you'll never do it again?" Judy says.

"I'm not the way I used to be. I don't want to hurt nobody. I've made a lot of changes," Rachael replies eagerly.

"I stabbed somebody, too," Cristina volunteers, tears streaming down her face. "I was like the fifteen-year-old who has never confessed. I didn't own up to my offense for two years. When I did, it was a release. It feels good to say, 'This is what I did, this is where I need help.' The truth is going to be there, no matter how much you lie to yourself."

" 'The truth will set you free.' Have you found that to be true?" Ric asks.

"Yes," Cristina says.

"I'm here for aggravated robbery. It could have been murder," a tearful Keisha blurts out. "I'm glad you were kind enough to do this."

"You're not here for our pity," Elena observes, typically forthright. "You're here to help us."

"That's right. We don't need your pity," Judy agrees. "Our dream for you is to get out and lead happy, productive lives."

"Sir, miss, what is Parents of Murdered Children like?" Elena asks.

"There's people in the group like us, who have been through trials and seen the killers go to prison," Judy says. "There's people who know who killed their child, but the killers were acquitted. There's people who don't know and may never find out who killed their child. It's mainly about having a place where you can go and sit next to someone who knows what you are feeling."

"Do they all go to places like Giddings and talk to girls like us?" Elena asks.

"No," Ric says. "Many of those folks are angry."

"Do they hate us?"

"I wouldn't say that," Ric replies. "I'd just say they are real angry and they've decided to stay real angry. I understand that. But I found that for me, if I walk around hating the two guys that killed Katy, it makes me bitter, rude, short-tempered. It makes me a jerk. If I turn those guys over to God to deal with, then I can go on with my life, such as it is."

"I'm glad you were kind enough to do this for us," Michelle says. "Meeting Katy made me see; I mean, I knew, but more so now, how the things you do affects others. I was sitting here thinking, I wish I could bring her back. But she is alive, in a way. She's affecting us."

"Why are you here?" Ric asks Michelle.

"I took a butcher knife and chased my brother," Michelle replies.

"Would you have used it if you'd caught him?" Ric asks.

Michelle starts crying; she nods yes through her tears.

"Is he okay?" Ric asks.

Michelle nods again. "He has his first job, working as a bag boy. I'm hoping he feels like he is worth something."

One at a time, the Capital Offenders girls come forward to hug Ric and Judy. They go to the table and spend a lot of time examining pictures and handling the shoes and asking questions, strengthening their connection to the Nesbit family. There is another round of hugs and good-byes and then the girls line up and Pamp and Hilgers march them back to the dorm. The Nesbits walk back to the social services building with Ann

Kelley and the TYC official, who were watching behind the one-way mirror. Kelley is energized by the way the girls responded.

"When you first started, did you notice that look of 'How can you be here?' " Kelley asks as they walk. "They've only known one way to deal with anger. You are showing them another way. You haven't used your anger to justify hating."

The Nesbits sink into chairs in Kelley's office, completely exhausted. But when Hilgers and Pamp arrive, they perk up, eager to hear how the girls reacted.

"They were almost completely silent," Pamp says, smiling. "When the girls are not talking, you know something has really hit them."

Hilgers is excited about Nicole. "She just told me, 'Today is the first time I realized what I did,' " Hilgers says. "With Nicole, it's been kind of a jailhouse thing. 'I didn't murder anybody, it's just aggravated robbery.' When she told you, 'I could have took somebody's life,' that is the first time she really looked at her crime."

The Nesbits have a long drive back to Ft. Worth. But before they leave, someone has a few last questions: Are Katy and Michael's murderers beyond redemption? Should they have been sent to Giddings and given a second chance? If they were here, would you be able to do what you just did?

"Would I, could I, do this if the eighteen-year-old who killed Katy was in that room?" Ric asks. He pauses for a moment, then says, "Mercifully, I'll never know."

In the next session, each Capital Offenders girl receives a black-and-red ribbon to signify that she has attended a victim impact panel. The black is for violence, the red for blood, and the girls wear the ribbons every time they go to group. In a very real way, Katy, Sara, Judy, and Ric have become members of their group. Until the last day, the girls sprinkle their speech with phrases like, "When Mr. Nesbit said . . . ," "Remember how Mrs. Nesbit told us. . . ," "I've been thinking about Katy. . . ."

1 0.

"THE BITCH THIS, THE
BITCH THAT"

A crime story begins with earliest offenses, and it is amazing how little the girls were when they took the first small step on the criminal path.

"Stealing, between ages five and six!" Elena replies when Mike Hilgers asks. She is on the edge of her seat, legs vibrating on the balls of her feet, eyes shining with anticipation. "I stole in stores, I stole at school, I stole cigarettes for my cousin Jay. I had money from my stepdad Leo. I didn't have to. Stealing was fun! I liked going into a store and not having to pay. I'd bring stuff home and tell Mom lies about where I got it."

There is a difference between reciting a crime and reflecting on it, and Elena is too hyper to do the latter. To slow her down, Hilgers asks the other girls how old they were when they first did something they knew they shouldn't.

"Fifth grade, stealing stuff," says Nicole.

"Sixth grade. Shoplifting," says Keisha.

"Third grade or fourth, using drugs and fighting," says Cristina.

"Twelve or thirteen, using drugs and selling," Michelle says, and so on around the circle, back to Elena.

"Do you see yourself reoffending?" Pamp asks her.

"I won't reoffend!" Elena says, all certainty and conviction.

"Part of a psychological evaluation is to determine risk," Hilgers says, referring to a detailed "psych eval" that is done when a student is eligible to leave the State School, an evaluation that helps determine whether she will remain in Giddings, be released on parole, or go to prison. "If you had to put yourself low, medium, or high, where would it be?"

Once again they travel around the circle, with each girl rating herself "low," except Michelle.

"I don't know. I'm being real. Sometimes in the cottage, I get so angry . . ."

"Anger and impulsiveness drive a lot of criminal activity," Pamp confirms. She watches Michelle stare across the room at the fiberglass soundproofing, then turns back to Elena.

"Other than stealing, were you hurting people?"

"Oh yeah! I was a bad little ass!" Elena says, flashing her big, slightly diabolical clown's smile.

The year she reached ten, her six older brothers and sisters, two of her aunts, and several uncles were active in gangs. By then, Elena despised her mother. It wasn't so much that Lucy was always away, working at one menial job or another; or that she drank and used drugs and was often unstable; or even that her reaction to most problems, large or small, was to hit the child who presented them. She didn't listen to Elena; did not respond to things she told her, like how badly the spray-addicted neighbors were treating her and her sisters. "She wasn't there for me" is the way Elena sums it all up.

Elena was already a risk-taker; she was stealing, but not to get things— for the thrill of taking them. Gangs offered far bigger thrills; gangs were the most dangerous game of all. Alienated from her mother and missing Leo, her stepfather, Elena needed to connect with someone. The fastest, surest way to bond with her older brothers and sisters was to join their gang. Since she felt like "a nothing; I didn't want to be," she also needed something to believe in. And that, too, gangs provided. Suddenly, Elena had a cause; she was "down for blue."

"The Crips were popular then. My brothers were Blue Devils, Blue Riders," Elena explains, naming Crips-affiliated gangs. "I was stealing all my clothes and wearing all blue—a blue rag"—a handkerchief—"blue Dickies. My mom beat me up, she didn't approve, but I kept doing it. To be a gangster, you had to do more than dress like one. To get initiated, you had to do a drive-by.

"We drove by the house. The gun was a forty-five and I was only ten and I couldn't hold it. My brother held it with me and I shot the gun. They dropped me off at home. I was really hyper. I slept in my brother's room that night."

"How were you different, after you done that?" Nicole asks. Her elbows are on her knees, her chin resting on her fists as she peers across the circle at Elena.

"I felt powerful! I was on top of the world! I got a big head! I'm really good, I shot a gun! I told kids at school, 'Don't mess with me, I'll kill you!' I wasn't going to kill them, but if somebody looked at me wrong, I'd beat 'em up. I thought everybody was out to get me. I'd get them first.

"When I was eleven, we dropped the Crips. My aunts were Banderas, they clicked us in. They dressed *chula*," Elena says, laughing as she makes dabbing motions beneath her eyes. "You know, do makeup underneath, so you look like a cat. They carried guns and sold drugs, crack, mostly, and they'd fight their rivals. I started selling and using and this is when I started getting picked up by the cops. But I only got arrested four times, for criminal trespassing and runaways. They'd send me home to my mom, I'd run back to my aunts. We called them O.G.'s."

"Original gangsters," Cristina says quickly. An "original gangster" in a street gang is roughly equivalent to a don in the Mafia.

"No, 'old girls'!" Elena says, smiling broadly. "They were thirty-seven, thirty-eight. You know prep schools? Their kids were 'gangster preps.' I've got five woman cousins and they were all down and my aunts would always make us fight. Once, Teresa hit me and I started to bleed. I don't like blood on my face and I got mad and started going after her. Other than that, I'd lose. I don't hit my family.

"Since I got locked up, everybody's always telling me, 'You're avoiding, you're avoiding,' " Elena continues. "That's when I learned how. My mom would get mad and hit me. Like once, she beat me for touching other people's stuff. She got real mad and screamed, 'I wish you'd never been born!' I said, 'I wish I'd never been born, too!' and ran to my aunt's.

My mom came and got me and then something else happened and I ran again and stayed with my aunt. Then something would happen there and I'd leave and go stay with my other aunt. Then I'd go with one of my brothers, then I'd go with another brother. I was avoiding!"

"Avoiding. That's what you did at the end of your life story," Michelle says.

The chill in the room is sudden. Elena glares at Michelle, who looks away and pretends not to notice, but her right leg is vibrating. Other girls shift uncomfortably. Elena jumps up and goes through her back-cracking routine, then takes off her black sateen jacket and puts it on backward. She sits in her chair, her arms folded under the jacket. It is as if she is trying to use the jacket as a cocoon—or a shield.

Finally, Elena answers Michelle.

"You mean Manny, my stepfather. About him molesting me," she says, and Michelle nods yes.

Elena's mother did almost two years in the Bexar County Jail for wrestling a police officer's service revolver out of its holster and firing a shot into the ceiling. When Elena and her younger brothers and sisters finally reunited with Lucy, they found they had a new stepfather, a man named Manny. When she got to Manny while narrating her life story, Elena said, "He was supposed to be a father figure to me. He wasn't supposed to do what he did to me." And then she stopped and would say no more.

The girls tried to move her forward, asking if she had ever told anyone. "I didn't; I was real isolated."

Had she ever retaliated?

"He threatened to kill me if I told my mom. I slit his tires. I did everything to his car."

Knowing Manny would surface during her crime story, the therapists were reluctant to push Elena further. They know that a rape victim goes through periods when she feels hopeless. But with love and care from family and friends, with work and therapy and good support, most rape victims, over time, come to see the event as a terrible aberration and the world as a relatively safe place.

Elena has never had much love, support, or care. She never felt safe until, ironically, she was locked up. With the exception of her stepfather Leo and a compassionate schoolteacher, she never felt close to an adult. She tried burying memories of the sexual assaults in drugs and gang aggression, and when that didn't work, she turned suicidal. She will carry what Manny did to her, and the weight will drag her down, unless she can face what happened and put some distance between the events and herself. The best chance to do that is now, in the group room. Both the therapists and her peers know that.

The girls start to probe, but Elena has hunkered down behind her black sateen wall.

"It's already happened," she declares. "He got his thrill. That was his, there's nothing I can do about it."

"Do you ever want to talk about it?" asks Cristina, herself a rape victim.

"No," Elena replies.

"Not even for help?" Cristina continues. "If we take baby steps and move around the surface gently? I know it can be real dangerous. I know it's real easy to get lost in feelings. Take my hand. Tell me when the water gets too deep. We'll stop."

Elena replies in a high and affected voice, her imitation of an airhead.

"It's like, 'Yes, I got molested. He did this and this and this to me. It's all better now.' "

Dropping down to her normal voice, she says bitterly, "It's not even like that. I can't just say it and get it over with. It's not so damn easy."

"So, what you're saying is, we made it seem easy because we were willing to dish it out," says Keisha, who had great difficulty detailing her own sexual abuse. Subtly, she is accusing Elena of violating the premise of the group: tell everything that happened and when it's my turn, I'll tell everything, too. She and Elena are close friends, but now they are "mad-dogging," their eyes flashing anger at each other.

Cristina is the poet in the group, and she comes up with a new simile. "We're like a flashlight. If you don't turn on the flashlight, you can't see where you're going. You're living in the dark, surrounded by all these thoughts and feelings, and it's not your fault. It will never be your fault."

"It's not so fucking easy to talk about something that hurts you," Elena shouts. "It's not so fucking easy."

"Don't upset yourself like that. That's not fair either," Michelle cautions in her thin voice.

"What's fair?" Elena shouts. "There is no fair."

Life has taught these girls one lesson—"There is no fair"—and so Elena's outburst does not impress. They sit quietly, plotting ways through her defenses.

"What does something like that do to somebody?" Mike Hilgers asks.

"Makes them feel worthless," Elena replies.

Hilgers gets out of his seat and sits on the floor, a move he makes consciously, therapeutically. The message is, I'm the only man in the room and I'm in a position of authority, but I don't want those things to be a factor. So, I'll minimize them, I'll sit below you on the floor.

"What's it like to be you right now?" Hilgers asks, looking up at Elena.

"Shitty. Really shitty. A piece of fucking shit."

"Is that what you're feeling?" Hilgers asks.

"I'm at a place right now where I just want to do something physical," Elena replies. "I feel like I want to kill somebody."

"You want to do what people did to you," Rachael observes.

Elena looks at Rachael and shakes her head in dismay.

"He got a thrill off of you and hurt you and now you want to hurt somebody and get a thrill," Rachael explains.

Elena turns thoughtful and finally nods yes, that's right.

"How's that going to thrill you?" Michelle asks.

"Hurt them so I can see their hurt," Elena says.

She jumps up and takes off her jacket, cracks her back and sits down, but does not put the jacket back on.

"I'm in a bit of a quandary," Hilgers says. "Part of group is to learn to do less avoiding, and part is learning how to cope with life and be more genuine. But part of me really respects our tendency to avoid. It's there for a reason: to protect us. And I wouldn't want to take that away from anybody."

"Why do I have to go through all this stuff?" Elena asks rhetorically. "If I talk about it, my feelings and thoughts will still be there. It might get worse if I talk about it."

"Have you ever tried to talk about it?" Michelle asks.

"No."

"You can't say that until you try," Michelle parries.

"There's no changing my thoughts," Elena says.

"Elena, do you care about me?" Michelle asks.

"I care about you."

"What if I just sat here and avoided talking about stuff that you knew would help me? Wouldn't it hurt you? Wouldn't you try to get me to talk about it?"

Cornered, Elena takes a cheap shot. "Sorry to disappoint you, guys," she says in a voice that is suddenly jailhouse-tough. "Sorry you're not going to hear a story that'll get you off."

Michelle whispers her reply. "Elena, that is not fair."

The sound of Elena slamming her palms on the armrests of her chair echoes off the wall.

"You want a manifestation or something? This is what fucking happened. Christmas Eve, he took me to my aunt's house and fell asleep in bed with me. When I woke up, he had his thing in me. Is that what you all want to hear? About the other motherfucking times, too? *Shit, man!*"

Elena hurls herself backward and her head hits the wall. She crumbles to the floor in a heap and lies there sobbing. Pamp jumps up and glances at Hilgers, who mouths, "Be careful." Pamp kneels next to Elena, but does not touch her. Michelle and Nicole arrive and hover over Elena, and Pamp begins speaking softly. Elena gets enough control to ask for Keisha, who is still angry over their exchange and is pouting in the corner. Keisha comes over and Elena reaches up and the two girls hold each other. Keisha helps Elena off the floor and the girls crowd around. Elena hugs them all, one after another. They are crying and hugging and blowing their noses, and when Pamp makes a joke about what a snotty group this turned out to be, they all crack up.

"We can have compassion for Elena, but we can't just leave her with that," an emotionally drained Jeri Pamp is saying after group in Mike Hilgers's office. "The greatest gift we can give her is helping her move her compass to accountability. Doing that tells her that her life has form and she can impact it. If we don't, she'll spend her life reacting to primitive injury."

On his way to work, as he often does, Hilgers bought tacos—eggs, beef, bacon, cheese, potatoes, and salsa wrapped tight in a tortilla, $2.25—made by religious Mexican ladies in a taqueria located in a bright pink trailer across from the Wal-Mart. He left them under a desk lamp to keep warm, and Pamp is unwrapping the aluminum foil. "We ask so much of them," she says quietly. "We ask them to set aside enormous injury and put down the best defense they have, their anger, and go ahead and have a life. And most do! This population is so treatable. I'm so proud to be part of that."

Pamp was once a successful Los Angeles television producer. Stylish and in her mid-forties, she grew up in an alcohol-ravaged family in San Bernardino County, west of Los Angeles. "I'm still close to my adolescence," she says. "I acted out all over the place. Got kicked out of Catholic school, did drugs." Pamp was married to a musician and through him got a close look at what may well be the sleaziest, most lowlife-riddled industry in America. Kids cannot run a con or try a hustle that Pamp cannot identify.

Ask Pamp if you have to come out of your childhood wounded to work with the population at the State School and she quickly replies, "No. If you come here wounded, you'll be looking for something and the kids will become a lab for your own stuff. They'll sense that—they're brilliant at picking up the clues—and they'll use it to manipulate you. It's important to be shored up before you come to this work."

Ann Kelley comes in and Hilgers reaches under the lamp for a foil-wrapped taco. This is the typical lunch in Giddings—therapists gathering in an office to talk about kids and what happened in group.

"Jeri is going all philosophical," Hilgers informs Kelley with typical wryness. "She's quoting famous writers."

Pamp flashes a smile. "Walking back to the dorm, the girls were talking about having bad thoughts, so I quoted George Bernard Shaw: 'We've all had thoughts that would shame hell.' "

"I'm ashamed I've barely heard of George Bernard Shaw," Hilgers says, and the therapists laugh.

At twenty-nine, Hilgers is the youngest therapist on the staff. Growing up in Plano, a sprawling suburb north of Dallas he calls "the teen-suicide/teen-heroin-use capital of the country," Hilgers died his black hair an albino white, like Johnny and Edgar Winters', and ran with a wild bunch that did property crimes, like breaking into construction sites to steal tools they could fence for money. He evolved into an excellent father who delights in his two young children, Maddie and Tucker. The Hilgerses invite Pamp to birthdays and holiday celebrations and he gives her daily updates on the kids. It is one way the pair keep from getting "crispy," the Giddings term for burnout.

"I try to keep things in balance and remember that most kids aren't like this," Hilgers says. "I've gotten good at turning it off. I use my commute as wind-down time. I don't want to saturate my family with stories from here."

Burnout and "compassion fatigue" are occupational hazards among the treatment staff. Larry Reue, the first therapist Linda Reyes hired, still holds the record for doing the most Capital Offenders groups, nineteen in ten years. Reue so loved his work, he thought he was invincible. The horrors couldn't touch him. And then, suddenly, Reue just couldn't do it anymore. At first, he thought he was suffering from burnout. It turned out to be compassion fatigue.

"People think of burnout and compassion fatigue as the same thing. I found out they are opposites," Reue said in Austin, where he now trains TYC therapists. "Burnout is when you shut down. Compassion fatigue is when you become super-sensitive. Police reports never bothered me. They're dry. I'd read hundreds. All of a sudden, I'd read one and start crying.

"It's the images; they accumulate. You can only absorb so much. I wanted all the horrors to stop. I needed a rest."

Pamp, Hilgers, and Kelley are tough-minded evaluators, which is part of how they survive. Recently, a young man was transferred to prison to serve a thirty-year sentence, because the trio were convinced he was a dangerous psychopath. They combined to fight JCOs and TYC administrators who thought the youth should be paroled. They do not consider themselves miracle workers who can transform lives. They understand the work they do is only the beginning.

"Therapy isn't an antibiotic," Pamp explains. "It's not six months of Capital Offenders and you're cured. It's not about cause and effect, either. It's not, 'Elena was sexually abused, therefore she is a criminal.' It's so much more complicated than that. It's a gestalt. The best we can hope for is, what happened today will start her processing."

"What's the likelihood she can be her own therapist?" Kelley asks. Turning each girl into her own therapist is the goal of Capital Offenders. Better yet, turning her into her own parent.

"She probably won't be worse off when she leaves here," Hilgers says. Pamp rolls her eyes; Hilgers can be so dry.

"This gives her a fighting chance," Pamp says.

Ann Kelley has an interesting way of interpreting "gestalt," the collection of physical, biological, and psychological phenomena that come together to produce antisocial behavior. She thinks it begins in teenagers as a quest for authenticity.

"Youth who grow up abused and neglected learn to hide themselves in coping," Kelley explains. "They have no conception of joy. They are at a loss for authenticity. How do you strive for authenticity if there is no feeling for bliss?

"Violence has to do with fraud," Kelley continues. "It's about trying to feel alive in an environment where you feel dead. It's feeling the most connected to life when you are taking extreme risks. It's the rush of holding a gun and having someone afraid of you: the rush, the immediacy. 'I'm so alive! I have the power to take the life of others!'

"Accountability and responsibility are not just a cleansing. They are about rounding out a sense of self," Kelley concludes. "The more you disclose, the more responsibility you accept, the more you learn about yourself. That leads to redemption."

———

Since Elena went through such an overwhelming emotional experience during the last group, it seems reasonable to think she might need days, even weeks, to gather strength and go on. In fact, the reverse is true. Kids are remarkably resilient, and by the next session Elena is bright-eyed and ready to go. Bringing pain-soaked memories into the light dries them out, makes them lighter.

Elena begins the group by describing the terrible cycle that is common to young girls who are being sexually abused. Her stepfather molests her, she runs away. Her mother finds out where she is, brings her home, and beats her up. She tries to tell her mother what is happening but fails. "I'd start, she'd be, 'There you go again.' And I'd be, 'Forget it, Mom.' When I finally did tell her, she said, 'It can't be him. It must be someone else.' " Again, Manny molests her; again, she runs away. The cycle keeps repeating until Lucy gives up and quits chasing her daughter.

"It was awful; I was having nightmares about Elena and I'd wake up screaming," Lucy recalled. "I felt her presence, I knew she was in danger, but I didn't know why. It was about that time I moved to Corpus Christi and wanted her to go with me. She wouldn't go and she was cussing me and telling me I couldn't do anything about it. It was awful."

By now, Elena's older brothers and sisters are in jail or in prison, and she ends up living in an apartment with three of her oldest brother's "associates." Sammy, Gabe, and Jimmy—twenty-five, twenty-eight, and twenty-nine—are hard-core criminals, ex-cons, active members of a gang connected to Nuestra Familia. Elena is fourteen.

The trio spend their days getting high on whatever is available and planning crimes that are half real, half fantasy. Gabe claims to have a wealthy uncle who owns a big ranch up in Colorado. The trio keep talking about doing a job and taking off to Colorado, where no one will find them.

They glide around Houston in an early-eighties Oldsmobile, casing places before deciding on an antiques store near the Greyhound bus station downtown. The store is owned by a young gay couple and has one employee, a grandmotherly black woman. Easy pickings.

"They said, 'Are you going with us? Are you down for la Familia?' " Elena recalls. "I said I was."

Elena was always ready to do a drive-by or jack a car. But she does not want to do this robbery. For one thing, the guys are so much older and really scary. And she kind of has a relationship with Florence, the black lady who works in the store. Elena hangs out in the bus station and often finds herself on the same downtown bus as Florence. They always say hello and exchange a few words. Florence reminds Elena of her grandmother.

One night, Elena waits for the ex-cons to get high and then tells them she knows Florence. She is hoping the gangsters will let her out, or perhaps decide to find another store to rob. But they just smile at her naïveté and keep sucking on joints and downing Budweisers. Hey, little girl, that don't mean nothing. She don't know your name. So what if she recognizes you? You'll be in Colorado.

But she reminds me of my grandmother, Elena says. The ex-cons choke on marijuana smoke and slap the couch. Hey, little homey. No one is going to hurt no grandmother. This is just a robbery.

Early the next afternoon, Elena and the three criminals amble into the antiques store. There are no customers. Florence is in a rocker, half asleep after lunch. Elena plops down on a big Victorian couch across from the rocker. Florence snaps awake, surprised to see her. "What are you doing here?" she asks.

Then her eyes widen in surprise and terror. Elena turns to see Jimmy holding a co-owner by the hair, bashing him in the face. Florence screams.

"Hit her! Hit her! Hit her!" Sammy yells.

Elena has a split second to decide: Will she protect the elderly lady, or will she do as she is told?

She jumps off the couch and socks Florence in the jaw. Sammy runs over, grabs Florence by the ankles, and jerks her out of the chair. Her head clips the edge of the chair and slams into the floor. Florence screams again.

"Shut the fuck up, bitch!" Sammy yells and kicks the elderly woman in the ribs. Then he stomps on her face.

"Get her jewelry! Take everything off her," Sammy yells at Elena. Elena drops to her knees and removes rings and bracelets. Sammy is kicking and stomping away. The co-owner's face is now a pulpy mess and blood is streaming into his eyes, but he sees what Sammy is doing and yells, "Please don't hurt Florence! She's fragile!"

Jimmy slams him to the floor, grabs some vintage 1940s ties from a rack, and uses them to bind the co-owner's hands and feet. He throws a necktie toward Elena. "Tie her up!" Jimmy yells.

Elena is winding the necktie around Florence's hands when suddenly, she freezes.

"She's not moving!" Elena yells.

"Fuck the bitch!" Gabe replies. He is emptying the cash register and watching the window. A car pulls to the curb. He alerts the other robbers, who watch as a young man gets out and walks to the entrance.

"Play it cool!" Gabe hisses.

The robbers drag the co-owner across the floor next to Florence and stuff a necktie in his mouth. They sit down in overstuffed chairs and do their best to appear calm, even bored.

A stylish young man comes through the door and removes his sunglasses. "Hey, everybody, is Bernie around?" he asks.

"One of the guys who owns the place?" Gabe replies. "He just went in back."

The young man nods and is passing the robbers when Gabe leaps up and thrusts a knife to his throat. The young man screams in terror. Sammy throws him to the floor and begins kicking and stomping, his specialty. The young man keeps screaming.

"Shut the fuck up, pussy!" Gabe commands.

Sammy kicks the young man until he is unconscious. He takes his briefcase and scurries around the store, filling it with jewelry. The other robbers grab whatever they can carry. The three ex-cons reach the door before they realize Elena is not with them. They turn to see her crouching over Florence, who has not moved. Gabe races back, grabs Elena by the collar of her World Wrestling Federation jersey, and yanks her toward the door.

Outside, she and Gabe flee in one direction, Jimmy and Sammy run off in the other. Within minutes, they hear sirens and slow to a walk. Elena takes off her wrestling jersey, throws it in a vacant lot, and removes the pins from her hair. She and Gabe keep walking as police cars race by.

"We made it safe to my aunt's house and went back out that night and looked for Jimmy and Sammy for hours," Elena tells the group. "We played it off that we were looking for dogs. Whenever we saw somebody coming, we'd whistle. Finally, we gave up and came back and called the city jail. We gave them Sammy's and Jimmy's names and asked if they were there. A deputy said, 'Yes, we have them.'

"They wrote statements implicating Gabe and me. When it came out on 'Crime Stoppers,' I was a twenty-two-year-old white female, stocky, with blue eyes and short hair. For two weeks, I didn't hide or nothing. I dyed my hair and braided it up. I'd go to the bus station and cops were everywhere and I'd just sit there.

"My mom, she had moved down to Corpus Christi and she came back for court. For me. I had an assault charge. I was hanging out in the bus station and saw her when she got in. She came up to me and said, 'Can I talk to you?' I said, 'I have nothing to talk to you about.' She said, 'We really need to talk.' I said, 'I'm busy.' She said, 'Since when are you busy? Listen, we can do this the hard way or the easy way. If we don't talk, I'll make a scene in front of that cop right over there.'

"I looked and there was a cop. So, we talked. She said, 'I heard what happened. Your brother Arturo told me. I hear it's on 'Crime Stoppers.' What are you doing, trying to be all big and bad?'

"The next day in court, I was sitting there drinking a Coke when my mom came up with my probation officer. He said, 'I hope you enjoy that. It's the last drink you are going to have in The Free for a long time.' "

Lucy remembers that day, too.

"It turned out, her probation officer was looking for her. She was a suspect," Lucy recalls. "He put the cuffs on her right there in court and I said to Elena, 'I always told you, if you can't do the time, don't do the crime.' "

When the girls realize the narration is over, the first thing they want to know is, What happened to Florence?

"She had a heart attack," Elena replies. "She was in the ICU for a couple of days. They were going to charge it as capital murder if she didn't recover."

"What did Florence look like, lying there on the floor?" Rachael wonders.

"When I hit her, she was, 'Oh my God! Please don't!' Then she looked asleep, like she was thinking, I'm going to die."

"Elena, hitting an old lady is about as chickenshit as it gets!" Jeri Pamp erupts, genuinely angry. She finds crimes against children and the elderly especially reprehensible.

Elena is banging her gray stocking cap on the arm of her chair.

"I had a choice!" she wails. "I could hit her and live. Or not hit her and die. I was in a scary situation! They were big guys and they were all riled up and I was scared!"

"Been there, done that." Cristina, who grew up in gangs, sighs. "Elena, you're justifying."

Justifying is a thinking error—rationalizing, deflecting responsibility.

"I had to do things in order to live!" Elena replies, her voice rising. "If I was big enough to be in a gang, I was big enough to take care of business. The people I did my crime with are in the second- or third-largest gang in the U.S. They could have put a contract out on me."

The girls aren't buying it.

"Why did you go in with those three men? Why did you agree to rob that store?" Rachael asks.

"I wanted acceptance!" Elena wails.

"Was the stronger reason the fear of dying?" Cristina asks. "Or was it getting power?"

"It was fear!" Elena insists, jumping up to tuck in her sweatshirt. "I see how fear can tie into selfishness, but I was really, really scared!"

"All the empathy you had for Florence didn't stop you from hitting her and tying her up," Hilgers observes.

"I couldn't! I didn't have control of Sammy, Jimmy, and Gabe!"

"That is such shit!" Pamp says. "You are not the victim of that crime, Elena! There were three victims and four perps, not the other way around!"

"What could I have done? I'd have been killed!"

"All those gang people, they're not going to be worried about you," Nicole points out.

"Those big gangs, they're strictly business," Cristina agrees. "They're not going to be worrying about some little Trece running the streets."

Trece, or the 13s or the Loco 13s, are a subset of la Familia. "You're sitting here thinking you didn't have control," Cristina adds. "But you gave them control! You gave them control!"

"You are not taking responsibility for your crime," Nicole asserts.

"That's not true!" Elena shoots back. "They had no evidence. They thought I was a twenty-two-year-old white woman! I could have gone free! I confessed!"

"You're acting like you confessed out of the kindness of your heart," Keisha observes. "If you'd done something earlier, before it happened, then, okay, I'd believe you."

"You could have gotten help," Rachael adds. "You could have called the police when they first brought it up."

Elena sinks into her chair. "I guess so," she says, her voice weary. "I guess I could have stayed home and been called a snitch. I guess I could have stayed home and died."

"You could have called anonymously," Keisha points out. "Come on, end the drama. Tell us really, why'd you do it?"

"I was thinking if I proved myself to them, then I could get things done. In my mind, I was thinking, I'm going to move up. If I can do this, I'll be able to get things done to people."

It is here, finally, that boys and girls do not differ. Boys and girls commit crimes for the same reasons: to gain power, control, and acceptance.

"You've got to understand, the way you all think about it and the way I do is two different things," Elena finally says.

In one voice, Pamp and Hilgers reply, "That's the whole point!"

Elena turns surly and stops answering questions.

"You're getting frustrated and shutting down, like we're the problem," Pamp observes. "We don't understand, we're all full of shit, you're just going to tune us out."

"You keep going back to yourself. It's always what could happen to you, not what happened to your victims," Michelle observes. "That's being selfish."

"I could have said, 'Kill the fucking bitch!' " Elena shouts. "I didn't."

"The bitch this, the bitch that," Cristina observes. "Tie the bitch up. Kill the bitch."

" 'I shouldn't be doing this.' *Pop!* You hit her in the mouth," Keisha says, miming the events. " 'I shouldn't be doing this.' You tie her hands a little tighter. If you'd said, 'Stop!' don't you think Florence might have a different attitude on you?"

"If Florence was in this room, you think she'd feel sorry for you?" Nicole asks.

"You made eye contact with Florence," Michelle says quietly. "You need to think about how she looked. You're running from it."

"In The Free, it is going to be different!" Elena yells. "I'm going to get counseling to work on my anger!"

"What do you think we're doing here?" the girls chorus.

When their laughter stops echoing off the walls, a somewhat concessionary Elena says, "I see I could have done something, even though I was in a bad position, too."

"That's your defense right there: 'I didn't have a choice,' " Keisha says. "You did have a choice, Elena."

11.

"STUPID WHEN YOU LOOK BACK ON IT"

It snows late in the afternoon on the day Elena tells her crime story, a rare event that has everyone talking about the big wet flakes that disappear as soon as they hit the ground.

By seven o'clock, it is wet and bitingly cold, and no one in the social services building wants to walk through the dark to the gate. Ann Kelley is one of a few administrators who rank high enough to drive a car onto the campus, so a group of therapists and secretaries scramble into her Jeep Cherokee for the quick ride to the parking lot.

At the gate, the first sally port slides open and Kelley pulls up to a security officer. But instead of looking in the car and running a mirror underneath it, he thrusts a radio in Kelley's hands.

"Two kids just ran from Cottage Ten!" the officer says. "Go back and drive around, see if you can spot them!"

Kelley backs up and pulls onto a narrow road that runs along the fence. She is turning into a parking lot when her lights catch a heavyset young man in a black sateen jacket, creeping along the side of the vocational building. He freezes like a deer in her headlights; his head darts one way and then another, then he whirls and runs back in the direction he came from. He reaches the edge of the building seconds before two security officers and a program administrator come around the corner. The youth practically runs into their arms.

Kelley drives on to Cottage 10, arriving just as Greg Rangel, the campus gang specialist, is apprehending the second youth. The boy tries to fight Rangel off and two security officers race up to help. One of them pulls a canister of pepper spray from his belt, aims it, and pushes the nozzle. His partner catches more spray than the youth and staggers away, gasping for breath. The officer covers his eyes with a forearm and drops to his knees in agony.

One of two doors to Cottage 10 is open and boys are crowding into the doorway, peering over the head of a juvenile correction officer. Word spreads that pepper spray has been used, and threats and curses echo off the walls. Meanwhile, Rangel is using TYC restraint techniques to take the youth to the ground. He rolls the boy onto his stomach and is about to put him in handcuffs when a JCO opens the second door to Cottage 10 and steps onto the landing. Boys pile up in the doorway behind him and peer into the darkness, trying to see what is happening.

"You get back in there and close that door!" orders Charlene Davenport, a secretary in social services who caught a ride with Ann Kelley. She marches to the door, waving a large green thermos she carries to and from work. "Who trained you?" Charlene demands of the JCO. "Don't you know better than to be opening a door at a time like this?"

Charlene has been at the State School for almost thirty years. She weighs maybe one hundred pounds and is something of a stand-up comic. (Telemarketers who call her home get a breathless woman whispering, "I told you never to call me here! Hang up and I'll meet you behind the diner in five minutes!") Youth who reach phase four are eligible for jobs on campus, and caseworkers like to send withdrawn kids up to social services to work with Charlene. There is no way a kid can stay in a shell around her.

"You boys, you know you're not supposed to be in that doorway!" Charlene shouts. "Get back in that cottage! Go on now!"

The boys scurry inside, followed by the chastened JCO, who quickly closes the door. Rangel has the boy on his feet and is moving him to a van when suddenly a youth charges past the JCO at the other door and races toward Rangel. Two security officers intercept him and wrestle him to the ground. "They were kicking your ass, homey!" he shouts, raising his head off the grass. "They can't do that!"

"I love you, *mejo!*" cries the boy Rangel is propelling toward a security van.

"Almighty Latin Kings forever!" shouts the boy on the ground.

Half an hour later, Cottage 10 is quiet and the campus is still. And that is what troubles Butch Held, the Giddings superintendent.

Two boys running out of a cottage is not classified as an escape attempt. Technically, it is "disruption of program," an offense that is punished by a night in security. Disruption of program does not become an escape attempt until a boy or girl touches the fence, a fact that every student at Giddings knows. There have been three such incidents in the last month. Taking off and leading staff on a wild chase is something you can do for the thrill of it, if the punishment is light.

"We have to be more creative in responding to kids who act like this," Held says in the brick ranch house TYC reserves for the Giddings superintendent, just outside the fence. "We have to make sure there's appropriate consequences for inappropriate actions. We've got to make kids take responsibility for their actions. We can't just put them in security for a night and then it's all over."

Within a month of the "escape that was not an escape," the TYC responded. Ann Kelley and Rebecca Thomas, an official in Austin, drafted changes in policy that raised running free on campus to a category-one offense, with consequences like serving thirty days in the security unit and an automatic loss of phase. Word quickly spread and within a few days, kids were no longer blasting out of dorms or classrooms.

"This is good, this will help us hold kids accountable," Held said when the changes came down.

"Holding kids accountable" is as close as Held comes to having a mantra. A college baseball player from Oklahoma City who joined the Peace Corps after he graduated, Held ended up in Colombia organizing recreation programs in prisons. He left Colombia with a lifelong hatred for prison guards or police officers or any authority figure who abuses power.

In a facility that detains delinquents, there is always tension between staff members who believe that security is paramount and youth should be treated as prisoners, and staff who believe that incarceration is an opportunity to deliver treatment. The two sides can become quite hostile, with treatment-oriented staff referring to security-oriented staff as "the Gestapo" and the other side responding with taunts of "bleeding hearts" and "marshmallows."

To Held, security and treatment are two sides of the same coin. "Custody and control have to come first," he says. "If kids don't feel safe, it becomes survival of the fittest and kids join gangs. That's how gangs recruit—join us, we'll protect you.

"But you don't want kids to just behave—all that teaches them is how to be good inmates. You want kids to understand why they got into this situation. That means treatment, and you can't treat kids if they don't feel safe. A kid has to feel safe before he will risk himself in treatment."

Ross Robinson, the assistant superintendent who has overall responsibility for campus security, says his job "calls for a level of paranoia that falls just short of commitment." At the weekly meeting of program administrators that Robinson chairs, he sifts through information Greg Rangel and other staff members have uncovered. One week, it is a drawing from an art class where all the numbers on a clock are fives (for the Five Deuce Hoover Crips). The next week, it is boys leaving their left shoelaces untied (in addition to colors, gangs identify with directions; in this case, it is the Latin Kings, who "bang to the left").

"Giddings has the lowest number of incident reports per one hundred students of any institution in the state, and the way to keep it that way is by staying on top of the little things, like making sure there's no litter on campus," Robinson tells his staff, week after week. "Major problems are often the result of neglecting the small details."

Beyond anything else, an institution fears concerted action, a planned event involving a large number of participants. The last one that occurred in Giddings took place on April 28, 2000, when groups of boys were marching across campus, as they do every day. Suddenly, Crips and Latin Kings broke out of formation and attacked each other.

Kids always know an institution better than the staff. They are there twenty-four hours a day—staff members work an eight-hour shift. So when the numerical code for "fight in progress" came over the radios carried by juvenile correction officers, gang members knew the fight that had been brewing for months was finally on. When JCOs opened cottage doors to see what was happening, boys charged out of dorms to join the battle. Twenty-two boys fought for twenty-seven minutes before the staff regained control.

Chester Clay, the superintendent at the time, first noticed something was wrong when small, scrawny boys kept arriving in the infirmary, claiming they were sick and wanting to spend the night. "The kids who didn't look like Greek gods weren't safe," Clay remembers. "Kids who look whipped, kids who aren't sleeping and can't digest their food, if they're safe, everyone is safe. I sat down and talked to them. 'What's up, man? Why aren't you working the program?' "

Clay learned that gangs were becoming predatory, beating up kids to force them to join. Before he could act, the fight broke out.

The incident that triggered the mêlée was a fight between a Latin King and a Hoover Crip that took place in the infirmary. The two gangs began plotting retaliation and it all may have remained just talk—or "bumping," in gang argot—if a girl who was "going" with a Crip hadn't claimed that a Latin King had dissed her. She kept pressuring her boyfriend to do something—what good is having a gangster boyfriend if his set doesn't step up when you get dissed? Veteran gang leaders on both sides tried to calm things down, but they were close to their release dates and their power was waning. The boyfriend pressured second-echelon leaders wanting to make a name for themselves, and they set up the brawl.

A gang specialist like Greg Rangel would much rather work with a veteran gang leader than an up-and-comer. The cardinal rule is, Never negotiate—that gives the gang leader power, makes him a player in determining events. Tell the gangster that if A and B occur, the consequences will be C and D. And if A and B do occur, make sure C and D happen soon thereafter. The young Turks were too intent on establishing their reputations to listen to Rangel or anyone else, and the Crips and Latin Kings had their battle.

Tami Coy spent weeks investigating the incident, preparing charts to illustrate how the fight was gang-instigated. She took the evidence to the local district attorney, who convened a grand jury. Coy testified for hours. Twenty-two combatants were indicted on charges of assault, conspiracy, and organized criminal activity. Twenty were convicted and sent to prison.

"The convictions sent a message not to do anything on a massive scale," says Clay, who left Giddings to become one of the TYC's top three officials. "Gangs are still very much there. Only now, they do isolated hits. A kid goes into the shower and comes out with a black eye. When a corrections officer asks what happened, he says he slipped. I've come to see TYC as a place where gangs and corrections staff have infiltrated each other's territory."

The most difficult task in youth corrections is trying to wean a youth from a gang. Tami Coy learned it can only be done subtly, by asking a youth the right question at the right moment.

"If you beat a kid over the head, it doesn't work," Coy says. "You try to be direct and keep it simple."

Coy will ask a gang-related youth, How many times did your homeboys visit when you were in juvenile hall, waiting for your trial? How many have written since you've been in the State School? How many have visited your mother?

The answer is always the same: Nobody visits, nobody writes.

When she senses a gang member is questioning his or her affiliation, Coy will ask, "If your gang tells you to do something and you don't, they'll beat you up. Would a true friend do that? How could someone who says they love you hurt you if you don't do something they want?"

Finally, there is the big question: Can you leave your gang? Coy springs it when a boy or girl expresses remorse for past actions.

"When a kid says he doesn't want to hurt anyone anymore, you say, 'If you really mean that, you have to get out of your gang. You can't just be inactive. You have to get out. If you don't, you will end up hurting someone."

Greg Rangel has a surprisingly balanced view of gangs: "Gangs are all the good things, going in all the wrong directions." Before a youth will leave a gang, she has to believe that she can achieve "the good things"—acceptance, respect, and love—outside her set.

"I don't view gangs completely negative. In their own way, gangs are very loving," Rangel says. "I see that in the letters we intercept. It's 'little brother' and 'little sister' and 'I'll watch out for you.' If someone attacked my loved ones, I would be obligated to show love by defending them. It's like a secret society.

"The big problem is, the way they deal with anger is violence, and un-necessary violence is always bad," Rangel concludes.

"Elena, what do you need to understand your crime?" Jeri Pamp asks as the next session begins.

"A role play," Elena replies.

Elena has been thinking about this and quickly turns into a casting director. Rachael is black and quiet; she will play Florence, the elderly victim. The thin, wan Hilgers will play Florence's coworker.

"I can picture Michelle, if she was in her old ways, being Gabe," Elena says. "He was angry, he was always, 'Shut the fuck up, bitch! I'm going to kill you, bitch!'

"Nicole, she did her crime for fun, she can be Sammy. He thrived off it. He got a rush out of hitting Florence. He liked stomping Richard, the guy who walked in the door. He liked telling him, 'Shut up, pussy!'

"Keisha can be Jimmy. He's cool, until someone does something he doesn't like. Jimmy timed the whole thing. It only took five minutes."

"Amazing, isn't it, how it only takes five minutes to change lives," Pamp observes.

The girls and therapists go into the small hallway to construct the play. Elena takes a chair to a corner and sits down to wait. The minutes pass slowly. Finally, Pamp walks in with Rachael. Rachael quietly arranges chairs and, assuming the role of Florence, sits down and pretends to be rocking. The door opens and the three thugs walk in.

"Where's the men's pants?" asks Michelle, playing Gabe.

"Right over there," says Hilgers, playing Bernie, Florence's coworker.

"What about the dressing rooms?"

"Right by the pants."

Cristina, playing Elena, sits down across from Rachael.

"What are you doing here?" Rachael asks. "I never see you except on the bus."

"Just checking stuff out," Cristina says.

"What are you thinking?" Pamp whispers to Elena.

"I'm going to hit this lady," Elena replies, intent on the drama.

"Were you into it?"

"I was shaking."

Nicole, playing Sammy, suddenly grabs Hilgers and holds an eraser—a knife—to his throat. The crime unfolds.

"You hit her, you punched her with your fist right on the jaw. What do you think that did to her?" Pamp asks.

"She screamed, *'Oooowwww!'*" Elena recalls, seeing the event in front of her.

"Do you think she remembers? Do you think she is carrying it with her?" Pamp asks.

"I think she'll have to be cautious forever after this. The fear is gonna be in her head. It's gonna be there for the rest of her life," a solemn Elena answers.

"Get her jewelry!" Nicole yells. "Strip her! Fucking strip her stuff!"

As Cristina removes rings and bracelets, Pamp says, "You say you had feelings for her, but look what you're doing. Does that look like empathy? You hit her and watched while she got kicked! Now you're taking her things! You didn't do a thing to help her!"

"Tie her up! Tie the fucking bitch up!" orders Nicole.

Elena covers her ears, then covers her eyes. Pamp pulls her hands away and makes her watch. Elena begins to shake and sob.

"I see her face over and over again," she blurts out. "I hurt somebody. It hurts. It's going to be there the rest of my life."

The reenactment ends with Elena wailing on the floor. It took a lot of energy to keep the front up, to act hard while all along she was hurting because she hurt someone. Two girls lift Elena off the floor and help her into a chair. The group waits for her to compose herself. Then, the role reversal begins.

Cristina will play Elena; Elena will play Florence, her victim. Elena does not want to do it. Two girls lift her out of her seat and place her in the chair that represents the rocker.

"So, you're a grandmother. How many grandchildren do you have?" Pamp asks.

"Two. Two grandchildren," Elena replies, hesitantly assuming the role of Florence.

The robbers enter the store. Cristina, still playing Elena, sits down across from the real Elena.

"Hey. I know you from the bus. How you doing?" Cristina asks Elena.

"What are you doing here?" Elena asks.

"Just checking out stuff. We might be going in together on an apartment."

The robbery begins. Cristina attacks Elena and Nicole yanks her to the floor.

"They're calling you a dumb bitch," Pamp says. "They don't give a rat's ass about you!"

Elena is crying so hard, she barely notices when Cristina grabs her hand and pretends to yank off rings.

"This is what it was like!" Pamp says. "This is what it felt like!"

When it is over, Elena is back on the floor, convulsing in sobs. Pamp motions the girls out of the room. Hilgers turns down the rheostat, leaving Elena alone in shadowy light, crying on the floor. Five long minutes go by before the door opens and Pamp comes in. She sits next to Elena and gathers her in her arms. Elena is limp as a Raggedy Anne doll.

"What's going on, Elena?" Pamp asks. Elena shudders and curls deeper into Pamp's arms.

"It really hurts, doesn't it," Pamp says.

She hands Elena a tissue and Elena blows her nose.

"It's how sorry I am," Elena says, trying to explain her tears.

"You made some stupid choices, girl," Pamp says.

Elena wraps her arms around her legs and buries her head in her knees and mutters something.

"The group is going to come in. They want to sit next to you. Is that okay?" Pamp asks.

Elena nods and the girls file in and line up to hug her. Then they sit in a circle on the floor.

"Are you okay with me telling what you just told me?" Pamp asks. When Elena nods, Pamp says, "Elena thinks she is a really bad person."

Keisha moves over and hugs Elena and they both start crying. Suddenly, all the girls are crying. Pamp and Hilgers leave the room to watch from behind the one-way mirror. Gradually, the girls collect themselves.

Rachael, whose dream is to become a hairdresser, scoots over and begins braiding Elena's hair.

"Why do you feel like you are bad?" Keisha asks.

"Because I am," Elena replies.

"Why in particular?" Keisha asks.

"Seeing her eyes cry out for help, and me hitting her just the same. I see that every time I think about my crime. That's why I try not to think about it."

"What are the benefits of this situation right here?" Keisha asks.

"I been kind of like a little kid with my crime, hiding my eyes," Elena says, her speech regaining some of its usual bounce. "Like when I went up to security the last time. Remember? I was upset about my little sister being pregnant and my mom being in an abusive relationship and not being able to leave because every time she tries, he finds her and beats her. When I went up to security, I pulled the blanket up over my eyes. I did."

"What do you see, now that you don't have a blanket and can't hide your eyes?" Keisha asks.

"How sorry I am," Elena replies, and starts to cry again.

"Well then, if you really, really, really are sorry, if it hurts so much you won't never hurt nobody ever again, how can you be a bad person?"

Elena is pondering Keisha's question when the therapists slip back into the room and the feedback round begins. Rachael goes first, stately and solemn, as if she is in church.

"Elena is judging herself just like I do myself. I stabbed a boy six times. One of those stabs just missed his heart. I almost took his life. He was beating me up every time he saw me, but he could beat me till my flesh came off and I wouldn't do it again. Nothing justifies what I did."

"It's very complicated to ask someone to forgive herself for doing something horrible," Pamp tells Rachael. "But part of not doing it again is not hating yourself."

When it is Cristina's turn, Hilgers asks what it felt like to play Elena.

"I had the same feelings I did when I did my crime-story role play," Cristina replies. "When I saw myself doing what I did, stabbing somebody just to prove I wasn't powerless, it was crazy. The type of thinking I had, it was just crazy. I felt so stupid and tired afterward."

"It is overwhelming, isn't it, when you stop and consider," Pamp says.

"It's stupid when you look back on it," Cristina replies. "You don't feel stupid when you're doing it. You're serious and intense. It's a real sick power trip."

"That's how I felt when I did my role play: sooooo stupid!" Keisha says.

"What do you mean when you say 'stupid'?" Hilgers asks.

"I robbed and beat somebody for acceptance. I was trying to prove myself to my co-actors, just like Elena," Keisha explains. "I did someone the same way I've been done. There's no good-enough excuse for things that happened to me and that's how I feel about my victim: there can't be no excuse good enough for what I did to him. I wouldn't accept an apology from my grandmother for beating me and he probably has the same mentality I do."

"So how are you not going to do it again?" Nicole wonders.

"Seeing myself in my role play and realizing the point I was trying to prove, I felt stupider than ever," Keisha replies. "What I did was pointless and proved nothing.

"I'm glad I came here," Keisha concludes with a sigh. "If I hadn't, I'd probably be dead or have six kids or be packing somebody's STDs," sexually transmitted diseases.

"If I wasn't here, I wouldn't be thinking of my crime," Nicole agrees. "You get that criminal life going and you're on the run and everything keeps you from thinking. I see role plays and I think, 'Dang! They look dumb!' Then I think, I looked dumb, aiming a pistol at a clerk's head and robbing that store. I wish people who don't care could see a role play and see how dumb they look when they're cronked."

"Cronked," as in "cranked up," is a reference to a crime-triggered adrenaline rush.

Role plays give the girls a chance to take one small but momentous step outside themselves and see themselves in action. They glimpse the forces that have shaped their lives, and that gives them a chance to shape those forces, rather than be shaped by them. If they look foolish to themselves, they'll take steps to stop acting foolishly. They are, after all, teenage girls.

"All the feelings which made us commit our offenses haven't changed," Michelle says as the group winds down. "All of us feel powerless. Just because we feel powerless doesn't mean we get to hurt nobody."

The group goes an hour long and the girls miss their lunch, so Pamp calls the cafeteria from the phone in the hallway and has lunch delivered to the cottage. The girls form a column and walk up the sidewalk with Pamp and Hilgers on either side. Both the girls and their therapists are too spent to bother with marching and calling cadence.

The girls take off their jackets and wash up for lunch, which arrives in Styrofoam trays. They are sitting at round tables, quietly eating and drinking milk from pint cartons, when there is a knock on the door and the JCO turns the key and lets Candace in. Candace grew up in the State School; she was fourteen when she arrived and is now twenty. As a phase four, Candace is eligible to work on campus, and has just completed her four-hour shift in the high school office. Candace is tall and slender, her long brown hair is in a ponytail, and her eyes—"my jewels," she calls them —are cobalt blue. Candace spots Elena and walks over and massages her shoulders.

"Elena, you do all right? You get through okay? You didn't hold nothing back?"

Elena nods and reaches up to pat Candace's hand.

"Good, that's good," Candace says. She squeezes Elena's shoulders and walks over to sit on a couch with big lavender cushions, where her startling eyes survey the Capital Offenders girls, eventually landing on Nicole. Nicole is white; Michelle is white/Creek Indian; Rachael and Keisha are black; Elena and Cristina are Latinas. Candace notices things like that.

"I took Capital Offenders twice," Candace says. "The first time, I was one of two white girls in the group. In the second, I was the only one."

Candace has spent six years watching racial issues ebb and flow inside the fence, and has come to see race as a big and not particularly interesting game. Candace says parents who use race to explain their lives are playing the blame game. She says teenagers who join gangs are playing the race game.

"When you first get locked up, everybody tries to dominate everybody, and it's the white group gets stomped on because in here, the white group is the minority and out there, the white group dominates," Candace explains. "Parents tell their kids the white group is to blame because it is dominant: 'I didn't go to school because back then there were no opportunities for people like us.' 'I didn't get that job because they gave it to a white.' That's parents playing the blame game. It's a way of not taking responsibility.

"Joining a gang in here is like joining a fraternity or a sorority in The Free," Candace continues. "You get to be in on secrets, you get to conspire against others, and then somebody tells you to do a hit, to punch somebody in front of everybody in the cafeteria, and you end up in security. You get 'props' from your gang when you get back to the dorm, and the other side retaliates, and it just goes on and on. That's the race game. The race game is a way of avoiding. That's all the race game is.

"There's more than enough bad shit to go around," Candace concludes. "Playing the race game just makes it worse."

Dr. Leonard E. Lawrence, chairman of the TYC board of directors, comes pretty close to agreeing with Candace. A prominent child psychiatrist with a commanding presence, Dr. Lawrence is a professor of psychiatry, pediatrics, and family practice at the University of Texas Health Science Center at San Antonio, and is a past chair of the Student Minority Affairs Section of the Association of American Medical Colleges. An African-American from Indianapolis who had his own troubles growing up, Dr. Lawrence is convinced that racism and poverty play a role in creating teenage offenders. He is just as convinced that is all they play: a role.

"Poverty or racism does not give anyone the right to perpetuate criminal behavior," Dr. Lawrence says. "Yes, there is discrimination in the recurring circumstances, in the hard but true fact that if you are poor and a minority, your opportunities for habilitation are diminished. We have to take those conditions into consideration, but we cannot use them to excuse criminal behavior. Too often, excuses are used as an explanation."

But how do you explain the fact that in Texas, there is an over-representation of minority youth locked away in the TYC?

According to the U.S. Census 2000, 52.4 percent of all Texans identified themselves as white, not of Hispanic origin (Latinos are difficult to
enumerate because the census treats Hispanic as an ethnicity, not a race);
32 percent stated they were of Hispanic or Latino origin; 11.5 percent
were black or African-American; and 2.7 percent were Asian.

In the census year, the TYC had 5,650 youths incarcerated in fifteen
secure facilities. Its racial composition did not reflect the racial makeup
of Texas. Only 25 percent of the TYC population were white; 34 percent were African-American; 40 percent were Hispanic; 1 percent were
Asian and American Indian. Clearly, the white population was under-
represented in the TYC; Latinos and African-Americans were just as clearly
overrepresented.

Texas is in no way unique; minorities are overrepresented in the juvenile justice system in every state in the union. The overrepresentation begins with arrests and increases all the way through the system, to the
exceedingly high percentage of minority youth sentenced to terms in state
prisons.

"In 1997, minorities made up about one-third of the juvenile population nationwide but accounted for nearly two-thirds of the detained and
committed population in secure juvenile facilities," Shay Bilchik, administrator of the OJJDP (Office of Juvenile Justice and Delinquency Prevention), writes in "Minorities in the Juvenile Justice System," in December
1999. "For black juveniles, the disparities were most evident. While black
juveniles ages 10 to 17 made up about 15% of the juvenile population,
they accounted for 26% of juveniles arrested and 45% of delinquency
cases involving detention. About one-third of adjudicated cases involved
black youth, yet 40% of juveniles in secure residential placements were
black. These numbers cannot be ignored."

The OJJDP found that in 1997, more than six in ten juveniles in
places where the doors are locked and guards patrol the halls were minority
youth. "Secure detention was nearly twice as likely in 1996 for cases involving black youth as for cases involving whites, even after controlling
for offense." More than three-quarters of youth admitted to prison in
1996 were minorities. Nationally, six out of every ten youths judges sent
to prison were black.

The OJJDP is careful to point out that these figures may be the result of factors other than racial discrimination. A detailed analysis to determine whether minority youth are, in fact, committing more serious crimes than white youth or discrimination is at work at all levels, "is not possible with the data that are available." But the OJJDP goes on to say that "there is substantial evidence that minority youth are often treated differently from majority youth within the juvenile justice system."

Those who study the juvenile justice system have a term to describe why "minority youth are often treated differently": race effects.

Race effects help explain why cases involving minority youth—in particular African-American youth—are disproportionately excluded from juvenile court and sent into adult courts. These kids often end up in state penal institutions, where chances for rehabilitation are slim to none. Building Blocks for Youth, a research group formed by an alliance of children's advocates, researchers, and law enforcement organizations, studied the impact of transfer and exclusion statutes on youth in eighteen adult courts across the country. Among the findings:

- Eighty-two percent of cases filed in adult courts involved minority youth.
- In nine of ten studied jurisdictions, minority youth were disproportionately charged in adult court. One dramatic example is an Alabama county where African-American youth accounted for three out of ten felony arrests, but represented 80 percent of the felony cases filed in adult court.
- African-American youth were overrepresented, especially in nonviolent drug cases sent to adult court.
- African-American youth (43 percent) and Latino youth (37 percent) were more likely than white youth (26 percent) to receive a sentence of incarceration (as opposed to probation or other lesser sentences).
- White youth were twice as likely to be represented by private counsel as African-American youth. Youth represented by private attorneys are less likely to be convicted and more likely to be transferred back to juvenile court.

It is difficult, if not impossible, for researchers to determine where racial discrimination ends and race effects come into play. Do cops patrol minority neighborhoods in urban areas because they use racial profiling, or because those areas are crime-ridden? Joblessness and one-parent families on welfare breed crime, and yet as the years pass, more and more minorities live in those conditions. "Increased urbanization, inequality, and class segregation have had a disproportionate impact on blacks in the past 30 years," write the authors of "Race, Ethnicity, and Serious Violent Offending," another report published by the OJJDP. "In 1970, one in five poor blacks lived in high-poverty areas; by 1990, the ratio was slightly more than two out of five."

The State School population are mostly minority youth from impoverished backgrounds who come through the gate seeing the world through the prism of race. Most have never developed a friendship with someone whose skin is a different color.

"You hear them when they first get here," said Jackie Urbach, who spent years working in the dorms. "Everyone thinks they are so different from one another. Hispanics, for example, are thought to be these exotic creatures with all these strange customs. But then, you put kids together and they find out they have a lot more in common than they ever thought. To begin with, so many of them have been abused."

A youth who openly declares himself to be a racist—"I don't trust nobody but my own kind"—is not likely to spark a fight, or even a debate about racism or discrimination. Instead, a staff member or a peer is likely to accuse him of "going racial" to avoid facing something buried inside himself.

"They make you look at why you are going racial," Candace says. "They ask you, What do you think going racial is going to accomplish? That's the question, right there."

12.

"I EARNED MYSELF SOME
DISTANCE FROM MYSELF"

A high school coach who has had twenty winning seasons displays his career on the wall for all to behold: championship pennants, play-off banners, plaques from the Rotary, citations from the mayor. Not Sandy Brown. When he slides into a booth in the Texas Grill, a chicken-fried place, he carries his career highlights in a large manila envelope.

The coach brings out letters he's received, one at a time, gives a capsule biography of the writer, then reads a line or two. "This young man graduated from Prairie View A&M. I sent him twenty dollars every month. It wasn't much, I just wanted him to know I was there. He writes, 'Thanks for the money. But more importantly, thanks for the love!'" The manager of a Wal-Mart includes a picture of his family and writes that he tries to treat his employees the way Coach Brown treats his players. The foreman of a construction company says if he hadn't played for Coach Brown, he'd be in prison.

After the letters come the treasures, mementos kids have given the coach over the years. His favorite is the last, a tiny box wrapped in gold foil and tied with a red ribbon.

"Candace," Brown says, slowly shaking his head. "Candace adopted me. Wasn't anything special I did. She just needed a father figure. She wanted to give me a Christmas present and she did not have a dime and anyway, there isn't anything in the State School you can buy for a present, so the box is empty. And that's the best part."

Reverently, Brown slides a note from under the ribbon and unfolds it. He clears his voice and reads: " 'You never can unwrap it/Please leave the ribbon tied. Just hold the box close to your heart/Because it's filled with love inside.' "

As the coach slowly refolds the note and slips it back under the ribbon, he starts telling how Candace won the state championship in the 300-meter hurdles. "You cannot do what Candace did," Brown says, gently pounding the table. "You cannot cut six seconds off your best time in one race. You cannot do that."

Winning a blue ribbon on the track at Baylor University in Waco is an amazing accomplishment for a teenage felon serving a ten-year determinate sentence. But then, Candace has been doing amazing things, legal and otherwise, since at least age nine.

A marvelous actress, Candace learned her craft to survive. She tilts her head a certain way, puts a lilt in her voice, and suddenly, the drab TYC institutional attire fades away and Candace becomes an oil patch debutante, prattling on about how the young men of today simply have no manners. She narrows her eyes, lowers her voice until she is as hoarse as a barmaid in a biker bar, and now she's talking back to a cop—"Don't fuck with me, Jack, I know my rights." Candace is also a gifted spin doctor, as brazen as any in politics, always presenting the hapless figures in her life in the most favorable light. Her father, for example. "My dad is the only man in my life that didn't try to touch me. I value that a lot." Or her mother. "I thank my mom for these precious jewels, my eyes."

Candace's mom and dad were drug dealers with large appetites for their product. High on cocaine or coming down hard, her father was dangerous. When Candace was five, he pushed her to the floor, breaking her nose and sending teeth through her lower lip. But he could be fun, too. Dad liked to play kids' games and make up funny stories, like the one about the clouds being cotton and planes taking people up there to pick it. And he did protect Candace—if only after the fact.

Candace's father prided himself on being a Good Samaritan, probably to prove to himself that, deep down, he was a good guy. One day on the street, he started a conversation with a homeless man and ended up bringing him home, so the guy could take a shower and spend the night in a warm, safe place. In the middle of the night, eight-year-old Candace staggered into her parents' bedroom, legs dripping blood and semen. The homeless man had raped her. Her father beat him half to death, then dragged him to a police station.

A year or so later, Candace's father left the apartment to do a drug deal and never came back. The police never did arrest a suspect and for years, Candace was sure the homeless man had done it. He had waited until he got the chance and then killed her father for beating him up and turning him in. It was all her fault.

Candace's only precious possession is a loose-leaf notebook filled with her poetry. Sitting at a picnic table outside the social services building, she thumbs through papers until she finds the poem she wrote about her father on the tenth anniversary of his death.

> Daddy
> I miss you so much
> Daddy
> If I could only feel your touch
> Daddy
> I wasn't ready for you to die
> Daddy
> Why can't it be a lie?

Candace is the oldest of three children from her mother's second marriage; the first marriage produced two daughters. Her mother has admitted injecting Candace with heroin when she was four or five, "to calm her down." Candace doesn't remember that, but has vivid memories of Mom making her kneel in a corner with her hands behind her back while pressing a penny to the wall with her nose. If the penny dropped, her mother beat her. These things happened when her father was still alive and there was at least a semblance of family life. Whatever strength her mother possessed crumbled when her husband was killed and she turned to prostitution to support her drug habit.

"My mom kind of disappeared after my dad died; she wouldn't come home for days," Candace recalls. "My older half sisters weren't living with us, so I had the caretaker role for my younger brother and sister. When I started stealing, it was out of necessity."

Candace followed the mailman, skipping along and humming whenever he happened to glance back, then riffling through the letters he dropped in a mailbox, looking for cash and money orders. Sundays she attended services in different churches and palmed bills from collection plates. Supermarkets and clothing stores she regarded as donation centers for her brother and sister.

"I'd get caught—you're always going to get caught—and I'd play innocent and pretend I was looking around for my mom, and when the guard or whoever was distracted and I saw the chance, I'd run. If they took me in the back, I'd give them my half sister's phone number. We had it all worked out. She'd pretend she was my mother and say she was crippled and couldn't come down and get me. This was the first time, I'd never done anything like this, and would they please just send me home? They almost always did."

Candace strolled down streets in Ft. Worth residential neighborhoods, watching for an elderly lady out working in the yard or an old man passing time on a front porch. When she spotted one, she'd march up with a big grin and announce, "Hi! I'm Candace!" The precocious little girl was as delightful as an unexpected breeze, and it was the rare grandmother or lonely widower who did not invite the sweet child in for something cool to drink. While the elderly person was in the kitchen fetching the drink, Candace cased the front room, grabbed everything she could carry that looked valuable, and ran for the door. She made her way up alleys and down side streets until it was safe to hop a bus and ride downtown, to a resale shop where the owner purchased everything she spread on the counter, no questions asked. Candace used the money to buy items that were too big to shoplift—orange juice, milk, laundry detergent.

Long before her period arrived, Candace had decided she was suffering from "the Curse—the Curse of being born to be hurt." By day, she was stealing, washing, cooking, and babysitting for her younger brother and sister. By night, she was trying to run off the men her mother brought home. "I'd steal from them, I'd cuss at them," she recalls, summoning up her street-tough voice. " 'You're the second guy who's been here tonight, you dumb fuck!' "

Some men said the hell with it and left; some stayed; and some who did came creeping into Candace's bedroom. When she heard the door open, she woke her little sister and told her to get ready to run. Then she got ready to fight the guy off.

Things were even worse after her mother married a twenty-seven-year-old with a voracious drug appetite. Her "stepguy" (Candace loathes him far too much to call him her stepfather) took her outside one afternoon, showed her a knife, and threw it at a tree. As the knife was quivering in the bark, the stepguy told Candace, If you don't do what I want, your head is that tree.

    He sneaks in easily without a noise
    Awakens her softly with his deep voice
    She feels his whiskers in her ears
    His nasty secrets are her worst fears

    Caressing, grabbing, stroking, squeezing
    It's not her fault, she was only sleeping
    The stench of alcohol is overwhelming
    He threatens her life if she thinks of telling

    Rubbing furiously up and down her chest
    Greedily fondling her tiny breasts
    Try pushing him away but he's too strong
    Oh my God! Where the hell is her mom!

    Start making noise so he'll hopefully leave
    Can't tell nobody, they won't believe
    She's scared and lonely, full of tears
    This mess has been going on for years

    Paranoia strikes and he runs away
    She's safe now but awake she stays

She feels so dirty and all alone
Why can't she sleep in her own home!

It's morning now and nothing's happened
Out in the hall, she hears him laughing
But school is awaiting and she must go
I must be perfect so no one will know.

Her mother divorced this pervert, but as soon as he left, Mom asked a friend to move in and share the rent. The friend arrived with her son, whom Mom promptly directed to Candace's room. "He was sixteen, I was eleven. It was, 'Mom, what do you expect?' I quit fighting it. I gave in to it and let it happen."

If Candace gave up the battle in bed, she did not stop fighting the Curse in its other manifestations. She had huge screaming matches with her mother and fought back by stealing, and consuming, Mom's drugs. The clothes she shoplifted for her brother and sister came from chain stores—generic was good enough for them. For herself, Candace selected items from the most exclusive stores. "I saw well-dressed, confident people and wanted to be like them, so I always stole high-class stuff. I never wanted to be white trash," she says.

But the Curse was always there. And when she was tired or frustrated or the drugs she stole from her mother were gone, she took it out on her little brother and sister.

"One day, I was wanting drugs and they were being loud and I threw my little brother into the wall, hard, and then I wrapped the telephone cord around my little sister's neck. I pulled it tight and held it until she turned purple. All of a sudden, I saw what I was doing and I ran into the hallway and sank down to the floor. I realized what I'd become: my mom. I never hurt them again. I've written letter after letter begging for forgiveness. So many, they've asked me to stop."

By age thirteen, Candace's days as a caretaker were over. "I was running away a lot," she says. "I didn't care about myself. I was promiscuous."

Candace spent hours in front of a mirror, artfully applying makeup to turn herself into a woman, years older than she was. She draped her girl's figure in expensive shoplifted dresses and went for slow walks down busy streets. She drew men like the sirens in *The Odyssey;* only Candace didn't turn men into swine. They were swine to begin with.

"Men in their twenties and thirties would pull over. Old perverts would pull over. I didn't care."

Could they give her a lift? Take her to dinner? That outfit she had on was real nice. Would she like another one like it? Candace accepted their offers and let things happen. It was on these "dates," as she calls them, that she perfected her acting skills.

"The older guys who picked me up and stuck around me were all the same: they all wanted 'Baby Doll.' Baby Doll is all about being dependent. I learned to play that role real good. Somebody would say, 'Let me buy you some clothes,' and we'd go to a store and I'd pick out something and they'd wrap it up. I'd pick up the box and go, 'Eeeuuu, this box is sooooo heavy.' The guy would laugh and pick it up for me. In a restaurant, I always waited for them to pull back my chair. If somebody didn't open a door, I'd go, 'Goooodnessss! Where was your mother?'

"It was mixed manipulation. Guys used me for sex, I used them for money. We'd go to a motel and do whatever. The guy would go take a shower and I'd steal his wallet, his money, his car keys, sometimes his car. That way, he'd have to call his family and explain where he was. I hated the way I felt about myself: an object, a piece of meat. But still, I was turning the Curse around to my benefit. I was getting something back."

Candace kept bouncing from place to place and one night she ended up in the apartment of a woman she knew through her mother. "Her name was Angel," Candace recalls dryly. "Far from it."

The first night Candace was there, she and Angel stayed up late watching movies and smoking marijuana. The next day, Angel introduced the fourteen-year-old to crack cocaine. "I remember that effect more than any other drug," she says, still amazed at how hard crack hits. "I immediately wanted more."

Angel and Candace reached an agreement: she could stay rent-free, in exchange for babysitting Angel's two children. But before the week was out, Angel asked Candace to turn a trick.

"I said no. I didn't like the label 'prostitute,' even if, technically, you know, I had. Angel said, 'If you are going to be living here, you need to find a way to pay.' I said, 'I thought I was taking care of the kids.' Angel said, 'That's nothing to me. You need to find a way to bring in money.' "

The next evening, two young men walked into the apartment. One was Derrick, a twenty-three-year-old plumber Candace had gone out with several times. Derrick had been calling Candace at home and had finally given up. The other was a friend of Derrick's, a plumber he was working with. Angel was the guy's cocaine connection.

Candace and Derrick walked out to his car, a huge cream-colored '81 Mercedes diesel, a hand-me-down from his parents. Candace told her story. "I need to get you out of here," Derrick whispered before giving her a kiss and driving away.

That night, Candace was in the room she shared with Angel's children when Angel appeared and said someone wanted to meet her. In the living room, Angel introduced her to a fat guy with gold teeth and small, mean eyes. Angel led Candace into the hallway and told her the scary guy was a very important drug dealer. She gave Candace two choices: have sex with him or get out. Candace went to her room, piled her clothes in a laundry basket, and swept past Angel and the dealer before they could stop her.

She was in the parking lot wondering where to go when the apartment manager appeared and asked what she was doing out there all alone. Candace told her story and the woman let her spend the night in her apartment.

"The next morning I heard it, the low rumble of Derrick's old diesel," Candace remembers with a grin.

Candace ran out to the parking lot and jumped into the Mercedes. Derrick had figured out how to take Candace away from her troubles.

"We got to do what we got to do to survive," he told Candace. Then he opened the glove compartment and showed her a handgun he had stolen from his parents. Derrick hadn't thought out exactly how they were going to use the pistol to survive, but Candace had an idea. She remembered hearing a news item on the radio about a couple that was apprehended after sticking up a string of convenience stores. Candace thought she could come up with a plan so perfect they'd never get caught.

Derrick loved it. He hated being a plumber.

They chose a target carefully and checked out surveillance systems. They mapped out an escape route and drove it until fourteen-year-old Candace, the getaway driver, had it memorized. They bought new clothes every morning and threw them away after every job. They changed motels every night. In three days, they robbed six convenience stores. In six months, they robbed 120.

Candace kept refining their technique. She strolled into an empty store and walked to the back to get a drink from the cooler. When Derrick came in, Candace counted to 1,004 and then started back up the aisle. She had about reached the front counter when Derrick pulled the gun and announced the holdup. Candace screamed and dropped her drink. Derrick whirled and grabbed her and held the gun to her head. "The girl is going with me," Derrick said as he watched the clerk fill a bag with money. "I got a friend watching outside; if you come out from behind the counter to see where I'm going, he's gonna call me on the cell phone and this girl right here will never go for another ride. And it'll be your fault."

It was one huge rush. Candace took to calling Derrick "Clyde"; she was "Bonnie."

"Getting ready to do a robbery was like being on top of a roller coaster, ready to take the plunge," Candace recalls. "I liked that the best. The drugs were good, the drugs were important. They helped us because we didn't want to live real. We wanted to be in a cartoon. We wanted to be ten feet high and bulletproof. We wanted to have fun and live happily ever after."

But after the one-hundredth ride, the roller coaster wasn't the thrill it once was. Convenience stores were just too easy. Candace craved a new challenge. One night in bed, she said, "Derrick, let's figure out how to take down a bank."

"But then I got sick," Candace says. "From when I was, you know, being promiscuous, I got a disease."

It was chlamydia, a sexually transmitted disease that is asymptomatic in its early stages. The disease announced its presence with itching and burning, but Candace ignored the symptoms and the chlamydia eventually turned into PID, pelvic inflammatory disease. Candace was bleeding vaginally and growing weaker. One morning, she could barely get out of bed. Derrick knew he had to get her to a doctor, but they had spent the money from their last score on drugs and the motel room. They couldn't do another robbery; Candace was too sick to drive the getaway car.

Suddenly, Derrick got an idea. He had walked off the job without giving notice, sure, but they still owed him his last paycheck. He picked up the phone by the bed and called his former employer; the check had been mailed to his forwarding address, his parents' home. Derrick hung up with a big grin. They would drive by his parents' house and pick up the check. They'd cash it, get Candace to a clinic, check into a new motel, and wait for the antibiotics to kick in.

Their timing, which had been impeccable, was turning incredibly bad. At one of the last stores they hit, a manager followed them far enough to scribble down a few numbers on the license plate. Only one old diesel in the database fit the numbers, and it was registered to Derrick's father. As the robbers turned onto the leafy street where Derrick grew up, his mother was standing at the front door, explaining to two plainclothes detectives that she had not seen or heard from Derrick in three months. Derrick tried to drive by quietly, but you can't do that in an old Mercedes diesel, and when the cops heard that rumble, they turned and the chase was on.

"It really wasn't a high-speed chase because the diesel wouldn't go that fast," Candace says with a little grin. "A bunch of squad cars were behind us and they had a bullhorn and were telling us to pull over, but we had drugs and the gun and we didn't. They finally forced us off the road. I told the cops I was sick and had to go to the hospital. They didn't believe me. I pulled out the towel I was holding between my legs and said, 'This ain't no fuckin' period!' They took me to the hospital. I was there four days."

The district attorney hit Derrick with every charge he could—armed robbery, statutory rape, harboring a runaway. Derrick was sentenced to forty years in state prison. His fourteen-year-old accomplice received a ten-year determinate sentence and was sent to the TYC.

"I arrived at Giddings with a group of girls on January fifteenth, 1997," Candace says. "I loved the campus, it was so beautiful, and I loved the staff. I made up my mind: this was going to be a new start."

For several years, Candace kept making false starts. She did well for a few months, then lost control and wiped out all her progress. Once, she assaulted a girl. But slowly, painfully, she discovered her life could be defined as a series of thinking errors. She was locked into feeling special—"No one could have had a worse life than mine." She blamed others—"The guys I stole from were asking for it. If they hadn't pulled over and come on to me, nothing would have happened." She was adept at downplaying—"We never stole from a person, just stores. We never fired the gun. We always said, 'Thank you' and 'Have a nice day.' " Candace seemed to think she was the star of a drama set in the State School. The staff and the other students were her supporting cast. As the years went by, the drama wore thin.

Slowly she began to emerge from herself, and when she did, Candace turned into a unique figure on the Giddings campus.

"Candace became a feminist, working for equal rights," says Sherry Whatley, one of her Capital Offenders therapists.

Candace saw that the only avenue students had to protest staff behavior was to file a grievance. But a grievance pits a student against a staff member; somebody has to be right and somebody wrong. Candace knew there were dozens of problems students and staff could work out together. She came up with the idea of "positive feedback," a system that allowed students to address problems without placing blame. She sold the idea to the administration, and a big "positive feedback" box appeared in the cafeteria. Students stuffed it with suggestions and Candace sent them on to the administration, and over time, changes were made. For example, phase four boys were allowed to walk across campus without an escort, but girls were not. Candace lobbied to get that changed, and it was.

"I have to care about this place, I spent what are supposed to be the best years of my life here," Candace says at the picnic table. She thinks for a moment, and then she smiles. "I never went to the prom. But I probably wouldn't have gone to the prom, anyway. I probably wouldn't have gone to high school."

Almost certainly, she would not have become a track star.

Candace was running laps in the gym during a physical education class when Coach Brown noticed her long, easy stride and challenged her to do as many laps as she could. She surprised them both by doing twenty, and doing them fast, despite wheezing slightly from asthma. Hey, Coach," Candace said. The boys play football and have a track team; why can't the girls have a track team?

"That was how it started," Candace recalls. "We had to go through a lot of procedures and we finally got the youth rights specialist involved, and we got it!"

At the very first girls' practice, Coach Brown put a hurdle on the track and asked Candace to jump over it. She was intimidated; she had never even seen a hurdle before. What if she tripped and fell? Then she thought, I've gone over a lot of hurdles. She tried it and sailed over.

That first year, there were six girls on the track team. The second year, there were nine, and one of them, Candace, qualified for the Texas Association of Private and Parochial Schools state meet in two events, the 100- and 300-meter hurdles. The hundred was her best event, but she tripped over a hurdle and finished fourth.

"Before the three hundred, Candace came up to me and said, 'Coach, I'm going to win this for you,' " Brown recalls. "Her times were about average for a Texas schoolgirl; she was lucky just to make it to state. I said, 'Candace, you just run your best race.'

"She came out of the blocks and burst ahead of the other girls. She's got a ten-meter lead and I know there's no way she can finish at the pace she's going. She's asthmatic. I grabbed her inhaler and cut across the in-field because I knew she was going to fall.

"Candace went wire to wire. She was ten meters ahead when she crossed the finish line. She collapsed and I got there and gave her two puffs from the inhaler. She looked up at me and said, 'I told you, Coach.' "

Candace ran a 49.1, six seconds faster than her next-fastest time.

"Sometimes, what you know can work against you," Brown says, taking a stab at explaining how she did it. "Candace didn't know enough about track to know she couldn't run a forty-nine. She wanted something so bad, she went way beyond her level of performance. You can't really explain it. You can only admire it."

Brown picks up the tiny, carefully wrapped present and puts it back in the envelope. He smiles to himself.

"What do you give a kid like that?" the coach asks. "You better give her everything you've got. Because that is what she is giving you!"

Candace sits nervously in a chair in a hallway outside the conference room where the Special Services Committee is meeting. The splendid actress has spent almost six years preparing for this appearance and now that the moment is finally arriving, she does not want to take the stage. She wants to go back to the cottage, crawl into her bed, and pull the covers over her head.

Inside the conference room, Ann Kelley is at one end of a long table, next to a stenographer. The high school principal, Ben Hauerland, is there; so is Tami Coy, the girls' program administrator; next to Coy is the institutional coordinator, who is in charge of placing youth leaving Giddings in group homes or halfway houses. A program administrator who represents victims is there, and so are two caseworkers.

One of the caseworkers formally presents Candace to the committee, summarizing her crimes and her time in custody. Candace has been in the TYC for seventy months and is currently at 4.0 on the four-point system. Candace experienced difficulty in discussing her issues in Capital Offenders and struggled to complete the program. Candace asked to repeat the program and did much better the second time. Candace has come a very long way.

The school principal delivers Candace's academic report, which he finds perplexing. She fails easy standardized tests and scores high on difficult ones. She has earned a GED, but easily could have her high school degree if she hadn't refused to work in a classroom.

Opening the mandatory psychological evaluation, Ann Kelley reports that Mike Hilgers, who did Candace's evaluation, found several traits that are consistent with a narcissistic personality disorder, including grandiosity and manipulation. Then Kelley runs through Candace's risk factors. Statistics show that when one or more of these dynamics are present, youth can go on to commit crimes after being released from custody.

There is a history of criminal behavior in Candace's family. She suffered both physical and sexual abuse at home. She has no support system;

her mother is living with a member of a motorcycle gang and using narcotics. Candace adjusted poorly to school and her worldview is limited.

On the plus side, Candace has a high IQ and has emerged as a positive influence on campus. She sticks to a task. She has earned a GED, completed Chemical Dependency, and completed Capital Offenders twice. She has never been a gang member. She has not been involved in a disruptive incident in years. Candace has matured to a great extent.

"I'm concerned Candace thinks life outside is going to be easier than it really is," Kelley tells the committee.

Candace comes through the door clutching the big three-ring binder every student brings to the Special Services Committee. It is a record of her years at Giddings, and Candace's is bulging with school papers, poems, letters of apology she wrote to her victims, certificates for completing programs, and finally, the all-important success plan.

Candace sits down at the end of the table facing the committee and flicks her long brown hair behind her shoulders. The school principal asks to see her binder; Candace pushes it toward him. He will peruse the binder and pass it along so that every committee member will have a chance to see it.

"As you know, we are the Special Services Committee," Kelley begins. "We can make one of three recommendations. We can recommend that you be released on parole. We can recommend that you remain in the State School for a longer period. Or we can recommend that you be transferred to prison. You're aware that's what we will be deciding?"

Candace knows all this. She understands "prison" surfaced only because Kelley is duty-bound to present it as an option. But still, the dreaded word throws her and she loses focus. It takes her a moment to nod yes.

"That's why we are here," Kelley says. "Tell us why you are here."

It is as if Candace is in the United Nations, waiting for a translation. She stares down at the table until things mesh and then she begins.

"I'm ready to leave," she says. "I'm here looking for your approval." She halts, then remembers something else she should say. "I've come a long way," she adds.

"How are you a different person than when you arrived?" Kelley asks.

"I came here so locked in my feelings, there was no way I could understand them," Candace replies, finding her rhythm. "Everything Giddings has to offer, I took advantage of. I earned myself some distance from myself. I understand my emotions and I understand other people's emotions. I had no self-esteem when I arrived. I've developed confidence. I've learned assertiveness."

"But you didn't take much advantage of what the school has to offer," observes Ben Hauerland.

The statement throws Candace. She has done extraordinarily well at the State School. Why aren't they praising her?

"I do care about education," Candace answers after a moment. "I earned a GED. But I don't learn in a classroom. I know that about myself. I put that in my success plan. That's why my career goal is what it is."

Candace is determined to go to a school in Austin and become a therapeutic masseuse. She envisions herself building a massage business and branching out to open a yoga salon and perhaps a health food restaurant. The businesses would be clustered around a glassed-in office, where Candace could watch all three enterprises at the same time. The architecture of this design led Mike Hilgers to flag Candace's narcissistic tendencies.

"Candace, are you really certain you want to work as a masseuse?" Tami Coy asks, expressing an uncertainty she shares with others around the table. "With your history of sexual abuse . . . are you sure touching people every day is healthy for you?"

"Oh, you're thinking of the wrong kind of masseuse, Miss Coy," Candace counters. "This is not a come-on or a front for prostitution or anything like that. This is therapeutic. It's got proven health benefits. Ask anybody from California. Everybody in California gets massages. It's coming to Texas—that's why I want to go to school in Austin. It's happening there first."

"What are the barriers you will have to overcome to make your success plan come true?" Coy asks.

"My mom's a barrier. She's married again, to an ex-con. It's the same kind of relationship she's had in the past and I'm afraid if I went home, I'd run away. They don't live too far from here and my mom is always promising to come and visit but she hardly ever has. Story of my life. So, yeah, my mom's a barrier."

"That's why your success plan is written the way it is," says Walter Stevens, the institutional placement coordinator, reinforcing the fact that Candace will not be going home when she is released. Stevens has been busy arranging to place Candace in the TYC halfway house for girls in Ft. Worth.

"What will you need to change to succeed?" Kelley asks.

"Well, drugs are still a barrier. I still relapse in my thoughts. I'm going to find a Narcotics Anonymous group and stay with it, probably forever. And I still struggle with low self-esteem."

"There are a lot of kids out there who struggle with low self-esteem, but they didn't do one hundred and twenty armed robberies," Kelley points out. "Why did you?"

"I was rejecting my mother. I didn't want any rules. I ran away. I was always running away. An unhealthy relationship with my co-actor allowed me to keep on running. I told myself the robberies were my only option. They allowed me to not go home, to keep doing drugs, to be with my co-actor, to keep on running.

"But I've stopped running," Candace says, nodding at the big binder that is making its way down the table. "You can't go through this place and keep on running. You can't look at all the stuff I've had to look at. You can't do Capital Offenders twice if you want to keep on running."

"No one is saying you haven't done well here, Candace," says Tami Coy. "But we have concerns. What happens when you're in The Free and you don't get exactly what you want? How is that going to be a risk for you?"

"I'm not sure what you mean," Candace replies.

"You manipulate to get the things you want," Coy says. "You know your patterns. Manipulating is an issue for you. How are you going to deal with that?"

"I know I can manipulate and make something happen," Candace replies. "But I've also learned that manipulation is short-term and self-defeating. To really accomplish something, you have to work hard and build trust."

When none of the committee members replies, Candace adds, "This isn't TYC-speak I'm giving you. I really mean it!"

"That's good assertiveness!" Kelley says, and everyone laughs at the TYC in-joke.

"What kind of job will you be wanting when you first get out?" asks Walter Stevens.

"Nothing you have to flip in the air," Candace replies. "Nothing you have to plunge into hot oil."

"Nothing where you have to say, 'Would you like fries with that?' " Stevens asks, his eyes twinkling.

"Help make us feel real confident about your success plan," Kelley urges.

"I really am scared of The Free," Candace replies. "I'm taking nothing for granted. I know probably you all are thinking I've got my head in the clouds. But I know if I take it a step at a time and work real hard, I can get there. And isn't that what dreams are for? I mean, they are like a blueprint, aren't they?"

The questions begin to wind down and Candace gathers her binder and prepares to leave.

"We will make a recommendation and send it to the administration. The administration will share it with you," Kelley tells her.

After Candace says thank you and leaves the room, the committee votes that Candace be released to the halfway house in Ft. Worth. The vote is unanimous.

The Texas legislature, which is generous in providing funds to support the treatment culture that flourishes inside the TYC, turns parsimonious when youth are ready to leave. There are never enough slots available in halfway houses; there is not enough money to continue treatment outside the fence. It is a bit like taking a whooping crane that has hit a power line to a highly specialized rescue center, nursing it back to health, and then releasing it into the wild and hoping for the best.

Three long months pass before there is room for Candace in the Ft. Worth halfway house. It is dead time she passes by working in the high school office and helping the girls in Cottage 1-A work on their problems. One afternoon, Walter Stevens calls to tell her to be ready to leave tomorrow. She goes to breakfast as usual the next morning and then returns to the cottage to pack everything she owns in a cardboard box. The girls gather around to hug her and cry and make her promise to write every week.

Tom Talbott, her caseworker, takes Candace on a final tour of the campus. She says her good-byes and hugs everyone she has come to know. Then she and Talbott take the long walk to the gate.

Talbott is reaching for the gate when it clicks open, as if by magic. He glances at Candace and smiles. That little click is the sound of freedom. They go through the gatehouse and out to the parking lot, where the TYC van is waiting to take Candace to Ft. Worth. Candace says good-bye to Talbott and gets in.

She had always thought leaving the Giddings State School would be an ending. Now she realizes it isn't an ending at all. It's a beginning.

EPILOGUE

THE BOYS

Ronnie was paroled to his mother, who was single and wasn't dating when he arrived. She was still working in the nursing home and taking care of Kenny, who was out of boot camp. "I decided I just wanted it to be me and my boys. Kenny and I grew very close while Ronnie was away, and I wanted for him and I to become that close," Marina says. She joined a church and when Ronnie arrived, the church threw a surprise potluck supper to welcome him back. Small-business owners in the congregation offered Ronnie a job, but he decided to work in the nursing home that had employed his mother for years. Within a year, he was head of the custodial crew. "I'm responsible for eleven people, can you believe that?" Ronnie asks rhetorically. "I had to fire somebody. Me! I fired someone!"

Ronnie has a girlfriend and a new car, and some weekends, he drives up to Oklahoma to visit his father and grandparents. "When I first went to my [paternal] grandparents' house, my grandmother came out and gave me a big hug. I don't know how she recognized me. She cried. As for my dad, me and him get along fine. He's a hard man to talk to about anything emotional. The closest it gets is, he'll say, 'It didn't work out,' about him and my mom. He still sits on the porch, but he's not doing drugs.

He's smoking three to four packs of cigarettes a day. I watch his hands shake lighting a match and think, That's my dad. I'm going to accept him for what he is." That also goes for the aunt who beat him so often when he was a child. "She lives across the street from us," Ronnie says. "She's re-married and she's in our church. We don't talk about what happened. There's still things I don't understand but I'm okay, I've found my peace with it. And I know she feels bad." And what about his brother? Has Kenny forgiven him? "Kenny is starting ninth grade. He's got a learning disability, he has to take things slow. I really hurt him a lot. I was messed up. Now, we talk and do things together. He tells me, 'You're a changed man. Now, you're my brother.' "

Like every player on the Giddings Indians the year the team played in the state semifinals, Ronnie received a copy of the wonderful documen-tary Holden Productions did on the team. "For the first few months, he wouldn't leave the house without that tape," Marina says. "He'd go out to the store—he'd take the tape. He'd go over to a friend's house—he'd take the tape."

Tran was paroled to his mother and father. During the final year of his stay in the State School, Tran kept trying to convince them to open a Vietnamese restaurant. They warmed to the idea and were able to secure a bank loan. The restaurant was almost ready to open when a drunk driver plowed into the family car, severely injuring Tran. He spent time in the ICU but has gone on to make a full recovery. The restaurant is a big suc-cess. The family is about to open a second, which Tran will manage.

Mark is somewhere in the Texas Department of Criminal Justice gulag, serving a forty-year sentence for murdering his sixteen-year-old girlfriend.

Daniel and his father reunited while Daniel was in the State School. Foot-ball helped. His father came to every game and took a keen interest in Daniel's play. Daniel was paroled to his father, who put Daniel to work in his car-detailing business. Daniel quickly moved up to a management po-sition. The business is thriving.

Antonio held up his arms in group one morning, looked around in mock-seriousness, and said, "Why can't I get no fucking job?" Everyone laughed. His arms were so heavily tattooed, it was difficult to spot skin the needle had not altered. But the question behind the joke was serious: Who would hire a tattooed gangbanger who had done a murder? The answer: Antonio's uncle, who has a roofing business. Antonio is thrilled to be out and leading a life that is free of gangs, violence, and drugs. His uncle says he is the hardest worker on the crew.

Johnnie is an apprentice auto mechanic, living in his own apartment, wondering if the past is truly behind him and he can trust himself to start dating. The grandparents who struggled to raise him are both dead but the good work they did is evident now in ways it wasn't when they were alive. When Johnnie wakes up in the morning, he tells his grandparents that today will be a good day and he will make them proud. Then he gets up and takes a shower.

Tim's life story turned out to be as much about his little sister as it was about him. Tim loves his sister. She was the only one in his family who wrote him, the only one who came to visit. That Tim had failed to protect her haunted him day and night. He stood by while an older cousin sexually abused the little girl. His sister never blamed Tim, something she made clear over and over again. She, it turns out, is brilliant. She got a four-year scholarship to Harvard, where she studied biochemistry. She transferred to Rice University in Houston so Tim could be paroled to her. He works at a Starbucks and goes to a community college.

Dwayne almost didn't make it out of Capital Offenders. During a search, JCOs discovered contraband—letters from a girl—hidden under his clothes. Dwayne swore the letters weren't his. After hours in a behavior group and increasingly convoluted explanations, Dwayne finally admitted that yes, the letters were his. This led to much discussion of why Dwayne felt he had to lie to deflect responsibility. Two weeks later, a JCO discovered another letter. Dwayne swore up and down the JCO was

lying—a very serious charge. The JCO couldn't produce the letter. Somewhere between his finding the letter and walking across the dorm to call
security, it had disappeared.

It was an intriguing little mystery and Frank Soto, Sherry Whatley,
and Jackie Urbach couldn't crack it, no matter how deep they dug. Finally, after something like four hours in group, Tran, with no warning,
blurted out, "The JCO left the letter on the shelf when he went to the
phone. I picked it up and went to the toilet and ripped it up and flushed
it down." Tran looked across the circle at his friend Dwayne and said, "I
did it for you." This led to several groups where the effects of Dwayne's
lies were explored in great detail—"Look at the position you put Tran in.
Think about how you could have damaged the JCO's reputation. Think
about all the hours your peers have spent in groups discussing this."

Dwayne spent a weekend in security but was not removed from the
group. While never a leader or a focal point, after he got out of security
Dwayne did much better than the therapists had expected and ended
up an active, alert group member. Dwayne was paroled to a halfway house
and is now working for a mail service in Houston.

Jerrold, the terrific running back, turned into a star defensive back. He
was paroled to a halfway house in Dallas that has a tradition of taking athletes. Staffers at the house called coaches from a local high school, a 5-A
powerhouse, to tell them Jerrold's story. They came by to meet Jerrold and
returned to take him to school and start him in the weight-training program. He spent his first summer lifting weights and working in a Kragen
Auto store. When school started, the coaches made sure Jerrold had a
tutor. He started every game at free safety and ended up making the All-
Conference first team. He graduated and is now going to a community
college and, of course, playing football.

THE GIRLS

Candace quickly ran into "issues," as they say, with sex. While living in the TYC halfway house for girls in Ft. Worth, she landed a job in a department store and soon was having relations with a young man who worked there. He provided her with a camera, which Candace took to the halfway house and urged other girls to pose in revealing positions. One of the girls reported Candace and for several weeks, it looked like she might be sent to prison. Candace was instead removed from the TYC halfway house and shipped to a Texas Department of Criminal Justice halfway house. There, instead of a bed in a comfortable room shared with only one girl, Candace slept in a bunk in a dorm. If she violated her parole in this setting, Candace would go directly to prison. But she did well and eventually was placed in the home of a retired couple in West Texas. The couple had taken in TDCJ parolees for years, but when Candace's stay was up, they notified the TDCJ she was the last. They intended to keep Candace. She lived with the couple and worked for a car rental company before moving to Houston. She now has two children by different fathers and spends her days caring for the youngest.

Elena spent more time in the TYC than any girl in her group, largely because officials determined that Elena had an anger problem that was not fully addressed in Capital Offenders. After six years in the TYC, a full year after the last girl in her group was released, Elena finally entered The Free. She moved in with her mother in San Angelo and for almost a year, she stayed mostly indoors. If she did go out, she'd get on a bus and notice that one of the passengers was a gangbanger. She'd convince herself that the gang member was "mad-dogging" her, or was about to "talk shit," and she'd get off at the next stop and walk the rest of the way home. She spent her days caring for her little sister's baby, after the fifteen-year-old returned to high school. Elena finally summoned her courage and started school to learn to be an aide in a nursing home. She began dating a young man who taught computer keyboarding there. They evolved into a cou-

ple, and Elena became pregnant and gave birth to a girl. She, her sister
and her child, and the baby recently moved into an apartment. "It's going
real good. We all get along. I love taking care of the baby. As soon as she
gets old enough, I'm going to get a job. It's like I told them in Capital Offenders. I won't reoffend, and I haven't."

Elena's mother has yet to take the GED exam again. "I've had some issues. Things keep getting in the way."

Jani ended up in prison. After the fight in Cottage 1-A, she repeatedly
made the same vow: "I'm going to be in the next Capital Offenders
group, and this time, I'm going to do it right." She seemed to be as good
as her word. She worked her way up through the phases and got A's in
school. The State School has a small volunteer program, made up mostly
of retirees who live in the vicinity. Jani asked to be matched with a volunteer. The two became close and Jani ended up giving the keynote speech
at the annual volunteer banquet. She got a standing ovation. And then,
for reasons no one could discern, Jani went back to being mean and
angry. She picked fights, disrupted groups, refused to work in school.
Anyone who tried to reach her got the same response: "Send me to the
pen, I don't care." The day Jani climbed into a van and left the State
School for a penitentiary, Mike Hilgers said, "I don't think there are too
many people here who are real broken up about it."

Keisha used to say she wanted "a life." That is what she got. She was
paroled to her grandmother, which did not seem like a good idea. Her
grandmother had used every excuse to beat Keisha. But it turned out
her grandmother had mellowed greatly and welcomed Keisha home with
open arms. For a while, she divided her time between her grandmother
and her father, caring for them both. Then she landed a job as a cashier in
a Wal-Mart and got her own place. She met a long-haul truck driver.
"He's a good man, a really good man. He's kind and he treats me right and
we have fun together." But "he's got two little kids and a wife who won't
take care of them. She's going out all the time and not there when she
needs to be. He can't depend on her, so it's me who ends up with the kids.
After I take care of them that woman will call me up and rag on me for

something I did. Can you believe that? I like the two of them just fine. I mean, they're great kids. But they ain't mine. And I don't need to be taking her shit and getting in the middle of their fights. I know, I just know, if I dedicate myself to taking care of them for the next ten years, I'll be resenting them and him. I already missed my childhood. I don't want to miss being young. And yet, I do care for him. So I don't know, I just don't know."

Nicole has her own apartment and her own car and is very proud that she pays for everything, working the 10 P.M. to 6 A.M. shift in a copy shop. She likes the hours because there are fewer people around then and that means fewer hassles. It seems that every time Nicole gets a new boss, he asks her out. She dissuades him, but he keeps upping the ante ("How 'bout I take you to New Orleans for a three-day weekend to celebrate your birthday the right way?"). Eventually, she says yes. The dates go nowhere, but do have one effect: Nicole ends up getting a new boss. She has a zest for life and more than anyone, keeps up with the girls she was incarcerated with.

Rachael is the mother of a baby girl and is pregnant again. The first thing she did when she was paroled home was become active in a Pentecostal church. There, she met a man a dozen or so years older than she was. She was working as an office temp and women began asking, "Rachael honey, are you pregnant or are you just putting on weight?" "Oh no, not me, I couldn't be," Rachael says she told them. "Then this one day I had such a hard time buttoning my favorite pants, I thought, Uh-oh, I better get myself to a doctor. Sure enough, I was pregnant. He's a real good man, he takes real good care of us. He's a very good provider, and me and the baby both care for him. I'm going to keep him."

Cristina went from the State School to a foster home. Her foster parents fell in love with the articulate young woman and ended up formally adopting her. Cristina took classes at a community college, intending to transfer to a four-year school and study psychology. She started going out with a classmate and ended up marrying him. She is now the mother of a baby boy. Back in the State School, Tommy, the wide-receiver football hero and Cristina's boyfriend, was heartbroken when he got the news.

Michelle pains me to write about. She is the young woman who changed the most in Capital Offenders, and the one who had the most insight. In a better world, Michelle would have finished her six-year sentence and gone directly to a four-year college on a full ride. All the Capital Offenders girls were excellent little therapists. None was better than Michelle. Her instincts and timing were flawless. It was easy to sit behind the one-way mirror and picture Michelle with a Ph.D., running a group. For reasons I'll never understand, Michelle was paroled back home to her mother, a deeply troubled woman. It didn't take Mom long to throw Michelle out for something petty—"She was disobeying me. I had to stop it before it got worse." Michelle called me—she had no one else—and I helped her get an apartment. For a while, she seemed to be doing fine. She'd get up in the morning and look around, amazed to be in a place all her own. She'd put on one of those silly uniforms and work in a cookie store during the day. At night, she did phone solicitation. She called every few days and then, I stopped hearing from her. Weeks later, Keisha called to say Michelle had a boyfriend and he had turned her out. She had invited Keisha to spend the weekend with her, but when Keisha arrived, Michelle tried to recruit her for prostitution. "She kept saying, 'You've got to do it, there's so much money.' I told her I'd think about it but that was just to get me out of there," Keisha said. "Michelle called after I left and I told her I had too much self-respect and wouldn't do that to myself. She was going, 'No, no, it's just short-term. We'll get some money and start an escort service.' The pimp was listening in. How I know is, all of a sudden his voice cuts in and tells her to hang up. And she did."

Michelle called me numerous times after that. She and her man weren't in the life anymore, she kept assuring me. They were passing a Bible church one evening just as services were beginning and they'd gone in and been saved. Now, they were following the Lord's way. The only bad thing was, her man was going to jail. His estranged wife had accused him of beating her up and they'd believed her, even though it wasn't true. Michelle was going to wait for her man. He was her true love. She even sent me his picture. At last report, Michelle was working as a waitress in a strip club in Dallas.

The writer lived in a trailer on some beautiful land, four miles out in the country from the State School. I'd come back after hearing a life story or a crime story and go inside and sometimes, I'd start to cry. I wasn't crying for myself; I was crying for these kids and their victims and for the pain we inflict on one another. Some stories more than others, Tran's and Michelle's in particular, completely wiped me out. I'd go outside and sit on the deck and watch the cattle make their rounds, and be filled with the sadness, the pain, the evil that the powerful inflict on the innocent; and then, innocence vanished, the pains the wounded go on to inflict on others. *Why doesn't it stop?*

We can deal with natural catastrophes, the Category Four hurricanes that swirl in from the warm oceans and the mammoth conflagrations that reduce mighty forests to ashes. They bring us together, help us re-create ourselves, make us stronger. What we can't deal with, what disfigures us, is the evil we inflict on one another. *Why doesn't it stop?*

I believe that if we can find a nonfascistic way to enter families and prevent domestic violence, we will change life in America. I believe that if the thousands and thousands of Ronnies and Elenas now doing dead time in prison had a chance to go through a Capital Offenders program, we could turn cell blocks into ghost towns.

Do I think it will happen? No. But it can happen. And I am grateful for the chance to tell the story of where it is happening, and why it works.

Note: I followed three Capital Offenders groups but was not able to tell a story from the boys' Capital Offenders Group B. Of the seventeen boys and seven girls I followed, two were transferred to prison. The other fifteen were released. None has been re-arrested.

ACKNOWLEDGMENTS

Stan DeGerolami was superintendent when I first visited the State School and carried my request to do a book to officials in Austin. Butch Held was superintendent when I arrived. The first thing Butch did was get me a badge so I could move through the gate and around campus almost at will. Whenever I needed help, Butch was there. Thanks for everything, Butch. Steve Robinson, the executive director, was an enthusiastic supporter who did much to help. I enjoyed many long, animated conversations with Dr. Ann Kelley. Dr. Linda Reyes knows as much about violent young offenders as anyone, anywhere, and was gracious in sharing her insights. Mike Hilgers was fun and candid and became a good friend. Watching Frank and Margie Soto day after day taught me a great deal about how dedicated professionals break through to kids who have shut themselves down. Miriam Goderich at Dystel-Goderich Literary Management got this book off the ground. Jane Dystel did a wonderful job editing the proposal and has watched its progress like a hawk. I am grateful to them both. Much thanks to my editor, Jonathan Jao, for his enthusiasm and careful work, and to my previous editors, Scott Moyers and Tim Farrell. Many thanks to Jill Wolfson for her support and great edits. Much thanks to Jessica Rose for her keen interest and encouragement. And to Bob Ingle, former executive editor of the *San Jose Mercury News* and the best editor I ever had, for his sharp eye and fierce intelligence. And to Karen Richardson for her fine copyediting.

NOTES

INTRODUCTION: "THE TOUGHEST PRISON IN TEXAS"

xiii   "right there where" Billy Joe Shaver, with Waylon Jennings, from "Tramp on Your Street," Zoo/Volcano Records, 1993.

xvi   "The juvenile crime rate began to rise" Malcom C. Young and Jenni Gainsborough, *Processing Juveniles in Adult Court—An Assessment of Trends and Consequences.* Washington, D.C.: The Sentencing Project, 2000.

xvi   "Criminologists like Alfred Blumstein" Alfred Blumstein and Richard Rosenfeld, *Assessing Recent Ups and Downs in U.S. Homicide Rates.* Pittsburgh: The National Consortium on Violence Research, Carnegie Mellon University, 1998.

xvi   "peaked and passed" See Young and Gainsborough, *Processing Juveniles.*

xvi   "received an average of thirty murderers" Chuck Jeffords, director of research, the Texas Youth Commission; also see the Texas Youth Commission website, www.tycstate.tx.us.

xvii   "Minorities are overrepresented" Bart Lubow and Dennis Barron, *Resources for Juvenile Detention Reform.* Baltimore: The Annie E. Casey Foundation, 2000.

xix   "an IQ of 121" Taken from Jerome's files. While the writer did not have access to the files, he was present at meetings where psychologists read from TYC case files. Jerome was tested while in the Marlin Orientation and Assessment Unit.

xxi   "one-third of all U.S. executions since 1977" See "Death Penalty Network," http://web.cis.smu.edu/~deathpen/.

xxi   "Butch Held" Butch Held retired in 2004 after more than twenty-five years with the TYC. He is now running a halfway house for federal white-collar criminals in Austin. Held is part of a tradition that goes back to the founding of the juvenile courts and one remarkable man, Judge Benjamin Lindsey (1869–1943), who was something of a Horatio Alger figure. As a boy, he was so helplessly poor, he once attempted suicide. He worked his way out and up, and when he became a judge, Lindsey did not look at the miscreants who appeared before him and think, If I could do it, they can, too. Instead, his childhood produced a compassion for the youth. But other than offering them a few kind words, there was little he could do. There was no separate court system for juveniles in 1898. Lindsey had to send them off to the same jails that held career criminals, muggers, cat burglars, and prostitutes.

One afternoon, Lindsey handed down a routine jail sentence to a young coal thief. The boy's mother began shrieking, piercing the judge's heart as well as his ears. She did not stop until he promised to look into her son's case personally. Lindsey visited the coal thief's family and found them living in a hovel so cold, he could see his breath. The father was lying in bed, dying of lead poisoning after spending his working life in a smelter. He had no health insurance; workers' compensation did not exist and the family was penniless. Stealing was the boy's pathetic attempt to keep his family warm.

Lindsey left the apartment asking himself if locking this boy up was the best thing for the youth, his family, and the community he was supposed to be protecting. The answers the judge came up with put him in the center of the Progressives, a political reform movement that was instrumental in founding a revolutionary new court in Chicago, in July 1899.

Hearings in the new court were to be informal and confidential, so no stigma would follow a youth throughout his life. They were presided over by a fatherly judge who had the youth's best interests at heart. If a youth was running the streets or the judge had to remove him from an abusive or criminal family, he placed the boy in a new facility that was for children only, a "home," and was presided over by caring custodians.

For more on Judge Lindsey, see Eric Goldman, *Rendezvous with Destiny: A History of Modern American Reform*. New York: Alfred A. Knopf, 1952. See also his autobiography, *The Beast*, written with Harvey J. O'Higgins. New York: Doubleday, 1910. For detailed descriptions of the founding of the juvenile courts, see Inger J. Sagatun and Leonard P. Edwards, *Child Abuse and the Legal System*. Chicago: Nelson-Hall, 1994; and Anthony M. Platt, *The Child Savers: The Invention of Delinquency*. Chicago: University of Chicago Press, 1969.

xxi   "the violent crime wave among juveniles" For analysis of this epidemic of violence and its precipitous decline, see *1998 Sourcebook of Criminal Justice Statistics*. Washington, D.C.: Bureau of Justice Statistics, U.S. Department of Justice, 1999; Jeffrey Butts and Jeremy Travis, *The Rise and Fall of American Youth Violence: 1980 to 2000*. Washington, D.C.: The Urban Institute, 2002; Alfred Blumstein, "Violence Certainly Is the Problem—Especially with Handguns," *University of Colorado Law Review*, www.saf.org/lawreviews/Blumstein2.htm, 1998, and Blumstein and Rosenfeld, *Assessing Recent Ups and Downs in U.S. Homicide Rates;* "Crack's Decline: Some Surprises Across U.S. Cities," National Institute of Justice, 1997, as cited in "Prosecuting Juveniles in Adult Court: An Assessment of Trends and Consequences," *The Sentencing Project Fact Sheet*, www.sentencingproject.org/brief/juveniles.html; J. Austin et al., *Juveniles in Adult Prisons and Jails: A National Assessment*. Washington, D.C.: Bureau of Justice Statistics, U.S. Department of Justice, 2000; John Hubner and Jill Wolfson, *Ain't No Place Anybody Would Want to Be: Conditions of Confinement*. Washington, D.C.: The Coalition for Juvenile Justice, 1999; and Wolfson and Hubner, "Trying and Sentencing Youth in Adult Criminal Court." Washington, D.C.: The Coalition for Juvenile Justice, 2002.

xxii   "Teenage superpredators" Elizabeth Becker, "As Ex-Theorist on Young 'Superpreda-
        tors,' Bush Aide Has Regrets," *The New York Times*, Feb. 9, 2000. John J. DiLulio,
        Jr., was a criminologist at Princeton University when he coined the term "superpreda-
        tor," which immediately had political currency. DiLulio was attacked by peers for
        "providing for what they thought were partisan politics." In 1996, DiLulio describes
        an epiphany while attending Mass, after which he "vowed to put the brakes on the
        superpredator theory and work on prevention." But by then, the "theory had taken
        on a life of its own." The Bush administration named DiLulio the first director of the
        White House Office of Faith-Based and Community Initiatives.

xxiii   "California Youth Authority ran recidivism" The 74 percent recidivism rate over a
        three-year period came from CYA statisticians working with data accumulated from
        1989 to 2001. It is the largest such study ever done by the CYA, conducted at the be-
        hest of—and first published in—the *San Jose Mercury News*. See "Where Hope Is
        Locked Away," Sunday, Oct. 17, 2004, mercurynews.com.

xxiii   "only 10 percent had been rearrested for a violent offense" From the Texas Youth
        Commission. Data released by youth commissions can be tricky and difficult to
        compare with data collected in other states. Fortunately, the TYC's data analysis is
        one of the best in the country. "States can play all kinds of games with data—and
        that's assuming they release data," said Howard Snyder, chief statistician of the Na-
        tional Council on Juvenile Delinquency in Pittsburgh, perhaps the country's most
        widely recognized authority on juvenile justice data. "Texas is far ahead of other
        states in both the amount and the sophistication of data it publishes. In most states,
        the norm is no data at all."

        Go to www.tycstate.tx.us, the Texas Youth Commission website. (Unless other-
        wise noted, statistics originating from the TYC can be located at this website.) Click
        on "Research and Data." Go to "Specialized Treatment and Recidivism." For the
        general population that went through only the resocialization program, the rearrest
        rate for felonies was 32.4 percent in 2003. The rearrest rate for any offense within
        one year was 52.8 percent. The data show clearly that specialized treatment programs
        like Capital Offenders have a great impact. In 2004, TYC chief statistician Chuck
        Jeffords found that "receiving specialized capital and serious violent offender treat-
        ment reduced the likelihood of capital and serious violent offenders being reincar-
        cerated for any offense, by fifty-five percent, and a felony offense, by forty-three
        percent." Thirty-six months after release, only 10 percent of the graduates of the
        Capital and Serious Violent Offender Program had been rearrested for a violent of-
        fense. Thirty-six percent were rearrested for felony offenses over a three-year period
        ending in 2003. Fifty-one percent were rearrested for any offense over a three-year
        period ending in 2003. "Any offense" can mean a technical violation, like failing to
        report to a parole officer or going outside a limited geographic area while wearing an
        electronic surveillance device.

CHAPTER ONE: "LOOKING LIKE PSYCHOPATHS"

8   "studies done by the U.S. Bureau of Justice Statistics" Kevin J. Strom, *Profile of State
        Prisoners Under Age 8, 1985–97.* Washington, D.C.: U.S. Department of Justice, Of-
        fice of Justice Programs, Bureau of Justice Statistics, Feb. 2000.

10   "cautious about ruling out kids" Linda Reyes on what makes a psychopath: "A psy-
      chopath is devoid of empathy and has no sense of obligation. People are there to be
      used. There is a physiological component to psychopathology. Some are born with a
      limited capacity for emotional attachment; in others, attachment failed. Combine
      low attachment with an abusive upbringing, and you can get a thrill-seeking psy-
      chopath."

14   "Listening to their stories" Reyes hit on the idea of having youthful offenders tell
      their life stories as a result of her Ph.D. training. She had gone through gestalt therapy
      and figured that if gestalt, with its emphasis on how past events affect present feel-
      ings, could cut through the cognitive defenses a Ph.D. candidate had erected, it could
      help a teenage offender cut through his defenses.

CHAPTER TWO: "I WANT TO RUN AND GET A KNIFE"

24   "poly-drug-addicted" To the public, a drug test is urinating in a bottle while a court-
      appointed official watches. But there are also sophisticated batteries of tests like SASSI,
      the Substance Abuse Subtle Screening Inventory, that are designed to ferret out how
      users conceptualize drugs. In SASSI, Ronnie offhandedly ranked drugs with the most
      important things in life ("I hate being away from my family and sex and drugs").

24   "conduct disorder" From the *DSM-IV,* the *Diagnostic and Statistical Manual of Men-
      tal Disorders.* Washington, D.C.: American Psychiatric Association, 2000. Conduct
      disorder is a psychological condition that applies only to children and adolescents
      and, according to the *DSM-IV,* the psychologist's bible, is manifested by "a repeti-
      tive and persistent pattern of behavior in which the basic rights of others or major
      age-appropriate societal norms or rules are violated." A youth has to have displayed
      aggression toward people or animals, used a weapon, employed force to steal from a
      victim, forced sex on someone, or destroyed property ("i.e., setting a fire with the in-
      tention of causing serious damage") to earn this diagnosis.

24   "Fry" Will N. Elwood, Ph.D., "Fry: A Study of Adolescents' Use of Embalming
      Fluid with Marijuana and Tobacco." Behavioral Research Group, NOVA Research
      Company, University of Texas School of Public Health, Houston, Feb. 1998; Texas
      Commission on Alcohol and Drug Abuse (TCADA), Austin.

26   "Choctaw Bingo" James McMurtry, Sugarhill Records, 2002.

CHAPTER THREE: "A STRANGER PASSING BY"

57   "The days when Ronnie earned silver and gold stars were over" Therapists in the
      State School have heard so many variations of stories like Ronnie's, they inevitably
      turn into child advocates. They know that while children may not be verbally sophis-
      ticated, they are still eloquent. They act out feelings, giving clues to what is going on
      inside them, and in a better world, adults would listen and respond, while the forces
      are still building. That happens in strong families; in schools where teachers are not
      so overburdened that they have the time and energy to focus on a child who is start-
      ing to flounder; in communities where neighbors are alert and caring.

"Intervention," Linda Reyes says over and over again. "There are some families where we have to intervene. The earlier, the better."

But the positive intervention Reyes has in mind doesn't happen often enough. What typically occurs is, when a kid starts yelling in a classroom or on a playground, all an adult hears is noise. When a kid attacks a classmate, an adult sees aggression. The adults label the kid—"She can't control herself, she's a troublemaker"; "He's a bully"; "He's a terror"—and punish the behavior without searching for its source.

63   "oppositional defiant disorder" *DSM-IV* diagnostic code 33.8. The diagnostic criteria are a pattern of negativistic, hostile, and defiant behavior lasting at least six months, during which four (or more) of the following are present: often loses temper; often argues with adults; often actively defies or refuses to comply with adults' requests or rules; often deliberately annoys people; often blames others for his or her mistakes or misbehavior; is often touchy or easily annoyed by others; is often angry and resentful; is often spiteful or vindictive.

CHAPTER FOUR: "NO AFFECTION OR CONCERN UNTIL I GOT LOCKED UP"

80   "20 percent of the students in Giddings are on antidepressant medications" Ross Robinson, superintendent, the Giddings State School. Prior to Giddings, Robinson was an administrator at the Corsicana Residential Treatment Center, a TYC facility that houses youth who have been diagnosed as having mental illness or who have serious and persistent emotional disturbances. "Around half the kids are on antidepressants or some form of psychotropics when they arrive" at the State School, Robinson said. "We work to reduce the percentage. Too often, drugs are used as a quick fix."

83   "eliminated the judge" At first glance, the move to lessen the traditional role of the judge in juvenile court seems unnecessary—and perhaps illegal. Judges have always had the power to remove the most violent and habitual young criminals from the juvenile system and send them to criminal courts, where they will be tried as adults. Before making such a momentous decision, judges are legally charged by the 1966 U.S. Supreme Court decision *Kent* v. *United States* to hold a hearing and take many complex, interwoven issues into consideration: Was it a violent crime? Was it committed in a heinous manner? What is the offender's previous criminal history, psychological condition, and family background? What public safety risk does the youth present? What have been the previous attempts at rehabilitation and how did the youth respond? Does the youth have any mental health or substance abuse problems that contributed to the crime? Is there a program or facility available that could reasonably assure public safety while also offering treatment?

Today, forty-six states and the District of Columbia allow judges to review individual cases and exercise some discretion in deciding which youths will be tried as adults. (Only four states—Massachusetts, Nebraska, New Mexico, and New York—do not have the judicial waiver process.) And while media accounts and tough-on-crime legislators have charged that juvenile court judges are legally unable to send youth into the adult system (or are resistant to doing so), that is not the case. Studies in South Carolina and Utah have shown that juvenile court judges did not reject appropriate requests, but rather approved eight in ten transfer requests made by prosecutors.

What has changed in recent years is that now the vast majority of youth who come into the adult system have been sent there without this crucial, individualized judicial oversight. Far more often than not, new legislation limits or eliminates the role of the judge.

In 1998, nationally there were eight thousand petitioned delinquency cases transferred to adult court by judicial waiver. This represents a mere 5 percent of all decisions made to prosecute juveniles as adults. Most youth now completely bypass the judge under new legislation, like direct file and statutory exclusion.

In at least five states and the District of Columbia, the prosecutor—not the judge—now has the primary power to decide whether a case will be heard in juvenile or criminal court. Also known as prosecutorial discretion or concurrent jurisdiction, this direct-file provision hands the life-changing decision to the very person whose role in the justice system is to press charges and convict.

83   "the pathways from the juvenile to the adult system" Office of Juvenile Justice and Delinquency Prevention, *OJJDP Statistical Briefing Book,* http://ojjdp.ncjrs.org/ojstatbb/html/qa087.html.25, Apr. 2002.

84   "At least twenty-nine states limit or completely eliminate" and "At least fifteen states and the District of Columbia" *OJJDP Statistical Briefing Book.* For a complete discussion of transfers from juvenile to the adult criminal courts, see Jill Wolfson and John Hubner, "Trying and Sentencing Youth in Adult Criminal Court," 2002 Annual Report of the Coalition for Juvenile Justice, Washington, D.C., Dec. 2002.

84   "Since 1997, at least thirty-one states" L. Szymanski, "Once an Adult/Always an Adult," *NCJJ Snapshot.* Pittsburgh: National Center for Juvenile Justice, 1998.

84   "Most dramatic of all" *OJJDP Statistical Briefing Book.*

84   "discounted the traditional age of eighteen" *OJJDP Statistical Briefing Book.*

84   "violent offenses jumped 78 percent" Bureau of Justice Statistics, *1998 Sourcebook of Criminal Justice Statistics.* Washington, D.C.: Bureau of Justice Statistics, U.S. Department of Justice, 1999.

85   "overall juvenile arrest rate declined" Butts and Travis, *The Rise and Fall of American Youth Violence: 1980 to 2000,* and *1998 Sourcebook of Criminal Justice Statistics.*

85   "researchers were using state-of-the-art medical technology . . . Jay Giedd" Margaret Talbot, "The Maximum Security Adolescent," *The New York Times Magazine,* Sept. 10, 2000.

85   "Psychologist Michael J. Bradley" Quoted in Joanne Trestrail, "Science Explains Teenage Brain," *Chicago Tribune,* Sept. 6, 2000; David E. Arredondo, M.D., "Child Development, Children's Mental Health and the Juvenile Justice System: Principles for Effective Decision Making," unpublished paper. See also http://www.brainplace .com, a website run by Dr. Daniel Amen, director of the Amen Clinics in Newport Beach and Fairfield, California. The site explains brain imaging and shows images of normal brains, the adolescent brain, the frontal lobes of a child diagnosed with ADHD, and brains that have been devastated by cocaine, alcohol, and other drugs.

85   "the brain is still forming" Says Marsha Levick, legal director of the Juvenile Law Center: "Strong rehabilitative programs will bear more fruit during adolescence

than later in life. Thus, the way corrections supervises teens—the way they counsel, educate, teach skills—will have a long-term effect on their behavior." *Testimony on the Proposed Standards on the Confinement of Youthful Offenders in Adult Correctional Facilities,* Juvenile Law Center, www.jlc.org/home/JLC@WORK/juvenile justice/ACA%20Testimony.html, Aug. 2000.

86   "at least twenty-two states have enacted" National Center for Juvenile Justice, *Juveniles Facing Criminal Sanctions: Three States That Changed the Rules.* Washington, D.C.: Office of Juvenile Justice and Delinquency Prevention, 2000.

87   "recommend that a youth . . . be transferred to a state prison" From 1997 to February 2002, seventy-seven determinate-sentence offenders who served time in the Giddings State School were paroled and seventy-eight were transferred to prison. During that period, the other thirteen TYC institutions sent 106 of 325 determinate-sentence offenders to prison, a transfer rate of 32 percent. Giddings has a higher rate because Giddings gets the most serious offenders. TYC figures.

CHAPTER SIX: "I FELT POWERFUL WITH THE GUN"

120   " 'old law' or a Type A violent offender" For more on sentencing in Texas, see "Sentenced Offenders" and "Juveniles Certified as Adults by Offense, 1988–2000," Texas Youth Commission website, www.tyc.state.tx.us/research.

133   "more loco than anyone else" When that everlasting need for acceptance gets translated into gang identification, the results can be deadly.

At the same time Ronnie was telling his crime story, Maxine Cooper, his caseworker, was campaigning to get an eighteen-year-old named Carlos, a Latin King who had been in the State School since he was fifteen, transferred to prison. Cooper is one of the most respected caseworkers on campus, tough, caring, relentless in her assessments. She began making the case for Carlos's transfer after a spot search turned up photos of Carlos throwing gang signs with four Latin Kings, one of the largest and more deadly street gangs in the country.

Two things about the pictures particularly disturbed Cooper. One of the pictures was of Carlos and his Latin Kings homeys throwing signs next to a white Mustang. It wasn't just any Mustang. The car belonged to a teenage boy that Carlos had shot dead. As it turned out, Carlos had killed the wrong man; the driver was not the rival gang member the Latin Kings thought he was. But the fact that Carlos had murdered an innocent person did not bother the Kings. Carlos had killed someone for the gang, he was down. That was reason enough for the Latin Kings to celebrate.

Carlos was part of the group that had just completed Capital Offenders—that was the second reason why Cooper wanted him to spend the next thirty years in prison. If Carlos were honest, if he were genuine about giving up his gang identification, he would have destroyed the pictures or, better yet, produced the pictures and talked about them in group. Instead, the half dozen Polaroids were his hidden treasure.

"Carlos developed some empathy in Capital Offenders," Cooper said when she explained her decision to pursue a transfer. "He won't want to kill you, but he will. Carlos is weak. He needs his gang. He'll kill you because he values the acceptance of his gang members more than he values your life."

CHAPTER SEVEN: GLAD THEY WERE HOME

145   "About half of all State School students do not return home" Just over 50 percent of parolees from the State School go to group homes, according to Walter Stevens, placement director of the Giddings State School.

150   "fewer youth are tried in criminal courts" In Texas, prosecutors can file papers sending youth directly to the criminal courts, where they are tried as adults. Harris County prosecutors do this much more often than DAs in any other urban county in Texas. In 1998, for example, 218 youth in Harris County were certified as adults and sent directly to the criminal courts; in Dallas County that year, prosecutors sent only twenty-eight youth to the adult courts.

  But that is changing. In 1995, the Texas legislature added eleven new offenses to the nine original offenses that made youth eligible for a determinate sentence, in part to discourage prosecutors from sending youth to the adult system. As news of the changes filtered into their offices, Texas prosecutors reacted favorably, and between 1996 and 2001, the number of youths certified to stand trial as adults in Texas dropped by 66 percent. And yet, Harris County still maintains its large lead. In 2000, Harris County prosecutors waved seventy-two youths into the criminal courts. In Dallas County in 2000, the DA sent only thirteen youths into the criminal system. See "Sentencing," www.tyc.state.tx.us/research.

150   "Napoleon Beazley" See "Napoleon Beazley #779, www.clarkprosecutor.org/html/death/US/beazley770.htm. This site is a fifty-seven-page account of the Beazley case, including court proceedings, newspaper accounts, and letters written to the parole board.

152   "letters back to Giddings" The description is based on letters written by youth to staff members in the Giddings State School. The writer requested a tour of the Clemens Unit, but TDCJ public information officers denied the request, saying they could accommodate only newspaper journalists working on a deadline.

152   "costs slightly over $100 a day . . . to house" Butch Held, superintendent, and Ricky Foster, chief business officer, the Giddings State School. The cost of incarceration figures in the Texas prison system come from "Statistics" and "Budgets" on the Texas Department of Criminal Justice website, http://www.tdcj.state.tx.us/.

CHAPTER EIGHT: "IS THAT MAN THERE?"

160   "a borderline personality" "The essential feature of Borderline Personality Disorder is a pervasive pattern of instability of interpersonal relationships, self-image, and affects, and marked impulsivity that begins by early adulthood and is present in a variety of contexts." From *DSM-IV,* p. 706.

163   *"Morales v. Turman"* See "Juvenile Rights in Texas Reform Schools," in *William Wayne Justice: A Judicial Biography,* by Frank R. Kemerer. Austin: University of Texas Press, 1999, pp. 45–48. Interview with Neil Nichols, TYC general counsel, who was Ron Jackson's first hire. The TYC recently renamed the Brownwood facility after Ron Jackson.

166   "apprehension specialists" Recidivism rates started going up, alarming state legisla-
       tors. Steve Robinson went back to the capitol to explain that the increases were due
       to such "technical violations" as a parolee missing a meeting with a parole officer or
       violating a curfew.

CHAPTER NINE: MEETING KATY

181   "Parents of Murdered Children" The national office is 100 East Eighth Street, Suite
       B-41, Cincinnati, OH 45020, www.pomc.com; e-mail, nationalpomc@aol.com.
       The POMC provides "support and assistance to all survivors of homicide victims
       while working to create a world free of murder."

CHAPTER TEN: "THE BITCH THIS, THE BITCH THAT"

206   "leads to redemption" There is a literary precedent for what happens in Capital Of-
       fenders: Charles Dickens's *A Christmas Carol*. Life has badly wounded Ebenezer
       Scrooge. His mother died giving him birth, and his father blamed him. His beloved
       sister died giving birth. Scrooge blamed the universe and felt completely justified
       being as angry as he was miserly. When the spirits appear on Christmas Eve, the first
       takes Scrooge back to his youth and shows him who he was. The second shows him
       what he has become. The third shows Scrooge his own bleak funeral and takes him
       to the lonely tombstone that will mark his grave—if he does not change.
           Scrooge cannot go back and change the past. No mortal can. But he can change
       and live in a way that is contrary to his past. Scrooge does, and thereby redeems him-
       self.

CHAPTER ELEVEN: "STUPID WHEN YOU LOOK BACK ON IT"

215   "pepper spray" Only four security officers on campus are authorized to carry pepper
       spray. Contrast this to the California Youth Authority, where every guard has a pep-
       per spray canister dangling from his belt.

219   "you have to get out of your gang" Leaving a gang behind, like an alcoholic's decision
       to stop drinking, can begin with "bottoming out." Jennifer, a girl in the Capital Of-
       fenders group that preceded Elena's and now one of the senior girls in Cottage 1-A,
       had that kind of moment. Like Elena, Jennifer was a Trece, a Loco 13. Her father was
       a lifelong Latin King who was shot dead on a street in Laredo when she was twelve.
       By sixteen, she had risen to become a trusted drug dealer for the Kings. She had in-
       formation on the death of another trafficker and could have avoided a TYC sentence,
       but refused to testify.
           Jennifer landed in the security unit twenty-eight times during her first two years
       in the State School. She was close to being transferred to prison when, one night in
       security, she began to see things differently.
           "I realized none of my gang buddies were there, I was alone," Jennifer said. "But
       then, I realized I wasn't alone. Mrs. Soto came by to see me and my caseworker and

others were there for me, too. I knew I had to change. I had to get out of my gang. If I didn't, I'd go to prison and my life would be destroyed. My dad never learned that, and he was found dead.

"I decided I was going to quit the gang and if my peers couldn't accept that, I'd take the consequences," Jennifer continued, sitting on a couch in the cottage. "Gangs are about getting acceptance, respect, love, power, and money. I decided I was going to try to get that from people who are not gang-related."

227   "According to the U.S. Census 2000" Demographic figures for Texas are from Census 2000, http://www.census.gov/main/www/cen2000.html.

227   "TYC . . . racial composition" "Who Are TYC Offenders," Texas Youth Commission, www.tyc.state.tx.us/research.

227   "Shay Bilchik" Administrator's Message, "Minorities in the Juvenile Justice System," OJJDP, 1999.

228   "race effects" Here's how massive social forces like poverty and discrimination can play out in the courtroom, where a youth's future is at stake.

Let's say a young black defendant is appearing on an assault charge. Let's say the judge is a white woman. She is not prejudiced; she simply grew up in a very different world than the young defendant. Her family was intact and loving, her neighborhood was middle-class and safe; she did well in college and went on to law school.

The father of the defendant was present at his conception but has been unavailable since. His mother is not in the courtroom. She has three other children and cleans houses for a living; if she misses a day of work, she misses a payday and may lose a client. She cannot afford to hire a private attorney. The boy has a public defender; she is not incompetent, but she is overwhelmed. This is one of fifteen court appearances she will make today.

In Jolanta Juszkiewicz's "Youth Crime/Adult Time: Is Justice Served?" Washington, D.C.: Building Blocks for Youth, 2000, an in-depth study on the effects of race in the juvenile justice system, researchers concluded that "African-American youth were significantly less likely to be represented by private counsel, and youth represented by private counsel were less likely to be convicted of a felony and more likely to be transferred back (from an adult criminal court) to juvenile court."

The judge looks at the youth's record and sees he has two prior convictions. Since the boy is in court without a parent, the judge assumes he has very little supervision. She decides the young man is a threat to reoffend, and, doing her duty to protect society, sentences him to the youth commission.

Let's say the next case on the judge's docket is a young white male, and he, too, is facing assault charges. His father and mother are with him, and so is a private attorney the judge knows and respects. This young man also has two prior convictions, but this attorney knows the system. The family is not wealthy, but they do have some savings, and they have taken out a second mortgage on their home to finance an alternative placement for their son—if his lawyer can sell it to the judge.

"Your Honor," the lawyer begins, "this young man and his family are fully cognizant of the damage he has inflicted upon this community. In recognition of that, the family is prepared to pay his tuition for a two-year placement in CEDU, one of the nation's leading emotional-growth schools. CEDU is located in California and Idaho, far away from the influences that have led this young man to your courtroom.

CEDU offers a highly structured environment and state-of-the-art therapy, and—I think you will find this most appealing, Your Honor—this plan will not cost the taxpayers a dime."

The judge is only too happy to sign the papers and send the boy off to the CEDU Academy in Sandpoint, Idaho.

228   "Building Blocks for Youth" See Eileen Poe-Yamagata and Michael A. Jones, "And Justice for Some: Differential Treatment of Minority Youth in the Justice System, 2000," National Council on Crime and Delinquency, www.buildingblocksforyouth .org/research.html. See also Jolanta Juszkiewicz, "Youth Crime/Adult Crime: Is Justice Served?" Washington, D.C.: Building Blocks for Youth, 2000.

229   "more minorities live in those conditions" "Race, Ethnicity, and Serious Violent Juvenile Offending," *Juvenile Justice Bulletin.* Washington, D.C.: Office of Juvenile Justice and Delinquency Prevention, 2000.

CHAPTER TWELVE: "I EARNED MYSELF SOME DISTANCE FROM MYSELF"

232   "injecting Candace with heroin" The admission appears in Candace's TYC case file.

234   Candace's poem "Sleeping Troubles" was first published in *The Beat Within, A Weekly Publication of Writing and Art from the Inside,* Vol. 7.3, p. 70. A weekly journal of prose, poetry, and drawings produced by teenagers in five juvenile detention centers in the San Francisco Bay Area and in other facilities for youthful offenders around the country, *The Beat* is published by the Pacific News Service, San Francisco.

INDEX

ABOUT THE AUTHOR

JOHN HUBNER is a journalist and author who has a
special interest in children and families. The father of
two teenagers, he lives in Santa Cruz, California.